POPPY
IN THE WILD

POPPY
IN THE WILD

A LOST DOG, FIFTEEN HUNDRED ACRES OF WILDERNESS, AND
THE DOGGED DETERMINATION THAT BROUGHT HER HOME

TERESA J. RHYNE

PEGASUS BOOKS
NEW YORK LONDON

POPPY IN THE WILD

Pegasus Books, Ltd.
148 W 37th Street, 13th Floor
New York, NY 10018

First Pegasus Books cloth edition October 2020

Interior design by Maria Fernandez

ISBN: 978-1-64313-542-7

10 9 8 7 6 5 4 3 2 1

Printed in the United States of America
Distributed by Simon & Schuster
www.pegasusbooks.com

For Mike and Babs, for all you do for lost dogs everywhere.

And for lost beings everywhere, may you find your way home.

Contents

Author's Note

I have recounted this story to the best of my recollection, which may be foggy given my exhaustion during the real time events. Some names were changed and some characters are composites for the sake of story and privacy. Conversations are relayed from my memory, my journal, and, more often, text messages, but sometimes cleaned up for the sake of the story and your ease of reading—because people hiking or sitting stakeout for a beagle aren't really worried about spelling or grammar, nor should they be. The dogs' comments, though—those are verbatim.

1

PLANS

This is how it's supposed to be.

That's what I was thinking as I cruised east on California's Highway 46, the part that takes you through the rolling hills—golden or green, depending on the time of year—always dotted with cows, more of them in the spring, when the super bloom also wraps the hillside in orange poppies and purple lupine. I always like this part of the drive. It makes me happy.

Soon enough, though, all would change. I'd get to the hundreds of pumpjacks—those rocking, smelly, environment-destroying oil pumps also known as nodding donkeys, oil horses, and thirsty birds (cute names for such nasty equipment, no?). Next, I'd drive past Lost Hills, the little company town built for agriculture workers by a billionaire in a failed attempt to appear benevolent. And then I'd hit Interstate 5 and the stench of the concentrated animal feeding operation where those cows, who once stood on the lush, beautiful hillsides, now stand in their own feces awaiting slaughter. (I am not going to think about how this drive might be symbolic of my life; you should avoid thinking about that too.)

Everything after Highway 46 made the drive worse for me, every month without fail. But in that moment things were as they should be: me, cruising down the highway toward home, Jimmy Buffett on the radio, breeze blowing through my hair, happy, oblivious cows trotting in line down the hillside to my right, and an adorable hound dog safely settled in a crate in the back seat of my Subaru Forester.

Okay, that's not exactly right. I mean sure, there was a dog in my car. There's usually a dog in my car. But this wasn't my dog and there was no breeze tousling my hair—I never leave the windows down when I'm driving. I can't stand the noise. Also, it was November and very chilly. And come to think of it, "cool wind in my hair" is an Eagles lyric, not Jimmy Buffett. Odds are also good it was NPR or an audiobook playing for the drive, not Jimmy or the Eagles, despite the desert highway I was on. Also, I said I was driving "home" and I really don't know if that's correct. "Home" is a very difficult concept for me.

As a child, I lived in houses in a variety of Southern California suburbs— North Hollywood, Sylmar, La Habra Heights, La Habra (the literal downward slide must be noted)—while my parents worked on their unworkable marriage, divorcing, remarrying, divorcing again. The houses were filled with enough anger and angst to rarely feel like "home." There was also the very 1970s "every other weekend home" with my father and his second wife (third marriage, if you're counting) in two more houses, with one more sibling added.

My mother remarried too, and I gained a stepfather. They lived in separate homes for a decade or so before finally buying a house together and then eventually packing up and leaving that house in California for another house in Missouri. I visited all those houses, of course, but they were not my home.

My father divorced again, and remarried two more times (four wives, five marriages if you're still trying to keep track, but in his defense, wife number three likely would have lasted had she not passed away from a brain aneurysm suffered while standing in her kitchen baking Christmas cookies). Each of these marriages brought multiple step-siblings and at least one move to yet another house, effectively ensuring there was no place that was "home" for me for holidays or any other reason.

During this spouse and house swapping, I went away to college, first living in a dorm and then an apartment, then switching universities and living, as one does, in two more apartments, before leaving for law school and yet more apartments. I never went "home" for summers, since it never felt like I had a home to return to (and really, why leave Santa Barbara?).

Hang on a second, I'm going to need to check on the dog in my back seat. "You good, buddy?"

The dog thumped his tail in response. All was good. Dogs are such easy companions, aren't they? Back to the story then, and the drive.

My childhood lessons were well learned in my adulthood, naturally, as I bounced from house to house, never living anywhere more than five years. I also married and divorced twice, never staying married more than eight years. (Every family has its traditions, right?) Each time, I chose to leave the spouse and the house-which-was-not-a-home and strike out on my own. In 2004, I settled in Riverside, California, sixty miles east of Los Angeles, in a townhouse I'd bought with the plan to live quietly with just my books, some coffee, and my two old beagles. Also, wine.

I'd practiced law in Riverside for nearly twenty years by then, though naturally I'd changed law firms a few times as well. (What commitment issues? What are you talking about?) Riverside made sense, so I lived there. And soon, against all carefully laid plans, I was dating again.

Chris was twelve years younger than me and was supposed to be a fun rebound relationship to help Teresa get her groove back post-divorce; he was not supposed to live with me in my crazy dog-lady world. But the universe rolled over me with a moving van of love, respect, and laughter, and fifteen months from our first date (which I did not know was a date) he moved in with me. By then my "living alone with my dogs" plan had already gone sideways anyway, as both my old dogs passed away within the first few months after my divorce.

I plan. The universe laughs. I'm a walking cliché.

Chris and I lived happily in that same townhouse for over a decade. It was a home for me, at least for a time. I adopted a beagle whom I named Seamus, and he lived with us for nine of those years, battling and beating one cancer only to then pass away from another cancer. In between his cancer battles, I had my own cancer battle—triple negative breast cancer, which is as frightening as it sounds. Spoiler alert: I survived. Despite our battles with cancer, mostly we were happy in that home. (Chris's zodiac sign is Cancer, and we hoped that was as close as he would get.) I'd even started my own law office. And we adopted two more beagles—Daphne and Percival (you're sensing a pattern, right?).

But by 2014 the townhouse no longer felt like home either. I'd been in a relationship with Chris for ten years by then—breaking all records, you'll note, and I'll note it's because we haven't married. (Right. Commitment issues. Let's move on.) We were doing great, but his business was taking him away from home often. My neighbors were cranky and complained about my dogs, and wayward leaves, and old pipes in the walls that pinged (or exploded, depending on who you believed) when hot water ran through them, and I was no longer enamored of a small, low-maintenance yard. I wanted room to stretch out.

I finally had a life I wanted to expand.

Chris and I decided to try something different. We chose a place to live and create a home on purpose—not because of broken relationships, or schools, or even jobs (and only a little because of bad neighbors). We chose a place we might want to stay for a long, long while (look, saying "lifetime" is scary; that's like taunting the universe and just begging it to knock me off as the moving van pulled away, likely over my prone body after I tripped on packing tape).

Chris was in the wine business, with an online wine shop that specialized in Central California wines. He could work from anywhere but made frequent trips to Paso Robles, the heart of Central California's wine country, and I joined him as often as I could. Until one day we realized how much we loved the area, and I figured out that I could probably have a law practice there as well. I practice estate planning (wills, trusts, business succession planning—getting a plan together for life's changes, because *people, life changes. It changes all the damn time*). Since I didn't go to court, I didn't deal with too many last-minute emergencies, and there were now these things called computers, and inter-webs, and horrid apps where you can see on your computer screen distorted versions of one another (and way too much nose hair) while having a phone conversation. I began to think I could have a second law office in Paso Robles.

The dog in my back seat let out a contented, long sigh.

"I know, buddy. I know . . . Paso is a beautiful place."

More tail thumping.

Dogs are just so easy.

At first, Chris and I spent a week or so a month in Paso (as it's often called—I suspect because no one knows if one properly says "Robe-uls" or "Robe-less" after "Paso"), staying at winery guesthouses or the occasional Airbnb, while Chris visited the wineries, picked up the wines he'd be shipping, and tried to pretend that tasting wine was just part of the work and not an awesome way to spend a day. I worked from my laptop computer while also trying to make connections with other professionals and maybe some potential clients in the area, and possibly sipping on some wine myself.

Eventually, we rented a townhome in Paso, finally finding one that would allow Daphne and Percival. I rented a small office downtown, near the park with all the cute shops and restaurants in easy walking distance. I kept my law office in Riverside of course, since that was our main source of income, and drove the 260 miles each way a couple of times a month—north on Interstate 5, then west on highway 46 on the way to Paso, then east on 46 and south on the 5 back to Riverside. (You're recognizing the drive we've been on now, right? The dog is still safe in his crate in the back seat. I haven't forgotten him. I could never forget him.)

In March 2018, two years after I opened my Paso office, we had a stroke of luck the kind of which I don't generally see or know exists, and found a house for rent high on a hill, overlooking vineyards, surrounded by oak trees covered in Spanish moss, in acres of gorgeous countryside, yet only eight minutes from town. And the landlord was more than happy to have us bring our two beagles.

When I met another attorney who split her time between two offices—her main office was in San Francisco—and who was likewise trying to establish a practice stronghold in Paso, we began to plot to find office space to share. Eventually we settled into the "penthouse" of the old Granary building downtown, with its wood-beamed ceiling, beautiful arched windows, pleasant views, and creaky old, unreliable elevator. I still split my time between Riverside, where I lived in the same townhome with the same cranky neighbors, and

Paso, where I lived in the beautiful hilltop house with Chris and Daphne and Percival, who had quickly adapted from suburban, sidewalk-strutting, townhome-residing, couch-loving city dogs to rural, trail-hiking, house-and-yard-dwelling, couch-loving country dogs. I spent two weeks in each place, more or less. Generally, I tried to squeeze in more weekend time in Paso.

Chris by then had changed jobs and was managing a winery tasting room downtown, which meant he was living in Paso full time. When I was in Paso, we could easily walk to each other's place of business, though there was much more reason for me to walk to his (wine!) than him to walk to mine (law! See? Not the same). Things were going well. Our life was gradually tilting toward Paso Robles. We were enjoying our country life and could easily envision one day fully transitioning our lives to that beautiful town.

Sounds like home, right? How could that be confusing? I'd finally figured out this concept of home.

Cue the universe and its laughter.

I was so content, so lulled by the rolling vineyards and luscious wines, I forgot everything life had taught me.

I forgot to expect the shit storm.

In the same month we moved into the rented house on the hill, I had begun negotiations to merge my Riverside practice with another law firm. This would have given me more freedom to build the Paso practice and the Paso life while giving me at least a few years of income security. Instead, in August my sweet, adorable Daphne, my beagle mini-me, my little Doodlebutt, was diagnosed with lymphoma. *More fucking cancer.* We fought it as best we could, as we'd done with the three prior cancer battles in our household, but Daphne passed away in October. And my law firm deal fell apart a week before that. Or maybe it was after. I don't remember. It wasn't important after the loss of Daphne.

I was reeling from all of that when my dad announced he was putting his home up for sale and moving from Palm Springs—a forty-five-minute drive from Riverside—to Springfield, Missouri, several states and a day of flights away. My mother and stepfather had moved to Springfield fifteen years previously, following my brother and his kids, just as my father was doing now. Both parents, in explaining their moves halfway across the country, had told me they were certain I would be fine. And I would be. I am. I *always* am. It's what I do. It's what everybody tells me I do. I graduated law school with little fanfare at the age of twenty-three just "fine," handled two divorces "fine," and survived breast cancer "fine." "You'll be fine" should be cross-stitched on every throw pillow on my bed and couch, not that you'd see it under all the dog hair, but I'm sure you get my point. And sure, I was fifty-five years old and what is known these days as a "grown-ass woman." (Why it's known as that is a mystery, though clearly my ass does keep growing.) At any rate, I was not dependent on my parents in any way. But my father's move had me wondering when I would see him again and how many more visits we might have.

It all was a great deal of loss pummeling me. The idea of home was slipping away before I had a chance to be comfortable with it. I did not feel fine and I did not have my Daphne Doodlebutt by my side to help me through. Dogs know when you are most assuredly *not* fine. Dogs are *there* for you.

Home is where the heart is? My heart is in my chest, where it belongs. Home sweet home? No. I'm more of a salt person. "Home is a place you grow up wanting to leave and grow old wanting to get back to." One out of two isn't bad, right?

All I knew about "home" is that home was where my dogs were. (Well, and Chris, but I was already forty when we met, so dogs had been a part of my life for much longer than Chris had.) And yet, there I was, headed to a house with no dog. A house that was therefore not a home.

That's why I was telling you that embellished story about me on that highway, breezing along with a dog and happy cows and all being right in the world. I wanted to stay in that moment where everything was nice, beautiful even. I want to tell you that part and hold on to that part. Because when I woke up that morning, before I set out on that drive down Highway 46 to wherever it was I was going, nothing was nice or beautiful. I had not planned on getting a dog, even temporarily—and this golden-eyed dog in my back seat *had to be* temporary. That was the only way this worked.

The thing was, we still had Percival. And I had already committed to adopt another dog. A dog who at that moment was not in my back seat but rather was in China, recently rescued from the dog meat trade, saved from slaughter and soon to be flown to California, with ten other dogs, all in need of rescue and rehabilitation. I told the rescue group I would foster to adopt one of those dogs. How could I not? (Seriously, *saved from slaughter.* You'd take in one of these dogs too, right?)

Because of that commitment, I had no business getting this third dog, the golden-eyed hound now in my back seat. But I couldn't help myself. When it comes to dogs, I can rarely help myself—I just help them. But I pretend I am in control. Watch. You'll see. It's ludicrous.

Hop in the car. You may as well come along for the rest of the drive.

❖

Now that you're settled in, we can pull off highway 46 for the infamous Interstate 5, the highway that makes a vertical slice through the entire state of California. We've got time. I can explain, both this dog in my back seat and the one saved from slaughter in China. Sure, I know, when I put it like that it sounds like a bit much, a little over the top, like maybe I'm truly a crazy dog lady. But try not to think of it that way. This is dog rescue. This stuff happens.

Chris would interject here *"It happens to you! It does not happen to normal people!"* But he would also laugh. At least I hope he would. He had a great sense of humor, and he'd need it. Because I hadn't yet told him about the dog in my back seat. (I will. *I will.* I'm just practicing telling you first.) In my defense, he does know about the dog coming in from China. He even almost participated in that decision.

This stretch of Interstate 5 is long and straight and boring. I'll try to tell the story straight without the long and boring parts, though there may be rest stops, detours, lane changes, and passing vehicles. We should watch out for truckers too. There's a lot of them. I wonder how many of them have dogs with them? That would make me like them more, give me patience for their chugging along at ten miles an hour up over the mountain pass known as the Grapevine. But I'm getting ahead of myself (if not ahead of the eighteen-wheelers sharing the road with us).

This is the drive I take four times a month. I drive from Riverside to Paso, stay two weeks, turn around and drive from Paso back to Riverside, stay two weeks, then repeat—260 miles each way. The plan had been that Daphne would accompany me on these drives. Daphne loved car rides and loved me. Percival hates the car, tolerates me, and worships Chris. So this plan made sense (*shut up, Universe!*). Chris and I would be apart two weeks every month, but that was what we needed to do to follow our dream and make this whole Paso thing work. We were okay with the plan, and even saw an upside: solitude.

Although I grew up in a noisy, chaotic household, I suspect the need for solitude is as much my nature as it was any nurturing that was or was not done. And now as an adult, with one noisy chaotic marriage behind me and another where solitude was frowned upon also behind me, I'd found a relationship that worked, in part, because of a shared love of solitude. It also worked because of our shared sense of humor, our mutual "black sheep" status within our respective families, and a general compatibility. In other words, it was the healthiest, happiest relationship either of us had ever had.

The arrangement Chris and I had was atypical, but it was what we had to do and it worked for us for the time. We both were comfortable enough with each other to admit we enjoyed the alone time. We agreed the first week was great, and the second week edged its way into "absence makes the heart grow fonder" territory. Which is a very good thing because, with my law office merger falling apart, we would need to stick to this two-week routine for the foreseeable future.

But as I said, that plan, like all my plans, had involved a dog. Once Daphne passed and I was confronted with the loss of my road trip buddy and two weeks a month without a dog every time I went down to Riverside, I knew I was in trouble.

Sure, I would only be completely dog-less for those two weeks, and then I would return to Chris and Percival. But they were exactly that, *Chris and Percival*. Percival was so firmly, insistently, obsessively Chris's dog, he almost didn't have time for me. When I came back to Paso after my two weeks in Riverside, Percival would greet me, but then he would immediately launch himself into Chris's lap and commence licking Chris's face, holding Chris down, and doing everything his thirty-pound body could do to prevent me from getting anywhere near Chris. His message was clear: Chris was his and he was Chris's.

That made my dog-less state even more difficult. Though I had chosen Percival, and Chris had been the first to fall in love with and insist on adopting Daphne, the dogs had plans of their own. Daphne, it turned out, was the dog version of me—a bit of a loner but fiercely devoted to those few in her circle, serious until she wasn't, and not one to engage in slapstick, foolish fun. Maybe a bit of a misanthrope. Chris called her "the Commissioner" for the way she controlled Percival and other dogs she encountered. As far as I knew, he didn't call me that, but it wouldn't be entirely unfair if he did. Percival was Chris: social, outgoing, convinced the world loved him (and right about that), with a distinct fear of missing out (FOMO, as I believe the kids call it), but also with a fierce independent streak that often saw him leave a room to spend time alone, usually in a sunny spot (yes, Chris too; solitude is our family thing). They chose us. And they chose well. As is usually the case with dogs, their instincts were better than ours.

Daphne was my girl. Percival was Chris's boy. So while we'd both lost a dog, I'd lost my teammate too.

Chris understood, without being offended, that I could be without him for two weeks a month but *not* without a dog. In case you don't understand that, just know that I can text and talk to Chris by phone, but that's much harder with a dog. I know. I've tried. Though Chris is very good about sending me photos of our dogs in our times apart.

I struggled a lot in the days after our sweet Daphne died, especially since I was down in Riverside and she was at the vet in Paso Robles when she passed. I had been working a lot and was in the throes of due diligence on the possible law firm merger. We had thought it was easier on her to be in the Paso Robles home with fewer stairs and easier access to outside. We had also thought she was doing better and responding to the chemo. We were wrong. We were wrong about all of it.

Two days after I had departed to Riverside, kissing Daphne's sweet face and promising to be back as soon as I could, she collapsed. Chris rushed her to the emergency vet and she died later that same night. I never got to see her again. (And now you'll need to give me a moment; I'm pulling off the highway to gather myself, and maybe douse my pain in french fries.)

When I had finally stopped crying enough to talk, I told Chris that when the time was right, I wanted to adopt another dog, for me mostly, but also for Percival. I thought he would like a buddy. Though Percival and Daphne's relationship had been very much annoyed big sister/annoying little brother, and she may have bossed him around a time or two, I knew he needed to be around another dog. Percival, like most beagles, is a very social dog, and I didn't want him to start to pine for his sister.

"I want another female, but one who doesn't look like Daphne," I said. "That would be unfair to the new dog and would break my heart on a regular basis."

"That makes sense," Chris said.

"And I want to call her Poppy."

"Poppy," he answered, in a posh, clipped British accent. He was mimicking the way the name was said on the mockumentary *Almost Royal* starring the comedian Amy Hoggart as Poppy Carlton, 58th in line to the British throne. The show and the way the name was pronounced was the reason I wanted to name the new pup Poppy. I wanted to always smile when I said her name.

"Exactly."

"I like it," he said. "I think another girl will be good for all of us."

"The universe will send us a male dog now, you know that, right?" I said.

"Absolutely."

The day after that conversation at the end of October, I had thought I would get a jump on the universe, even though there was nothing about my life to date that would indicate I could one-up the universe. Quite the contrary. But I am blind, deaf, and ridiculous when it comes to dogs—or eternally optimistic if you want to put a happier spin on it (frankly, I don't do happy, but you have at it). I began scrolling the Facebook pages of my favorite beagle rescue groups (are you seeing another pattern here? No? Me either). Soon, I saw a photo that pulled all my heartstrings, unraveling every emotion (or, you know, both of them).

Beagle Freedom Project, the same rescue we had adopted Percival from, had rescued eight beagles from the dog meat trade in China. The photo showed all eight, small and frightened, newly arrived at the Los Angeles International airport, being held carefully by the rescue volunteers.

Beagle Freedom Project had made its reputation rescuing animals—mostly beagles—from laboratories that test on animals. They do it legally—no breaking and entering—and work diligently to get the animals out, rehabbed, and adopted once the laboratories are done doing whatever it is they do in the name of outdated science (mostly in the name of their continuing grant money). But recently, BFP, as it's known, had begun working with a group of brave women in China trying to stop the dog meat trade. The rescuers step in and force the breeders to release the dogs instead of taking them to the market, where they'd be sold for their meat. Horrifying to even imagine.

BFP doesn't know the real names of the women, who are part of a groundswell of animal advocates in a country that is still very much behind the times on animal welfare. In addition to dog meat "festivals," China still requires cosmetics be tested on animals—animals like Percival, who'd been rescued by BFP from an animal testing laboratory in Northern California—before the products can be sold in China. These women will stop trucks carrying the dogs to market and strong-arm people into giving up the dogs instead of selling them. I'd love to see how that's done but, under the circumstances, limited information is released. But I know BFP and its concern for the dogs, and I know how strong an animal advocate's commitment to saving a dog can be. BFP supports the rescue efforts by providing vet care, spay/neuter services, and transport of the dogs to loving foster homes and then, at long last, to forever homes in the US, all while continuing to work to shut down the dog meat markets worldwide.

Looking at the photo of these recently rescued pups, it's hard to imagine anyone would want to slaughter and eat them (you may have noted, I feel that way about the cows in the hillsides along the highway too). One beagle, with long droopy ears, a sad face, and the tan and white coloring commonly called "lemon," drew my immediate attention.

Without much forethought, I emailed the rescue asking if she was available. She wasn't. Happily, those dogs all had homes already lined up. It was too soon for another dog for me then anyway, and it had been an impulsive act. I was a bit relieved. I was already regretting having asked when BFP emailed that there was another group of dogs coming in from China in about a month's time. There were eleven of them: ten females and a male, several with the tan and white "lemon" coloring. Just like that, I was back to thinking about getting another dog.

I had never had a lemon beagle, though for many beagle-obsessed folks that's a favorite coloring (and one is either beagle-obsessed or beagle-abhorrent, there is no middle ground). I had always preferred either the standard tri-color (brown, white, with a black "saddle" marking on their backs) that both Percival and Daphne were, or the blue-tick tri-color (the "ticking" refers to a blend of the colors in the fur that gives a mottled appearance) of Seamus. A lemon beagle would be distinctive from Daphne and Seamus, unique from all my other dogs. A lemon beagle would be what I had asked the universe for. *How perfect!* When life gives you lemons, get yourself a lemon beagle, right?

With Chris's agreement and his standard joke about having no choice in the matter when it came to dogs, I had quickly agreed to foster to adopt one of the girl beagles. I said I preferred a lemon. Beagle Freedom Project was happy to accommodate us since they preferred experienced fosters who would understand what the dogs needed. "Foster to adopt" meant that our intention was to adopt, but the foster period would allow us all (dog, humans, rescue) to determine whether we were a good match. We had Percival to think about as well, and wanted to make sure the dogs got along.

The dogs coming in from China would be unsocialized, traumatized, and in need of a lot of love and patience, just as Percival had been when he was freed from the laboratory at eighteen months old. At the time we adopted him—six years prior—he feared loud noises, particularly beeping noises, was prone to night terrors, and would chew his own feet until they bled. He soon became a highly social, happy dog whose only signs of past trauma were his hoarse howl, a result of the lab severing his vocal cords (they apparently don't want to hear the dogs' screams), and the number tattooed in his ear, identifying the lab where he had been and the tests to which he was subjected. While Percival loved nearly all humans and all dogs, he wasn't always a fan of sharing his personal space. He and Daphne had numerous tussles and moments of *"Moooooom, she's/he's touching me!"* There was no way to know how he would react to Poppy, or her to him.

Nevertheless, I knew some of what was ahead for us. We had a lot to prepare for. But I was looking forward to it. The ensuing months would be difficult—for us and for Poppy—but it would all be for a good reason—to give a dog a good, happy, healthy life—not another health battle or terminal illness. I could use a win, and so could Poppy. But before she could be ours, our Poppy girl had to get vet treatment in China, clear USDA requirements, and be flown to the United States. She would not be arriving until sometime in December, still a full month away.

That is how I came to commit to fostering and possibly adopting a dog to be named Poppy. A dog that would be arriving within a month. A dog Chris had agreed to as well. A dog that was not the soulful-eyed hound in my back seat.

That explains Poppy to you. But there are still a few hours of driving left and it's probably time for me to explain this quiet, handsome dog in my back seat to you. This, in turn, will help me explain him to Chris, who last saw me, dogless, backing down the drive, ostensibly on my way to Riverside to patiently await and prepare myself for Poppy's arrival in a month's time, blissfully unaware of this handsome, golden-eyed stranger in my back seat.

2

COMMITMENTS

🐾

And now come the true confessions of a dog addict:

When I woke that morning, packed my bags, loaded the bags and myself into a car that had no dog in it, and prepared to leave on this journey you've now joined me on, I found I couldn't. Instead, I sat in my car contemplating whether home was the place I was leaving or the place I was driving to. Or did I have a home at all now? Because without a dog, I am all kinds of melodramatic about life.

And therein was the problem that afternoon, as I sat in my car wondering where home was. Is there a home without a dog? There is not. We've been over this. Poppy would be arriving in a month, but what was I supposed to do in the meantime? What was I supposed to do for those two weeks in Riverside?

I sat there in my car, in the driveway of our hilltop Paso home, slumped and still, putting off my dogless departure. Making matters worse, it was November—the beginning of the holiday season I hated—cold, with a wind dipping the temperature further. Holidays have a sad history in my family. Holidays are when rollover car accidents (me), motorcycle accidents (my brother), comas (same brother), brain aneurysms (stepmom #2), cancer (my dog Seamus, me), death (my stepdad's parents, my second stepmother), and family arguments resulting in divorce (everyone) happened. There were a lot of hospitals for the holidays throughout my life.

This was another reason I did not want to be alone. But there I was, sitting alone in my car on a gravel driveway.

I reached for my cell phone to call my friend Charlotte. She would have the answer to my heartache. Charlotte would have just what I needed to get through that next month, or at least the next two weeks.

Charlotte ran Meade Canine Rescue, a dog sanctuary she'd founded just outside Paso Robles. At any given time she had forty to forty-five dogs—mostly seniors, many blind, some with cancer, handicapped, or with some other old-age ailment that caused them to be overlooked at the shelter, or "owner-relinquished" by the disappointing humans who should have cared for them in their golden years. She didn't do it all alone, of course—there was a caretaker on the property and volunteers—but mostly, it was Charlotte. Without tireless, devoted, passionate Charlotte, there was no sanctuary. So of course she couldn't answer the phone at just that moment. I left a message and remained sitting in my car, forlorn and frozen, but unwilling to move.

I stared at my phone screen, as though I could will it to ring. Where Charlotte lived, as one must with dozens of dogs, was way out in the countryside, past the little town of Creston, past the horse farms, past the cattle ranches, well into the oaks, and back over the rolling hills, with spotty-at-best cell phone coverage. After a few minutes, I convinced myself that was reason enough to call her again. This time she answered.

"Hey, Teresa," Charlotte said. "I saw you called. I was out walking the dogs."

The mental picture of that made me smile. Charlotte "walked the dogs" by walking the sanctuary property. The dogs who could, and sometimes that included a dog in a handmade wheelchair, followed her Pied Piper–style around the ten acres of hills.

"I knew you'd be busy. But I'm about to head back to Riverside. Remember me talking about maybe fostering for you? I can come pick up a dog and bring it with me down south for two weeks. Anybody need a little TLC and time away from the masses?"

"Uh, me?" she said. Probably a true statement, but I knew she was kidding. Charlotte went nowhere without dogs. Even on the rare occasion when she went into town or when she met me for lunch, the car would be filled with dogs—a half-dozen old, tiny Chihuahuas, a beagle or two, and her own Quie Quie, a beautiful blue merle dachshund mixed with something, Corgi maybe, that gave the dog upright ears and baby-blue eyes. Seeing Charlotte arrive for a casual dinner, a friend once joked it was like a clown car, only with a never-ending stream of dogs.

"Let me think. I know we have several who could use some time alone," she said.

"Okay, I'll just head over. You can figure out which one while I'm on my way."

"Oh! I know the one. We have the cutest little blind dog. A black little fluff ball. You'd never know she was blind."

"Black little fluff ball" immediately made me think of my childhood dog Tippy, a black cockapoo (half cocker spaniel, half poodle) my parents gave me for Christmas (the one solidly good Christmas memory I have) when I was five years old, the year before their first divorce. He was named Tippit after running around the house knocking over the cocktails that had been set on the floor next to the chairs where my parents and the neighbors sat. He was my dog for my entire childhood, and to the extent I did anything childlike in that childhood, it involved my Tippy-poo. He moved with me to every new house we moved to until he died at seventeen when I was in my second year of law school. Ever since Tippy, I thought all dogs lived that long, though none of the more than half-dozen dogs I had in my life since were that lucky. All dogs *should* live that long.

"Okay, yeah. I've never had a blind dog, but sure," I said. Blind dogs weren't my forte; dogs with cancer had become my forte. I'd even written two books about dogs with cancer (Seamus and then Daphne). But this was a foster dog, not "my dog." The fact that this dog wasn't a beagle had some appeal. I would be less likely to fall madly in love and be heartbroken when I had to return her. Or so I told myself.

But as I drove to Meade Canine Rescue, I tried to envision a blind dog in my Riverside townhome, with its multiple levels, and open, modern stair railings. Even the courtyard, where dogs come and go from the doggie door in the laundry room, was tiered; she would have to go up three tall steps to get to the yard area unless she did her business on the terracotta tile patio. But what if she needed grass or dirt? There were stairs everywhere.

Would I have to carry her?

I knew what that would be like. I had spent the two previous months panicking and imagining Daphne, weak from the chemo treating her lymphoma and anemic from kidney disease, falling over the stair railing that suddenly looked so irresponsible and unsafe. She had collapsed once in the hallway, not quite passing out and not quite a seizure, but I had rushed her to the emergency vet nonetheless. A few days later when it happened again, she had required a blood transfusion. Despite an old back injury, I carried her up and down the stairs and kept my bedroom door closed so she wouldn't leave the room in the middle of the night and head down the now glaringly dangerous stairs. I had not slept through a night since Daphne's diagnosis and subsequent passing. Having a blind dog in the same house would mean more sleepless nights, more carrying a dog up and down stairs, more back pain, and more angst. I would be terrified the entire time.

I could not take a blind dog. I couldn't. As much as I loved dogs, my love would not be enough to give this dog what she needed in addition to that—safety and security. Canine chaos is the only kind of chaos I can tolerate in my life, but even for me this would be too much.

Charlotte greeted me at the gate, along with the merry band of beasts that usually followed her. Petite and blond with bright green eyes, Charlotte always managed to look funky-chic, even walking across a dirt play yard with a ragtag group of dogs at her heels. She wore a bright green velvet jacket and a vintage bucket hat, a Willy Wonka of dogs. Personally, I found Meade Canine Rescue more magical than a chocolate factory. (Sorry, did I just make you hungry? Didn't we just stop for snacks? Go ahead. Grab one. Chocolate if you'd like.)

"I'm sorry, Charlotte, I want to foster a dog, I do, but I cannot take a blind dog. Not in my house," I said.

"Oh, Teresa, you won't even know she's blind. Honestly, she gets around so well, they all do. Dogs are amazing. Well, you know that."

"I do. But my house is dangerous for a blind dog. I just don't think it's right. I would be scared to death. Is there someone else I could foster?"

Charlotte began to look at the yard full of dogs, her hand to her mouth, thinking, watching. "Oh, what about Bubbles? Bubbles could use some alone time. She always likes to spend time in the sun just by herself."

I knew Bubbles. She was a large beagle appropriately named given her Kardashian-esque rear end, which might have been larger than my doggie door. I was going to say "Okay, sure," when a beagle I had not seen before walked up. He looked up at me with the soulful hound eyes I knew so well, except his were golden. He didn't jump or howl or shy away. He merely looked at me, his expression simply "Well, hello there," with a touch of "Please consider me."

"Who's this guy? His eyes are gorgeous," I said.

Charlotte turned and looked down at the new arrival. "Oh! Yes, Roe! This is Roe. You could take him. We just got him this week, so we don't know much about how he is. You could let us know."

"He's so handsome. Where'd he come from?"

"He was a hunting dog, left chained up in the backyard when he wasn't taken out hunting. Then the hunter died, and his wife didn't want the dog. You know the story. A neighbor convinced her to let us have him. He was covered in fleas and ticks. Oh, he was such a mess, poor guy. But we got rid of the fleas and ticks. His skin will heal."

I bent down to pet Roe and he immediately sat, still looking me directly in the eyes, so earnest. His tail was nearly hairless, rat-like, and patches of fur were missing on his back, behind his ears and on spots on his legs. The exposed skin was dry and scaly. Sweet, beautiful soul.

"You want to go home with me, Roe?" I said.

I could be remembering this part wrong, but I'm pretty sure that's when he got his own leash and walked himself to my car, where he quietly and quickly hopped in the moment the door opened, and settled himself into the crate. I hopped in too (the car, not the crate). Charlotte handed me a spray for Roe's skin, and we headed east on Highway 46, warm air blowing out the vents and NPR on the radio. I think you joined us right about then.

The drive to Riverside typically took from four to five hours. That gave me plenty of time to think about how things should have been, appreciate that momentary happiness with Roe in the back seat, and consider that I'd just picked up a foster dog without talking to Chris, the person with whom I was trying to create this life in Paso Robles and with whom I shared a house, that we were making a home.

I thought of it, if one could call it "thinking" rather than reacting, this way: Percival was with Chris, Roe was my foster dog for a few weeks, and then Poppy would arrive and Roe would return to Meade Canine Rescue and eventually be adopted. This is a beautiful plan. My logical side loved this plan, even if my emotional side—teeny, tiny, and only making appearances when dogs are involved—knew there was a problem.

Chris would have reason to be concerned with what I'd done. I was working on ignoring that by carefully repeating the plan in my head (and to you) convincing myself it made total sense, while knowing it did not. It really did not. Even as I attempted to shove the emotional side back into the dark recesses of my brain where I usually kept it, I knew—Chris, usually the more emotional, less logical of the two of us—would see the flaw in the plan. You might not.

We can't have three dogs. The homeowner's association rules for my Riverside townhouse only allowed for two dogs, and our lease in Paso also only allowed two dogs. So Roe would *have* to be a temporary foster. I would have to be a foster dog parent. Which was where the flaw was.

It was me. I'm the flaw in the plan.

See, fostering requires one to let go of the dog, to send the dog on to be adopted by someone else, and I already loved Roe. Chris would know that I already loved Roe, because Chris loved and knew me.

I'm an easy mark, sure. But there was just something about Roe's open, hopeful expression and those golden eyes. He was effortlessly loveable. Also, he was a dog, and I love dogs. That dog walking down the street? I love him. The dog in the car next to me at the stoplight? I love her. The dog in the dog food commercial? *Love.* You've been posting your adorable pups on social media? Know that I have a serious love affair with them that deepens with every photo you post.

Dogs are love. Dogs are life. Which is why it's so devastatingly brutal when they die. And as much as that hurt, crushed, and immobilized me, I could not imagine a life without dogs. Apparently, I could not imagine two weeks without a dog. Thus, it makes sense I had a dog in my back seat and another one that would be coming in from China in a month. *I had to.* You understand, right? May I offer you a french fry?

I had two more hours driving to prepare for my discussion with Chris wherein I could convince him I was and would remain a temporary foster for Roe. You're welcome to help.

More of my rationalizing disguised as critical thinking: Roe needed some recovery time and loving care. I needed the companionship of a dog. It was a good thing for both of us for two weeks. That's how fostering works. Very straightforward. That's how it's supposed to be. (You may have noticed I have a thing about "how things are supposed to be.")

That all sounded highly logical, and Chris knew me to be a logical (sometimes to the point of annoying) person. But he also knew my common sense often abandoned me in the same way my low, gruff voice abandoned me for baby talk whenever a dog was near. He knew that, and I knew what his response to my logical and yet deeply flawed argument would be. His objections would not be baseless.

I had a history.

I was what is jokingly referred to in the dog rescue community as a "foster failure"—someone who was supposed to foster a dog but ultimately could not give the dog up and adopted instead. It's a success really, but also an indication of just how attached I get. Daphne had been my "foster failure."

Since I learned what fostering was and how important it is to rescue work, I'd always wanted to foster, but Seamus too preferred his solitude and did not want other dogs around. So up until he passed away, fostering wasn't an option. When I saw Daphne on that Facebook page, I knew my chance to foster had come.

City and county shelters in California, particularly Southern California, continue to overflow with abandoned and stray animals. Killing—or in more euphemistic terms "putting the animals to sleep"—to make room for yet more animals is done in horrifying numbers (the ASPCA estimates over 650,000 dogs per year in the United States, with about 175,000 of those in California, a state with one of the top five euthanasia rates). Private rescue groups such as Meade Canine Rescue, and the one that saved Daphne, can pull animals from these shelters, give them the care and medical attention they need, and most importantly give them the time they need to eventually find a home of their own, or at least a place to spend their final days knowing love and care—and knowing that they matter. But once the rescue is full, or if the animal for one reason or another can't be around other animals, the animal needs to be placed with a foster: someone who can help care for and socialize the animal, learn their true personality (never accurately on display in the high-stress shelter environment), and give them a temporary safe place to be until a forever home can be found. And there are some rescues that have no physical location, but instead coordinate a foster care system until adopters are found. Simply put, fostering saves lives.

That's why I fostered Daphne. That's why I wanted to do it again. To save the dogs and myself.

I looked at Roe, curled up and sleeping contentedly in the crate as we drove through the last stretch of freeway before we were home. There was no way this could be wrong.

"Good boy, buddy. We'll have a good two weeks together. Get you rested and well fed, and that skin taken care of. It'll be good for both of us."

And then I'll have to take you back to Charlotte's, where hopefully someone will adopt you soon, you sweet boy.

I reached my hand into the back seat and put my fingers in the crate. Roe moved his head toward me, and I gave him a little scratch behind his ears. "You're a good boy, Roe. You're a very good boy. We'll be home soon."

Already, I was trying to figure out who I knew who lived nearby and needed to adopt this dog so I could have regular visitations.

⁂

Roe had no trouble in the crate in my back seat. He had likely been crated a lot in his life. Though the french fries I stuck through the vents probably helped him appreciate the accommodations a bit more.

Roe was thin, especially for a beagle. It wasn't hard to imagine that he had been likely only thrown some low-quality kibble once a day in his old life. I would get him to a healthy weight on good food (more than I could say for myself), but in the meantime a few fries wouldn't hurt.

When we arrived in Riverside, he hopped out of the car and, true to his hound nature, began the serious business of sniffing every inch of my townhouse and yard. (You may want to get out and stretch now too; the drive is over. Seriously, get out of my car.)

I knew that dogs received important information through this sniffing process and I hoped that what Roe was learning was that many beagles had passed through here before him and lived happy lives, filled with toys and treats, good food, and plenty of love. The things I hoped for his future.

Once inside the house and with my car unloaded, I sat on the couch and patted a space next to me, inviting Roe to join me. He looked at me with those inquisitive yellow-gold eyes, not understanding what I meant, but wanting to be a good boy anyway. I petted his head and assured him he was the good-est boy. Then I picked him up and put him on the couch next to me, where I could continue to pet and assure him. I could feel each rib as my hand passed over his wispy fur.

"Made it home safe," I texted to Chris. "I picked up a foster dog from Charlotte," I casually added.

"Just tell me it's not a beagle."

"Ummmm. It's not a beagle?" I texted him a photo of Roe, who was definitely a beagle.

Exploding head emoji, dog face emoji, bourbon on the rocks emoji. Words were apparently not necessary for Chris at that moment.

Shrugging girl emoji. I probably should have followed with a few glasses of wine emojis. Or actual glasses of wine.

"What about Poppy?"

"Poppy won't be here for a month. Roe is a foster. I'll keep him until Poppy gets here. That way I get a dog too. He already makes me feel better." Not that he had done anything dramatic; just being a dog was enough. Roe had slept most of the way home but occasionally would sit up and look around.

I would reach back and pet him through the crate side vents and he would lean his head into my hand. Totally adorable. And slightly dangerous when driving (sorry if that scared you), but *I had a dog*!

"We can't have three dogs."

"I know. He's a foster."

"He's a beagle. You will be a foster failure."

"No, I won't. I can't. I've already agreed to Poppy and I know we can only have two dogs. Roe is a foster."

"Yeah, you keep saying that."

I looked down at Roe, nearly asleep now at my side. I petted his dry, patchy-skinned head. He met my gaze. *And oh, those eyes.* He looked so grateful for even the slightest attention. "He's really sweet."

"Yeah. This is a disaster waiting to happen. Looking forward to your *Sophie's Choice* of canines."

"I needed a dog."

"I know. I know you do."

I meant it. I needed a dog currently and I was simultaneously committed to Poppy—whoever she was. Wherever she was. But in the meantime, why not help a lonely beagle who needed and deserved some love? (Okay, yeah, maybe there's a lonely person in this equation too. Maybe.)

When I stood to get a glass of water from the kitchen, Roe leaped from the couch and renewed his thorough investigation of my townhome—nose down, tail high, sniffing at a fevered pace. Eventually he found the large basket of dog toys and after a few sniffs he stuck his head in and nudged the contents around. He grabbed a toy, bit down, shook his head, flung the toy, and then poked his head in for another. It must have looked like a treasure chest to him.

"Go ahead, Roe-Roe, play away." I grabbed a toy and threw it. He pounced after it, retrieved it and returned to the treasure chest. This time, though, he dove all the way in, turning and sitting in the toy box. I couldn't help but laugh. Then I saw what I had not seen before.

One of my favorite photos of Seamus had captured him in that same basket of toys, where he had jumped in and settled, buried up to his neck in fluffy, brightly colored toys, presumably to get warm. He looked like E.T., the alien in the toy closet from that movie long ago. And now I could see it in Roe too. He had the same mottled coloring, though where Seamus had been a "blue tick," Roe was a "red tick," with mottled red and white fur. Still, memories of Seamus flooded back. Seamus had been so much trouble but so full of personality and so incredibly smart. He stole food with a combination of stealth and brazenness that left you stunned just long enough for him to swallow whatever he'd grabbed off your plate. He howled his demands in his raspy, whiskey howl, his already large eyes bugging out of his head in outrage, until you gave in to whatever it was he wanted—food, attention, food, a walk, food, belly rubs, toast. You had to love him. And love him we did.

Seamus was Chris's first dog. He had not grown up with dogs and before me, before Seamus, Chris was not a "dog person." Seamus had been the dog that turned Chris into a devoted dog lover. Not quite as obsessed as I was, but I liked to think that was a work in progress. Percival was certainly doing his part.

I texted Chris a photo of Roe in the toy box. "He looks like Seamus."

There were a few minutes before I got a response. "So our new dog is Roe?"

No. Roe is a foster. A really cute foster, but a foster. We had Poppy coming home in a month, and Poppy needed us. Repeat to self as necessary. Ignore that I was the one who had said the universe would send us a male dog.

"He's a foster," I texted. "Goodnight, baby. We're going to bed."

"Goodnight. Love you."

"Love you too."

I went upstairs to change clothes and Roe followed me, constantly looking up at me for reassurances I was more than happy to give. "Good boy, buddy. You're fine. You're allowed. Good boy."

Back downstairs I gave Roe a small meal and then settled in on the couch. Usually when I had a new dog, whether foster or adopted, I slept downstairs on the couch for the first few nights, with the dog in a crate or on a dog bed next to me, so I could easily get them outside to do what we called their "dirty business." But Roe had no interest in a crate—who could blame him?—and minimal interest in staying on the dog bed. Instead he climbed up on the couch, crawled up on my chest, curled up, and fell asleep.

I knew I would be spending another night in an awkward position, not moving, limbs going numb, contorted for the comfort of a dog. And I didn't mind at all. *He's a really, really sweet dog.*

Universe, you are a tricky little bitch.

3

RESCUES

※

Sometime in the middle of the night, Roe moved down to curl up near my feet at the end of the couch. This gave me at least enough freedom to move around a bit and return the circulation to my limbs. After a few adjustments, we both fell asleep hard. Usually a new dog in a new environment means I'm up and down all night, letting them outside, bringing them back in, following them at a distance as they make their way about the house sniffing and investigating, or just petting and reassuring them that they are safe now, things will get better, easier. This was not the case with Roe. He just wanted to sleep, and no amount of my own movement altered that.

Until the sun began to rise.

I am not a morning person. Never have been. People told me that when I had kids that would change. That's one of the reasons I never had kids. People told me when I went to work at a big law firm that would change. That's one of the reasons I'm no longer at a big law firm. Not being a morning person is one of the reasons I have my own law office, where I can and do tell my clients I can't be responsible for any legal advice given before 10:00 A.M. But Roe had not gotten the memo. Roe woke with the first glimmer of sunlight and stretched his long, thin self forward and backward in the aptly named downward dog position, only with his front paws on my stomach, which I do not recall being part of the pose. Then he hopped off the couch—my cue to shuffle him outdoors and up into the terraced area of bushes and dirt. He followed easily, greeted the first bush he saw, and flooded it with a stream of attention. He kicked his legs behind him to cover his business, then trotted back down the steps and into the house, where he nimbly hopped back onto the couch, sat, and looked at me with his open expression clearly saying, "I like this. This is good. What's next?"

"More sleep, buddy? How about more sleep?" I said, as I struggled to get back under the blanket on the couch.

Roe stared at me a bit longer, then got down from the couch and went back to his treasure chest of random (and mostly shredded) toys, sorting through the neon remains of Christmases past.

"Okay, buddy. You're new here. You'll learn. We're big on sleep. We sleep past sunrise."

He squeaked a toy in response. Why is it that all beagles have such beautiful, expressive eyes that allow them to get away with everything? Roe, with his patchy skin and missing hair, had an extra element that made me want to do all I could to make him feel better. So, I got off the couch.

"All right, buddy. You win. Let me get you some breakfast."

He wagged his wiry tail. It's a beagle thing to understand the word "breakfast." I imagine it sounds to them the way "coffee" or "wine," or, well, "breakfast" sounds to me.

I knew I had dog food in the house. We had not expected Daphne to pass as soon as she did. Because of her illness, I had ordered specialty foods, a blend of frozen venison and squash, recommended by the holistic vet we had consulted. I had hesitated, squirmed, and initially resisted, since I'd been vegan for seven years by then (a choice originally made in light of my cancer diagnosis but maintained because of my love of animals—all animals). Ultimately, and more easily than I'd like to admit, I bought the food for Daphne. There was enough left over in my freezer to feed Roe for a week or so, and he certainly looked like he could use a special diet himself.

I warmed some food up as Roe danced at my feet, the beagle nose in overdrive. It was tempting to give him mounds of it, but I knew to be careful not to upset his digestive system with too much. We'd both pay for that. He'd not likely ever had food this rich.

He devoured the meal instantly and looked up at me, working that golden gaze, in the Dickensian beagle version of "Please sir, I want some more."

"Sorry, buddy. Can't do that right now."

I had my coffee, while Roe once again went outside and sniffed around the courtyard. My heart still ached and the thought of Daphne, gone only two weeks by then, choked me up. But it helped to have another dog nearby and particularly one who needed and deserved so much love and attention. I liked being able to focus on Roe.

I decided to take him for a walk. Daphne's harness was too big for him, but one of Percival's fit well enough. Roe was a bit taller than Percival, and Percival was thin for a beagle, but Roe was even thinner. *Poor guy.* He stood still while I arranged him in the harness and clipped the leash on. Instantly and easily, he walked with me as I headed for the front gate.

The sun was still rising as we walked. The air was cool and damp. Roe sniffed at everything—every planter, blade of grass, and weed. He even sniffed at the air. He pulled at the leash a bit, but mostly walked just a bit in front of me and regularly looked back to check he was doing things right. I continued to say "good boy" for the entire walk, because he was and because that was the extent of my vocabulary at sunrise on one cup of coffee.

Thankfully, given the early hour and my grumpy neighbors, Roe didn't howl on our walk as beagles are prone to do. Seamus had been a zealous howler, and Daphne notified all passing dogs that she was head bitch in charge anytime we went out for a walk (or if a dog dared pass by our house when she was outside). Beagles howl at other dogs, rabbits, squirrels, clouds, the stupid humans who don't bring them food quickly enough, food itself, the potential for food, and, most especially, if they feel they have not been given enough food or attention. Or maybe those are just my spoiled beagles. But Roe had not howled. As I thought about it, I realized I had yet to hear him make a noise at all. He didn't even snore. Daphne had been a heavy snorer, along with her enthusiastic howling.

Ah, yes, I remembered. Daphne also had not made a noise, other than the wheezing from her kennel cough, until what seemed like the very minute we agreed to adopt her. Then she was all howls at all the dogs (and cats, and mailmen, and birds, maybe spiders) all the time. Maybe Roe was just biding his time too.

I brought him to work with me—another perk of having my own law office. Seamus had come to work with me so often his photo was on my website along with the rest of the staff. Daphne had come to my office in the beginning, but her howling at the turtles in the pond in front of my office (and easily seen from the windows) made that untenable. Plus, once we had gotten Percival it seemed unfair to bring only one of them in, and Percival did not like the car. But I'd begun bringing Daphne to work with me again when she got sick, so I could keep an eye on her, get her the medications on time, and spend as much time as I could with her. (By then, she did not even have the energy to howl at the turtles.) Thus, my office was set up for a dog: dog bed, water bowl, toys, treats, and an extra leash. And I can't remember a time when I didn't have a regular supply of dog waste bags in my purse, because I am classy like that. Roe made himself at home quickly, curling up on the bed in the sun rays by the window.

We followed this routine for days.

My clients loved Roe, and he would generally join us in the conference room, happy to get a head pet, an ear scratch, or sometimes simultaneous ear scratches from the particularly exuberant clients. I told everyone who came in that he was available for adoption. And nearly everyone said, "Why don't you just keep him?"

It was hard not to think about that. Roe was a very easygoing dog whose main goal in life, it seemed, was to please. His companionship was salve to my heart, and the way he slept smashed up against me, always needing to be touched, near, safe, was exactly what I needed then too.

But I was soon distracted by a much bigger dog issue.

🐾

Just before I was about to return to Paso with Roe, I saw a Facebook post from my friend Geraldine. Fires were raging. She had been evacuated from her

Corral Canyon house in Malibu with all twenty-three of her rescue dogs. She and a few folks staying in the Airbnb on her property had driven the animals to her Mexican restaurant, Lula Cocina, in Santa Monica and were camped out in the patio. The drive from Malibu to Santa Monica, normally an hour at most, took them five hours—which meant most of the residents of Malibu were on Pacific Coast Highway, also fleeing the fire. How frightening that must have been. Transporting multiple dogs can be difficult enough—stressed-out dogs was a whole other level, especially if one is trying to outrace flames. That's combining two of my biggest fears: fire and any danger to dogs.

Geraldine likely shared those fears as she also rescued dogs and had in years past had a home burn down. I knew Geraldine to be a resourceful person—she owned and operated several restaurants and had a commanding personality—I hoped that would see her through. She was also unstoppable, as this fire was about to prove.

There was a video, taken on the patio of her colorful restaurant, terracotta tiled floors covered with crate after crate of dogs, some dogs loose, many wagging their tails, the bright teal, lavender, turquoise, and yellow walls incongruous under the circumstances. And there was Geraldine in the middle of it all. She was tall and thin, with gorgeous, long, thick red hair, wearing leggings and boots and a big sweater, conducting the chaos. But she had to be terrified. And exhausted.

My mind boggled: how does one evacuate twenty-three dogs? And these weren't just regular, domesticated house dogs. These were rescue dogs, from a variety of mostly difficult backgrounds. And yes, Geraldine too has a soft spot for beagles, which is how I met her. A few years earlier she had hosted a fundraiser benefitting Beagle Freedom Project at her gorgeous hilltop estate in Malibu, the one she'd just fled. We'd become friends because of our dog rescue efforts, love of wine, and, as it turned out, love of Paso Robles. Geraldine and I met Charlotte around the same time, and the three of us had been meeting and working together to find ways to collaborate on rescuing more dogs and raising more funds for the never-ending sanctuary work ever since.

Eventually I reached Geraldine and learned that an acquaintance had offered her and the dogs shelter in her backyard in Santa Monica. I marveled at someone willing and able to take in a near stranger and twenty-three dogs, but such was human nature and the bond between dog lovers. I knew this. I would do this. (And I hope I would remember to ask Chris first, but I'm less confident of that last part. Because, dogs.)

Not quite a year earlier I'd offered the Paso Robles condo we were then renting to yet another beagle-loving, dog-rescuing friend when the Thomas fire ripped through Ojai and forced her to evacuate. I was worried that Karal might not have any place to go where she could bring her dog. As it turned out, her dog had passed away shortly before, but she did need a place to stay, along with her human roommates. She and her roommates (a married couple, their child, and the husband's brother and bandmate) stayed for ten days or so, while we were in Riverside sequestered for the holidays. When we returned, the only signs they had been there were the thank-you gifts they'd left and a very clean condo. Well, those were the only signs until three months later when we moved from the condo to our hilltop house and found a pair of one roommate's boxers, a lacy thong belonging to another, and finally, children's cotton undies with cartoon characters imprinted—all fallen behind the dresser. We'd guessed they were in a hurry to get home, and who could blame them.

Now Geraldine was a victim of another devastating fire, and again, members of the rescue nation had stepped up to help. Geraldine was safe; the dogs were safe. But the fire was enormous and only 10 percent contained. Geraldine's home was still threatened. The caretaker's home at another of her properties—this one in Cornell, which she'd only purchased a year ago to create an animal sanctuary—had burned to the ground.

All of this was still heavy on my mind as I drove Roe and myself back up to Paso Robles. I wanted to help. Maybe take in one or two of the dogs? But I also had told Charlotte we would keep Roe until Poppy arrived from China (I was not ready to let him go; you're surprised, right? Charlotte did not seem to be. *Hmmm*). Roe would be meeting Percival soon enough, but we had no idea how he'd do with other dogs. There was also Chris to think about. He'd agreed to have Roe stay with us until Poppy arrived, but how many dogs could I subject Chris to? (A lot, as it turned out.)

✦

With only fifteen minutes to go before we'd arrive at our house in Paso Robles, I suddenly realized it was time to give some thought to the introduction of Roe and Percival. For the two weeks I'd been in Riverside with Roe, Chris had been in Paso Robles with Percival. It now occurred to me that Percival, while perhaps missing Daphne, was probably ecstatic to have Chris all to himself. He would likely barely tolerate my return and the subsequent loss of at least a small bit of Chris's attention. What would he think of Roe? I'd been texting Chris photos of Roe, regaling him with stories of Roe's handsomeness and calm, eager-to-please demeanor, but that didn't help Percival. Percival was clueless that he was about to have a roommate.

I called Chris. "We're about fifteen minutes away."

"Oh, great. You made pretty good time," he said.

"I did. Only had to stop once. I'm thinking Roe and Percival should meet outside. Can you bring Percy-pie out and walk him around? When I get there, I'll get Roe out on a leash and they can meet as we walk."

"Good idea. Neutral turf."

We needn't have worried. Roe and Percival sniffed each other, danced around, pranced around, and immediately began to tug at their leashes to walk and play and get on with life. After a short walk, we took them into the house and let them off leash.

Both dogs immediately assumed the play position, tails wagging rapidly. They chased each other, spun around, rolled around, leapt over one another, and zoomed about the house.

"Apparently Percival has always wanted a brother?" I said.

"Seems so," Chris said.

"I don't think I've ever seen him so active."

They ran and played until both grew tired. Then Percival hopped up on the couch and Roe followed immediately, sticking as close by Percival as he had by me. That night, they slept smashed up against each other like long-lost brothers. Their legs got tangled up, and various body parts were used as head rests at one time or another, but neither seemed to care.

When they woke, they both stayed on the bed, near each other but available for petting, which Percival let us know by pawing at our hands. We obliged.

"You're right, he's a very easygoing dog," Chris said.

"He is. Super mellow. I think he's just so happy to have some creature comforts in life. And some attention," I said.

"And another dog to play with."

"And sleep with."

"Poor guy. His skin looks so sad."

"That's a two-week improvement. I've been giving him coconut oil and spraying this moisturizing oil on him that really seems to be helping." It was the spray bottle Charlotte had handed me as I was leaving with Roe. I didn't even know what was in it. She just told me to spray his bald spots, and I did, because I knew Charlotte always knew what a dog needed.

Both dogs suddenly stood, looked at each other, and simultaneously jumped off the bed. They trotted, side by side, down the hall and into the laundry room—also known as the "dog room," where the feedings took place. Percival had clued Roe in already, from the looks of things.

"Beagle Boys have declared it breakfast time," Chris said. We both followed them, like the dutiful human guardians we were.

I was both amused and amazed at how easily these two had become "brothers." "It's like they've lived together for years."

"It's true. They are the Beagle Boys. Maybe Percival only likes boys. Maybe we should be keeping Roe. Why mess with a good thing?" Chris looked at me with those long-lashed baby-blue eyes of his, every bit as mesmerizing as Roe's golden eyes.

I had worried about me getting attached to Roe, but I hadn't thought about Percival, let alone Chris, getting attached. And I had not forgotten my off-the-cuff statement that the universe, joker that she was, would bring us a male beagle. But I'd also finally received the email with the details for picking up the dog we were calling Poppy. The dogs would be arriving from China on December 6. Just over two weeks away. I suppose I could have backed out then logistically, but my heart and my head were moving forward—fostering Roe and adopting Poppy was the right thing to do. The Beagle Boys would have three weeks together. That would be enough time to get Roe healthy, adjusted, and happy. Then he could get adopted.

When Roe finished eating, he sat and looked up at me. "What's next?"

Next was taking Roe to our Paso Robles vet for his check-up. Dr. Edsall and I served together on the Cancer Support Community board locally, and he'd been the one who had attentively treated Daphne in her final months. He was happy to see I had another beagle.

"What's this guy's story?" he said, as he knelt down and petted Roe's head. "He's got gorgeous eyes. Dontcha buddy? Hey, who's a good-lookin' boy?"

"I'm fostering him for Meade Canine Rescue. He was a hunting dog. When the hunter died the wife didn't want the dog anymore. She left him in the backyard, chained up, and covered in fleas and ticks." I bent down to pet Roe too. Even though I knew he couldn't understand the story, and he was of course aware of all he'd been through, I hated revisiting how badly he'd been treated. I hated he'd ever been treated like that. "The neighbor convinced the widow to give the dog up to Charlotte."

"Ah, the poor guy. I can see all the skin problems, but that will clear up with a good diet and some time, now that the fleas and ticks are gone."

"He already looks better, and it's only been two weeks."

Dr. Edsall lifted Roe onto the metal table and began to examine him, running his hands over him, lifting his lips to see his teeth, checking his heartbeat. Checking his heartbeat again.

Uh oh. If he does it a third time, I know it's an issue. I have extensive experience with vets making serious diagnoses.

I had noticed a cough, but I figured with all Roe had been through, that was understandable. Dr. Edsall moved the stethoscope and listened again. *Damn.*

"He's got a bit of a heart murmur," he said.

"He does?"

I had a beagle many years ago, Roxy, rescued at eight years old, who passed away at the age of twelve from congestive heart failure after years of a worsening heart murmur. She died quickly in her sleep, the only one of my dogs to die at home, but that didn't make those words any less frightening to me.

"It's low grade. A two or a three. Nothing to worry about, just something to keep an eye on."

"Is that why he coughs?"

"Could be." Dr. Edsall moved back to examining Roe's teeth. "See this?" He moved Roe's lips and exposed his bottom teeth, ground down to stubs. "That's from chewing and biting at the fleas and ticks, and probably the chain he was on. Sadly, we see it a lot when a dog gets infested like he must have been."

My heart was crumbling for this poor dog. "Oh, Roe-Roe. I'm so sorry. You deserve better." I stroked his head.

"He's a great dog. Probably only about eight years old, too. And look how calm and well-behaved he is. You should keep him!"

Vet-approved, and with a heart murmur. *Oh, this was going to be hard.* I have a penchant for the hard-luck dogs; you may have noticed this. I'm sure a therapist would have a field day with why that is, but I can save my money. I see myself in these dogs. I'm not a lucky person myself, and I hadn't been able to depend on too many folks in my life either. I don't want to say I needed rescuing myself, but I finally knew what it was like to have that one person you could count on. In other words, I had great empathy for dogs in need.

On my way home, I called Charlotte to give her the report on Roe. Though I paid the vet bill, Roe belonged to Meade Canine Rescue. She'd need the report, and I needed to remember I was fostering this dog.

I told her about the heart murmur. Characteristic of Charlotte, she took it in stride.

"Oh, we've had plenty of those. Low grade is good. We'll keep an eye on that. I've had dogs survive a long time with heart murmurs."

Charlotte was magic with dogs. She'd had dogs survive a long time with all sorts of terminal conditions.

"I hope he's lucky like that. Poor thing is due some luck."

"Oh, I have a feeling he found his luck being with you." She laughed. I tried to laugh too, but it may have been a cringe.

I filled her in on the rest of the vet visit and how Roe with his beautiful golden eyes and calm demeanor had charmed Dr. Edsall too.

Charlotte had been told Roe was ten years old, but it didn't surprise either of us that his prior home had not kept good records or didn't know or care how old he really was. Was ten just a guess? Did they know? Whether he was eight or ten, he had a lot of life left in him.

Then Charlotte switched topics. "So, have you heard about Geraldine?"

"Oh my god. Geraldine. I can't believe she evacuated with twenty-three dogs!"

"You know she's going to Laurie's ranch, right?"

"The ranch in Lompoc?" Laurie was yet another beagle-loving animal rescuer. She had a dog, Indie, from Beagle Freedom Project as well, and she knew Percival before I did—back when he was with his foster mom, a friend of hers. Lompoc, where Laurie and her husband, Roy, had a second home, a ranch, was about two hours south of Paso Robles. Chris and I had visited them there once with Daphne and Percival. Daphne and their beagle, Homer, had run the well-fenced property together for the entire weekend, digging holes, howling, and chasing rabbits and rodents. Percival explored the property for a bit, but much preferred the couch, deigning to go outside only to chase Indie, who looked so much like him it was easy to assume they'd come from the same breeder—purpose-bred to be sold to laboratories. (My beloved beagles are the preferred breed for animal testing laboratories due to their compact size, short hair, and happy-go-lucky temperament.)

"That's the one. They're caravanning up there with all the dogs. Geraldine needs help of course. Laurie, and her friend Jane, and a few others are helping to take the dogs up and getting her some groceries, but they can't stay with her. Can you imagine? Alone with twenty-three dogs in someone else's house?"

Geraldine normally had paid help around her home: caretakers, gardeners, dog walkers. But she'd now fled her home, and they had too. No doubt their own homes and families were in danger as well. "I cannot imagine. No." I said.

Charlotte and I quickly sorted out that Laurie and Roy would not be staying there with Geraldine, and that Geraldine would need a lot of help. Charlotte told me she was going to join Geraldine for a few days, but had to leave on

Wednesday—the day before Thanksgiving. Charlotte would also be bringing some dogs from her own rescue with her, so her caretaker at *her* rescue wouldn't be left with quite so many dogs in Charlotte's absence.

Geraldine already had twenty-three dogs at someone else's ranch, and now Charlotte would be showing up with another eight or ten. I couldn't even be surprised. Dog women are serious about their dogs. I know this. I am one of them.

I also knew I needed to help.

"I'll talk to Chris. We don't have plans really for Thanksgiving. We probably could stay a few days with her." The plans we had involved a day in our pajamas eating the vegan paella Chris made for the last several Thanksgivings since we stopped going (or being invited) to any sort of family Thanksgiving gathering. These were plans that could easily be changed.

"Oh, that would be wonderful. Oh, she'd appreciate that, Teresa. Can you do that?"

"I think so. The ranch isn't far. We'd just need to bring Roe and Percival with us."

"Well what's two more dogs? That can't be a problem."

What's two more dogs, indeed.

❖

Chris was bemused and slightly terrified when I asked if we could spend Thanksgiving with Geraldine at Laurie's ranch with twenty-three traumatized rescue dogs. But he's a good human, so he knew that when a friend is evacuated from their home due to fires, one helps that friend. The twenty-three dogs were just a bonus.

Well, to *me* they were a bonus.

Thanksgiving with twenty-three—no, twenty-five dogs with the two we'd be bringing—was such a welcome development because that kind of canine chaos would likely keep me from thinking about why it was we had no plans for Thanksgiving. On this most family-oriented of all holidays, we were decidedly short on family. My family was now centered in Missouri.

I had a younger sister still in California, but we had different mothers and she'd long ago chosen to spend holidays with her mother and that side of her family, and I'd long ago decided that spending holidays with my father's second ex-wife and her third husband and his family was more discomfiture than anybody should have to deal with. Though Chris's family was only about an hour's drive away from our Riverside home, Chris had not been in touch with his parents or sisters for a year or so, and this did not seem to bother any of them. He had floated away, and they had waved from the shore. We didn't know what they were doing for Thanksgiving, and we had not been invited.

Over the past few years, I'd come to think of both of our families as "loosely knit," as opposed to the more commonly spoken of "close-knit" families. Chris and I were each dropped stitches—the stray, looping piece of yarn that hung furthest away from even the loose other stitches that held our respective families together. We messed up the patterns, as it were. The pattern can be repaired of course, but it takes some expertise to do so, and our families were not knitters, so to speak. Thus, we dangled, part of the pattern, but easily cut off. Lately I'd come to think the only thread that held us together with our families was simple DNA. That didn't seem enough. Better to focus, instead, on our found family, even if some of them had four legs.

Why not spend the holiday weekend at a ranch, with a friend and twenty-plus rescue dogs?

Since Wednesday was his day off from the wine tasting room he managed, Chris took Roe and Percival and headed out that afternoon to what I was gleefully calling "Rescue Ranch" and Chris was less gleefully, but every bit as ardently, referring to as "Feces Farm." I was being optimistic and maybe even, dare I say, fun. Chris was being realistic, or so he insisted. Strange. Those are not our usual outlooks.

I still had some work to finish up, so I would join them Wednesday evening. Before I left my office, Charlotte called.

"Tag, you're in," she said. "I left Geraldine this morning. She's alone until you get there."

"Chris is already there. I'm leaving soon." Whatever defects there may have been in Chris's upbringing, he was raised a gentleman. In the old-fashioned but good way. He'd take care of Geraldine. He'd be polite. He'd probably even wind up cooking, despite Geraldine being a talented chef. And he'd take care of those dogs, too.

I could hear dogs in the background as Charlotte spoke, but that didn't tell me a thing—Charlotte always had dogs with her. She could have been at home, in the car, at the hair salon, at a wedding (true story), and she'd have a dozen dogs with her. "Okay, good. I left this morning. I really needed to leave last night but she begged me to stay. Oh my gosh, Teresa, it's madness there."

"Twenty-three uprooted, stressed, old, sick dogs? How can this be a problem?"

"Right. Well, right. Yeah, it is. And Geraldine is the most stressed of all."

"Of course."

"But there's not twenty-three dogs. Ziggy was so stressed he picked a few fights and two dogs were bitten, so Ziggy and one other one—I can't even remember which—both were sent to temporary fosters. She's lucky people stepped up."

"Oh, poor Ziggy. I was looking forward to seeing him again."

Ziggy was a big shepherd/chow mix–looking dog whose human moved away and left him with her mother and young siblings who could not handle him. He was a dog I'd transported on a drive from Riverside to Paso Robles, dropping him off with Geraldine at the property where the caretaker's house had now burned to the ground. I had not seen Ziggy since, as is often the case in transporting and fostering rescue dogs. It would have been nice to see him, but perhaps not under those circumstances. Not if he was stressed.

"Okay, so *only* twenty-one dogs," I said.

"Right. Yes. Only twenty-one. I think that's right."

I of course was being sarcastic (Charlotte was not). As excited as I was, I couldn't imagine how we were going to feed that many dogs and get them all settled in to sleep at night. There were not kennels at Laurie's ranch. The dogs would be loose in the house and yard. It seemed unlikely twenty-plus crates had also been evacuated from Malibu. I thought of Chris, the formerly non-dog guy, now there dealing with that scenario, and a very stressed-out Geraldine.

"I'm sure she has a system," I said.

Charlotte paused. "You'd think that. But, no. Help her with that, Teresa. I think she's overwhelmed, and she just doesn't want to be alone. I can't blame her. But I had to go."

"Okay, well, Chris is already there. So she's not alone."

"She's not. Okay good. Well, good luck."

I could hear the concern in Charlotte's voice, and it wasn't unlike the concern in Chris's voice when I'd mentioned our new Thanksgiving plans. But all I could think was "So many dogs! This will be the best Thanksgiving *ever*." And one month after Daphne's passing, I could think of no better way to soften my pain than caring for a needy group of rescue dogs and a human friend.

I quickly packed sweatshirts, long-sleeved T-shirts, yoga pants that had never seen a day of yoga, jeans, boots, tennis shoes, a baseball cap, and some toiletries. Another joy of this long weekend would be that fancy clothes and makeup would not be required. No attempt at perfection, no put-ons, no expectations. No family tensions. I could just be all about the dogs.

Despite some holiday traffic, the drive was easy. The last several miles had me driving in the dark in wide open, desert terrain. Once at the gate of the ranch, I called Chris. He and Geraldine made sure all dogs were inside the house before coming out to open the large gate and guide me in on the gravel road, up to the ranch house. I parked on the side of the house, where my car would stay untouched for the next four days, except for those occasions when a blind, flipper-footed dog bumped into it.

Chris grabbed my suitcase and a few bags of groceries I'd brought and then, at the front door to the ranch, turned to look at me, blue eyes twinkling, mostly with mischief but with some shock mixed in. "Get ready. You're not going to believe this."

4

THANKS

Chris opened the door to the Rescue Ranch house, and I was immediately surrounded by dogs—beagles, a basset hound, a shepherd mix, terriers, more beagles, a pit bull mix, and some indistinguishable mutts. It was loud, crazy, and chaotic. The only kind of loud, crazy, and chaotic I can tolerate, mainly because deep down, I love it.

Chris struggled to make his way around me and through the excited menagerie to put my suitcase in our room. I dropped to the floor to pet every dog I could reach. *Hello, Georgie girl! Oh, Toots, you little cutie. And there's Peaches—so pretty, baby girl. Ariel, Coco, all you sweet babies! Chico, you handsome boy!* I petted, kissed, and scratched as many dogs as I could as quickly as I could.

Soon, Percival and Roe ran up to greet me as well. I had not immediately noticed them, as they'd both quickly assimilated into the pack.

After a few minutes, I stood and looked around the house. It was much as I remembered—a small cozy place with an open living room, a stone fireplace and mantel in the corner, a large kitchen opening onto the living room, with a bedroom and a bathroom on each side of the living area. Only now the floor was covered in dog beds, each with a dog or two, sometimes three, and a frenzy of dogs dancing around at my feet. Laurie and her husband Roy had five dogs themselves, so I guessed some of the beds were theirs. But Geraldine must have managed to bring dog beds with her when she evacuated, or more folks from our little rescue nation had brought them. Dogs were spread out on the beds covering every inch of the living room floor, and another four dogs were settling back in on the L-shaped couch (it could have been five dogs, six even; trust me, it was very hard to count dogs). The fire was going, and Geraldine was in the kitchen sipping a glass of wine. Twenty-three dogs (her twenty-one rescues and the two of ours) in a two-bedroom house and all looked idyllic.

"This is my idea of heaven," I said to Chris as he joined me in the living room.

"I know it is. And that terrifies me," he said, eyes wide but with a smile. I have a blind spot for dogs. Chris, thankfully, has a blind spot for me.

"Let's get everyone outside so we can start getting their food and medicine ready," Geraldine said. "Open the garage door."

This was the part Charlotte warned me about. There was no system. We had to feed twenty-three dogs at once. There had to be a system, didn't there? I wondered how many also needed medication. From the looks of the crew, probably a lot of them.

I moved down the short hallway to the door leading to the garage. Once in the garage I could see there were ten large dog crates, some with pillows in them. But only ten. They wouldn't all be eating in crates. I hit the garage door opener just outside the door, and the most agile of the dogs, including Roe and Percival, ran out into the yard. Several others trailed behind, including Jack, an old, flipper-footed, somewhat deaf and blind, black and white beagle mix who occasionally bumped into things but seemed quite determined to continue to enjoy the outdoors.

The weather was cool and crisp. It wasn't raining and there was enough lighting to see the front yard where most of the dogs had congregated. A few, again including our two, insisted on running about the entire fenced acreage. Luckily, I knew the property was securely fenced, or I'd have been panicking about potential escapees. Beagles are notorious escape artists, but Roy and Laurie, the owners of the ranch, are experienced beagle parents—this yard was definitely secure. I had to remind myself of that several times over the weekend when I tried to count dogs and came up short. It is not easy to count twenty-three dogs in motion, especially when half of them are beagles.

Chris joined me outside and handed me a pooper scooper. "I've already done this about a hundred times, so you're up."

"Right. Twenty-three dogs means a lot of poop. You have made that point a few times."

"And they don't nicely go out to the ends of the property to do their business. It's mostly right here on the front lawn."

"Great. Got it."

I got to work. From the looks of things, each dog was constantly pooping. Chris had already done rounds and I was still only able to go a few feet before scooping up another pile. (An entirely different, perhaps more authentic, "dealing with shit" at Thanksgiving?) But even trailing around in the dark scooping up dog poop, I was content. Seeing these rescue dogs so happy and playful after all they'd been through not only in their past but in these last few days was rejuvenating. The resiliency of dogs never fails to inspire me. And let's face it, I could use a little resiliency myself. So what if it comes with a little (fine, a lot) of dog poop?

Geraldine stepped on to the porch. "Come help me. Get some of the dogs in the crates so we can feed them in there." She had a pronounced Irish accent that clipped some of her words, and she spoke very directly. That combined with the fact that she ran a restaurant empire often meant she spoke in commands. I'll take directness over passive-aggressive or just plain passive any day. (Are there alternatives? Hmm. Discuss amongst yourselves. I'm not aware of any.)

"Which dogs?"

"Any of 'em. Just make sure Rocco is one of 'em. E's a bit food aggressive."

I moved back to the garage and began to corral dogs into the crates. I could see there was a bit of a system—ten crates would allow ten dogs to eat separately. Did we feed them ten at a time? That might work. But how would I keep track of which ten were already fed? There were so many beagles and many of them were very hard to tell apart. And beagles especially were not about to admit they'd already had dinner and defer to their unfed compatriot.

No, the beagles would be sneaking into the crates scarfing up as many meals as we put down. At least Rocco—a big Rhodesian Ridgeback and German shepherd mix—would be easy to identify. I grabbed his collar and led him into an extra-large crate. He seemed to know this meant "food." He went easily in, turned, and sat, watching expectantly.

Geraldine had set up a feeding station on top of one of the crates, a make-shift table of sorts. She scooped kibble into bowls and handed them to me. I took each one and slid it into the crate. Once the ten crates each had a dog and bowl of food, she kept handing me bowls.

"Just put these down for the rest of them?" I said.

"Yeah. Just spread 'em out. It's all we can do."

This would be interesting. No wonder we needed to crate Rocco if the others were going to be on a sort of honor system.

Chris had taken our two into the bathroom to be fed separately. They definitely were not used to eating with this many dogs around and could not be trusted not to steal food, and that was not likely to go over well. Plus, they ate a different brand of food, and switching their diet for four days would wreak havoc on their digestion, bad in any situation but more so with this many dogs traipsing around.

I placed bowls of kibble on the ground, as far apart as I could, and was quickly trailed by eleven hungry dogs. I'd maneuver to get the bowl directly in front of one dog who would quickly stick its snout in the bowl and begin snarfing up food as I twisted to redirect any nearby snout to another bowl. Twist, place bowl, twist, step, quickly place a bowl, turn, step, place another bowl, step over a dog, twist, place a bowl, cha-cha-cha. Somehow, it worked and everyone got a bowl. Geraldine and I stood in the midst of this ragtag gang of dogs, ready to redirect if someone tried to venture from their own bowl. They were then herded outside until eventually we were able to open the crates and release all the dogs. I may have yelled *"Release the hounds"* more than once. (Come on, you know you would have too.)

As the dogs emptied their bowls, the dishes were picked up and stacked back on top of the crate. The whole process took less than twenty minutes. Impressive. I think if we had been feeding twenty people it would have taken days. But maybe not. Geraldine did run restaurants. I couldn't help but think there would have been more fighting had this been a human family of twenty-plus (or is that just me?).

"Now it's time for their medicines," Geraldine said.

Okay, right. There's more. I followed her back into the house.

The medicine routine was much more elaborate as the dogs had a variety of health conditions that required differing ministrations. Some medicines were simply squirted into the dogs' mouths; others were pills rolled into a special meatball concoction Geraldine had made and stored in a large container in the refrigerator. The trick would be getting the right medicine in the right dog, since the meatballs were sure to bring many volunteers, including those ever-sneaky beagles. Thankfully, there were no needles involved, and with a little maneuvering, hip-checking, and collar-holding, we were able to get all the correct dogs properly medicated.

"One last run outside," Geraldine said.

We marched outside with the dogs. Again, those that could joyously ran about, chased each other, and the beagles among them howled enthusiastically, including our two. I smiled watching them and laughed out loud when five or six of them came careening around the side of the house and ran figure eights on the lawn, slipping and sliding, rolling over and springing back up to rejoin the chase. I chased them for a bit and snapped about sixty-two hundred photos on my phone, but it was getting cold and we still had to get dinner for ourselves.

While Geraldine and I corralled the dogs into the house, Chris did one more round on pooper scooper duty. I don't think he was singing "Feces Farm is the place to be . . . farm living is the life for me" the way I'd been singing "Goodbye city life!"

Fed, medicated, exercised, and having done their constitutionals, the dogs settled back in the house. Five went back into Geraldine's room, which also had three large dog beds in addition to the now dog-covered human bed. Percival retired to our room in his usual Garbo-style "I vant to be alone," and the rest of the dogs clambered onto dog beds or parts of the couch. Roe chose the back of the couch so he could continue looking out the window and dreaming of his next ranch romp.

While I initially worried there weren't enough beds and comfortable spots for everyone, the dogs seemed to figure it out quickly enough, and soon a symphony of snores could be heard.

I'd lost track of time—seven? Eight? Nighttime was all I knew. We'd been busy since I arrived.

After our own dinner, the humans wiggled into spots on the couch (picking up a dog and then putting the dog back down on our laps after we sat), anticipating spending a relaxing couple of hours drinking wine, snacking, talking, listening to music and doggie dream noises.

"Thank you, guys, for being here," Geraldine said, curled up in the corner of the couch, cradling a glass of wine.

"No problem at all. I love it. This is perfect. I mean, not the fire and the evacuation and all, but this is a pretty great night," I said.

Geraldine and Chris both looked dubious.

"I'm sure ya 'ad better things to do," she said.

"I can't think of anything better. And honestly, we had no plans."

Even though I knew that being with either of our families would have been messy, tense, and generally unenjoyable, it still hurt to think we truly had no Thanksgiving plans. And I was very much grieving Daphne. Yet the truth was, this was a good place to be. For me, and for Geraldine and the dogs. Mostly I felt warm and content. If I could just not think too much about what we're not doing, who was not there with us, where we were not welcome, I'd be fine. I'd be better than fine if I could just stay in the moment—like these dogs were doing, like dogs always do.

There's nothing like an evening spent fireside, with friends, a glass or two of wine, and a whole lot of dogs to soothe one's heart and mind. I sunk down into the couch, leaning up against Chris and petting Toots, who'd snuggled in on my lap.

We were all in bed by ten, much earlier than Chris and I normally went to bed. But we were exhausted. I fell into a deep, peaceful sleep, with Roe up against my right leg, and Chris and Percival to the left of me.

I woke with the sun. I didn't mean to stay awake; I was only going to step out of our room and cross the hall to the bathroom, but this seemingly simple act started a chain reaction, waking a household full of dogs. A herd of them headed toward me, with the *taptaptap* of their nails on the floor, and a breeze stirring from the rapid wagging of a dozen tails. I was instantly energized. It's hard to resist that many wagging tails, wiggling butts, and wide brown eyes. I ducked into the bathroom and got the door closed with only two of them joining me. When I came out, the furry crowd awaited me, tails wagging and heads tilted. The decision to stay up was an easy one. I could always nap later, and it was unlikely they were going to settle back down. They clearly had expectations.

After I threw on my yoga pants, T-shirt, sweatshirt ("Eat Plants. Drink Wine."), and tennis shoes, I opened the front door, let the dogs amble out (or in Roe's case, race out), and went back inside to make a pot of coffee. I watched the dogs from the large front window while the coffee brewed.

The sky was a beautiful mango orange with streaks of lavender. Cacti pricked the horizon. The dewy, green lawn, surprisingly lush for what it had been through these last few days, was dotted with tri-colored dogs, black and tan dogs, white dogs, big dogs, small dogs, floppy-eared dogs, roly-poly dogs, jumping dogs, lounging dogs, happy dogs, and streaks of bright color from their collars. I poured a cup of coffee and headed outside, warming my hands on the mug.

I sat on the wooden bench on the front porch as the dogs continued to run and chase, or meander and sniff, or sit and watch—whatever they liked. Why had no one ever said to me, "You'll be a morning person when you have twenty-three dogs to care for"? I might have looked forward to it. I might have even believed them.

Eventually, Percival came out, leaving Chris and Roe sleeping in our room, and joined me on the bench. He's a playful pup, but he loves humans and one-on-one time most. He is also a very handsome dog. He has dark brown, almost black, almond-shaped eyes, that looked to be rimmed with eyeliner, and a perpetual puppy look to him, even though he was seven years old—mid-life for a beagle. His joyful personality and confidence—he knows he's loved by all—only added to his charms. Given his devotion to Chris, though, I did not get a lot of one-on-one time with Percival. This was a special treat.

"Hey, Percy-pie, you doing good?" I scratched his chest and he looked up at me, tongue flicking in his half-kiss way. "Yeah, this is pretty nice, isn't it?" I rubbed his head, scratched behind his ears, and he leaned into me. We both watched the sun continue its rise as the other dogs sniffed and roamed about.

Soon Roe came racing up to us, stopped in front of the bench, and stood looking at Percival, wagging his tail rapidly and doing a half-bow—a clear invitation to play. Percival leaped from the bench, and the Beagle Boys were off and running. *Happy Thanksgiving, boys.*

I grabbed a second cup of coffee and my journal, but I didn't write then. I wanted to simply watch these dogs.

The next three days went on like this. We had no meal schedule, or any schedule at all, except for what needed to be done for the dogs: the regular feedings, treats, constitutionals, and medications. In between all of that was the pooper scooper patrols, which seemed never-ending, just as Chris had predicted, but lent their own contemplative realism as counterpoint to the idyllic scene.

Chris made the vegan paella for our Thanksgiving dinner, following our tradition for either Christmas or Thanksgiving the last couple of years. All other meals were a buffet of items, brought out on the kitchen island, and prepared haphazardly whenever someone felt like it. There was a lot of time to sit, read, journal, pet dogs, cuddle with Chris and the dogs (occasionally just one or the other), and sip coffee or wine, depending on the time of day (or more to the point, depending on whether anybody cared what time of day it was, and we did not). All the things I love most in life. It was easy to give thanks.

On Friday Geraldine spent most of the day on the phone with insurance companies. The fires were out, and her home had been spared, but it was covered in the pink phosphate fertilizer sprayed from planes as fire retardant. It was not yet safe to return. The Cornell rescue property had been partially burned, and the caretaker's house was a total loss. All people and animals had survived, however. Even the peacocks had been safely evacuated. We listened to her on the phone repeating to the various insurance companies what the damage was and what she needed. I was glad we could at least help in some small way, especially since being there was thoroughly enjoyable (okay, maybe not the poop patrol). Nothing like massive fires to give one a sense of gratitude for the simple things. (Days later, when Geraldine returned to her pink phosphate-covered home, she sent me a photo of a large decorative rock with the word "Gratitude" carved in it—covered in bright pink phosphate. Kind of on the nose, universe, dontcha think?)

When Percival got overwhelmed at the ranch or just needed his quiet time, he'd come back in the house, head to our bedroom and curl up on our bed. We noticed that Roe regularly came in and checked on him. Sometimes Percival would then leave with Roe and return to playing on the ranch. Other times, Roe would hop up on the bed next to Percival and they'd both nap. Less often, Roe just checked in, they would signal each other that all was fine, and Roe would return to his explorations while Percival continued to rest, or meditate, or whatever it was he did in his necessary alone time. They seem to have an understanding, and they had formed a team amid this rescue dog-pile ranch. I was also becoming attached. (Okay, fine. I'd been attached the moment I saw Roe.)

"These dogs are awesome together," Chris said as he joined me on the front porch Friday evening and handed me a glass of wine.

"I know. It's amazing we haven't had any dog fights and everyone—well, everyone except Rocco and Baron, is getting along."

"No, I meant Roe and Percival. You've noticed they're bonding, right?"

Right. Yes. I had. "Yeah. Hard to miss that."

He turned to look at me. "I really think we should adopt Roe. It's like it was with Daphne. Why not take the dog we know is easygoing and gets along with Percival? They're great together."

I looked away. "I know. But I said we'd foster to adopt Poppy. And I want another girl—one that can come and go with me. Roe and Percival will always want to stay together."

"And they should. I know you always want to help the dogs with the difficult pasts, but it's okay to do things the easy way sometimes. You know BFP has a ton of people lined up to adopt those dogs. Poppy will find a home. Roe's older and has a heart murmur. He needs us."

"I know," I said. I took a sip of wine. "I know he does. And you're right. He'll have a harder time getting adopted than Poppy will."

On cue, Roe bounded up and hopped onto the bench with us. He looked to both of us, turning his head to look us each in the eye. *Oh, those eyes.*

Chris said what it seemed Roe was thinking, "Please just consider this."

"I will. I am." I petted Roe and he snuggled in next to me. But soon Percival too came out of the house, and with one quick exchanged glance, Roe leapt from the bench and the Beagle Boys were off and running.

Chris looked at me with one eyebrow raised.

"I know. I know," I said.

Early Saturday morning, Chris left to return to Paso Robles. He had to work Saturday afternoon—winery tasting rooms are busy on holiday weekends. I stayed behind with Roe and Percival and of course Geraldine and her crew of twenty-one. We continued our semi-routine, though now with Chris gone I had to be the one to separate and feed Roe and Percival in the bathroom, then leave them in our bedroom before feeding the rest of the dogs with Geraldine.

By then the dogs had also fallen into a pattern—each dog had its place in the living room or one of the bedrooms. Mr. Man, a chubby beagle, often staked out the couch and attempted to keep off any trespassers, but we assured him that couldn't happen. Without any influence from us, he had already decided Roe was cool and willingly shared the couch with him, without so much as a grumble. But the other dogs required us to run interference to get them a spot on the couch.

Georgie, a beautiful basset hound, patrolled the kitchen searching for food, and she often stood up on her stubby back legs, stretching her long body as far as she could to sniff at the countertops and perhaps reach some morsel of food. Ariel, another beagle mix—perhaps with pit bull—could always be found trailing after Geraldine. And Jack, the blind, deaf, and flipper-footed black beagle, usually chose the bed nearest the door and was frequently the first one to want to head outside. He never went far and often went in circles, but his joy in the outdoors was obvious. We kept a more careful watch on him of course, as occasionally he'd bump into a car tire or a table leg, and sometimes he'd get himself stuck somewhere he couldn't find a way out of, but always he wanted to explore. We let him. *You go, Jack. You be you.*

I was especially happy to see one of Geraldine's adopted beagles, Maddie, being comfortable on her selected dog bed, shared with another beagle, and allowing me to pet her from time to time. Maddie was a dog I had helped Charlotte rescue, along with eighteen other hounds, from a hunter who had dementia and had stopped caring properly for these dogs long before his family noticed. The younger dogs in the group were nearly feral; the older ones were frightened but far better socialized and willing to trust humans. You could almost tell by the age and behavior of the dogs when the hunter's mental decline started.

Charlotte had been contacted by the hunter's son after a neighbor alerted him to the problems with the dogs and the human. The son gave Charlotte all of twenty-four hours to take the dogs or, he claimed, he would start shooting them. No rescue can prepare for an influx of that many dogs that quickly without a lot of help. Charlotte had called me; I called Lisa Price, who ran Priceless Pets, another rescuer with a penchant for beagles, and the next morning at sunrise Lisa and I were in a van stacked with crates and headed to Meade Canine Rescue to pick up as many of the dogs as we could; the rest would stay with Charlotte until they were adopted. The dogs were gorgeous—beagles and coonhounds, all tri-colored, varying ages (the hunter had stopped spaying and neutering the dogs), and all scared. We'd only been given the names for two of the older dogs, so we gave the rest wine-related names: Pinot Grigio, Merlot, Roussanne, and so on, naming them as we picked them up and put them into the crates in the van. At the time, I was reminded of one of my childhood pastimes: I collected little plastic horses, dogs, and farm animals together with my best friend, Suzanne. We would spend hours painstakingly naming each one of them and arranging them on the "farm" we'd set up on a patch of grass, and I would come up with their backstory. That was the entire game. With those hunting dogs, though, the stakes were a little higher.

With the traumatized hounds all loaded in crates in her van, Lisa and I had driven back down to Southern California and her rescue, Priceless Pets, where her husband and daughter had met us and helped safely unload and settle in each of the fourteen dogs we brought back. I didn't get home until after one in the morning and, as usual, didn't mind in the least.

Geraldine eventually adopted Marsanne from the group of dogs that Charlotte kept and changed her name to Maddie. Maddie had taken a long time to adjust, choosing mostly to just stay in Geraldine's bedroom in her Malibu home, safe on the bed without interacting with any other humans. That was why I was particularly pleased to see that she was not traumatized by the evacuation. She was hanging out with the other dogs and willing to be petted, though I could see she was skeptical, so sometimes I just sat next to her, letting her be.

Coffee on the front porch as the sun rose and the dogs roamed was something I quickly came to look forward to. So much silence and possibility—peaceful and hopeful. I journaled a bit, and sometimes I walked around with the dogs, but mostly I sat and watched the day awaken through the mist.

On Sunday morning, my last morning there, this hour of bliss was also my time for contemplation about Roe and Poppy and what "the right thing to do" might be.

Chris was right, and I knew that. Roe was an easy dog and seemed already to belong to us. Just like that, we'd created a pack. I began to wonder if I could fulfill my commitment to Beagle Freedom Project instead by fostering Poppy until they got her adopted. BFP, wisely, liked to have fosters who were experienced with dogs with traumatic pasts and who had another dog that could teach the new rescue how to be a dog. Percival even seemed more "dog-like" with Roe around—well, except for his Garbo moments (that was very human, and something to which I could well relate).

Even after only a week of them together, I couldn't imagine breaking up the bromance that was Roe and Percival, and frankly, that plaintive look of Roe's and the way he insisted on sleeping right up next to me would make it hard to break up my own love affair with this dog.

I rolled the facts around in my head. Roe's heart murmur diagnosis likely did mean he would have a much harder time getting adopted. Older dogs with a preexisting condition were not the first choice of most adopters. Whereas

Poppy, a two-to-three-year-old beagle rescued from the Chinese dog meat trade by an organization as well-known as Beagle Freedom Project, would, as Chris had said, no doubt have a long line of people waiting to adopt her. If there is one thing I had learned in my years of rescue work, it's that people love a good backstory. And there was the obvious fact that Roe and Percival really enjoyed each other's company.

Maybe we could get away with having three dogs until Poppy got adopted. A month? Two months?

This seemed reasonable to me. Charlotte hadn't asked when we were bringing Roe back, and other than my one or two social media posts saying Roe was available for adoption, I don't think there was any effort being made to get him adopted. She likely knew we'd be adopting him, but I'd let her know for certain. Right after I checked with our landlord in Paso Robles. They were dog people, but our lease allowed two dogs. I'd need to ask if we could foster a third for a little while. And if I took Poppy down to Riverside with me each time, there would only be one dog in Riverside every two weeks, so no violation of the homeowner's association rules. This could work.

I took a sip of coffee, still hot, with steam rising in the cool morning air, and watched the dogs play. If I could live a life just like this—quiet ranch home, beautiful vistas, and twenty-three rescue dogs as family—I'd do it in a heartbeat. I'd rescue them all.

We'll just start with these two.

5

TRANSITIONS

In most places on an early December morning, damp gray air, intermittent drizzles of rain, and temperatures in the low sixties, would be considered mild weather. But we were in Palm Springs, land of palm trees, mid-century buildings, bright colors, and celebrities of old. Palm Springs—where the average December temperature is supposed to be seventy degrees, with clear blue skies, and abundant sunshine. That's why people spent winters there. But because I'd planned with a tight time schedule, it was raining (the universe thing again). And we had been awake since 5:00 A.M. So I was complaining. A lot.

Fortunately for Chris, though, I was complaining only in my head (though my face was probably giving it all away; it always does). After all, Chris had awoken and driven us both out to Palm Springs that morning, and it wasn't his father we were helping. He was there to support and help me. When we dealt with our respective families, we preferred to do it together.

My Thanksgiving weekend joy and sense of calm had dissipated quickly. I stood in the middle of my father's mostly empty home, waiting for the movers to arrive, pack up the rest of his belongings, and take them on to my brother Jay's home in Missouri. I had promised I would see that it was all taken care of—assured my father he could just leave with his three dogs and all he and Jay could load into a rented U-Haul; I would get the rest of it sent to him when the house sold. I wanted to make the move easier for my father, as I could see he was struggling trying to make it all happen. He was seventy-seven years old, not the easiest time to be making such a life change.

But who leaves Palm Springs, California, and moves to Missouri in the early winter? That decision was probably another clue that Dad was stressed and not thinking things through. Too late to worry about that, though. He had been in Missouri for almost a month, and the house had sold much more quickly than we had anticipated. So, there I stood, coffee cup in hand, looking around a nearly empty house, wondering if I should take some personal item just to have something because, well—because who knew?

I had been away at college when my maternal grandmother died and consequently had no mementos of her—what my grandfather didn't keep went to my older sister and my mother, in that order. When my grandfather himself died I was a new lawyer, living in Riverside, not far away but far enough, apparently; he left me a small cash gift, listed twelfth in his will, well after my mother and siblings, the Catholic Church, a neighbor, and, as I remember it, any random stranger walking by. (A part of me knows he did this based on his perceptions of need, and no doubt because he thought I was "fine"—as everyone knew me to be, always. The other part of me is hurt. But I'm totally over it. Totally.) I don't even know who got his personal items; I have only a few photos given to me by my mother as a peace offering much, much later, when she also gave me a ring of my grandmother's. My dad's parents died when he was two years old, so even he didn't have any mementos of them.

Like I said, loosely knit. I had to grab on to whatever thread I could—a few memories of my dad.

I texted my dad and asked if I could keep the tin bar signs: COSMO LOUNGE: WHERE SMART PEOPLE MEET, ROYAL KNIGHT DISTILLED DRY GIN, and AIRPORT 90 PROOF STRAIGHT WHISKEY, along with a metal reproduction of Elvis's *Girl Happy* movie poster. My dad worships Elvis, and during the seventies my parents had a red and black bar and game room, complete with shag carpet, a pool table and juke box, the customary neon bar signs, an animated Hamm's beer sign, and other alcohol-related décor. This was in the last house my parents and siblings (the original two) and I all lived in together before my parents' second divorce—the one that took—when I was fourteen. Bar signs and an Elvis sign seemed fitting enough mementos. Although, as I thought about it, those mementos in the house I was then standing in were more than likely from his life with his fourth wife, who had left him and their dogs the day after his seventy-fifth birthday. These were not likely from my childhood at all. But they were my dad's. *Good enough. Beggars can't be choosers, and all that.*

I continued to pace in the near empty house. Here was another plan gone awry.

The movers could only come on that particular day: December 6. Naturally, this was the same day we had been told that Poppy and the rest of the beagles would be arriving from China. I was to come pick her up that evening—of course both things had to happen on the same day. Of course they did.

I had taken the day off work. My plan was to be up at 5:00 A.M., drive forty-five miles east to my dad's house, be done with the movers by noon, drive back home, take a nap, then head sixty-five miles west to Los Angeles to be at the designated rescue house by five that evening. The Southern California traffic gods would really need to be on my side for this one, but that wasn't likely to happen. The morning drizzle was supposed to turn to rain with a chance of thunder and lightning by evening. Any sort of inclement weather sent those same traffic gods into monastic retreat where they couldn't be reached and certainly not be bothered with the idiocy that is California drivers in the rain. This was probably one more reason I should have bowed out from fostering Poppy. But I did not. I could not.

When we had returned from the Rescue Ranch/Feces Farm the Sunday after Thanksgiving, Chris and I talked more about adopting Roe. We agreed, of course, to that much, but he still thought my fostering Poppy was a bad idea.

"You won't be able to let her go," he had said.

"I will. I'll have to. We can't have three dogs."

"Why put yourself through that? You're a foster failure. You'll be smitten in two seconds and want to keep her."

"But I can't keep her, and I really want to foster. I know it will be hard, but it helps save a life."

His face had remained skeptical, but he stayed quiet. At this point he'd been with me long enough to know that my plans were likely to fall apart, but neither of us could guess which way they would fall. I suppose that's why I kept planning, despite the overall uselessness of such behavior. The expression "a goal without a plan is just a dream" resonated with me, so I planned—even though it seemed that for me a goal *with* a plan was a nightmare.

Not seeing any choice, I had taken the day off work to handle the end of my father's California life and the beginning of Poppy's California life. Because such was my life.

The movers arrived right at 7:00 A.M. and quickly got to work. Chris and I showed them around the house, pointed out what needed packing, and then I sat on the lone recliner in the near-empty living room while Chris sat on a barstool, waiting.

"It was a good idea to leave Roe and Percival at home for the morning," I said.

"Yeah, hard to imagine them having to sit here on leashes with strangers coming and going, and it's not exactly dog-walking weather," he said.

"Hopefully we get out of here in time for us all to nap. What time are you planning to leave for Paso?"

"As soon as I can. The earlier the better." His voice echoed in the empty, tile-floored living room.

This made sense. That was the other thing we had decided—that I was going alone to LA to pick up Poppy. Roe and Percival, understandably, wouldn't be allowed at the home where the new dogs were arriving, and it seemed unfair to leave them in the car. Chris could hardly be expected to drive sixty miles from Riverside to LA to pick up one dog, then back to Riverside to pick up two other dogs, then back up 260 miles to Paso Robles—especially not on a day that started with a forty-mile drive into Palm Springs at 5:00 A.M. Instead, after our Palm Springs duties were over, Chris would take Roe and Percival north to Paso Robles and I would head west to Los Angeles to pick up Poppy. We figured two weeks for Poppy and me alone in Riverside would be a good adjustment period and not too overwhelming for her. I was worried she wouldn't have the guidance of either Roe or Percival during that time, but the logistics were difficult to work out. I needed to be in Riverside and Chris needed to be in Paso Robles. He'd only come down south to help with my father's move, not to help me pick up a foster dog he didn't think I should be fostering.

One of the movers came into the living room, "We can't pack these." He handed me a small, heavy box. I opened it.

"Okay, right." I handed the box of bullets to Chris. The look of the boxes struck me as oddly incongruous. Bright yellow and orange swirls and cheerful fonts didn't seem to go with "this is ammunition for killing." *Am I the only one that sees this? Is irony right and truly dead?*

The mover returned with two more boxes of bullets. "Sorry, we just can't."

I was not aware of this rule and wondered if there were also guns left behind. My father, true to his Southern roots, was an avid gun collector. My brother and I were both taught to shoot at an early age and proper gun safety along with it, but I still didn't like guns. I didn't even like holding the ammunition. Which was unfortunate because the movers brought me another four boxes.

"Is the safe empty?" he asked.

He was by now wondering the same thing I was—had dad at least taken the guns out of the large gun safe in his closet? Because if the movers couldn't transport ammunition, I felt quite certain they couldn't move guns. *He would not have left them behind. He would have to have taken the guns. Because I don't want to take guns with me.*

"Yes, it's empty." I said. *And it better be, because I have no idea how to open it.*

I looked at Chris and he shrugged. Not a lot we could do, as I didn't want to be driving home with a car full of guns. And I darn sure didn't want to be taking them with me to pick up a nervous little beagle. Jay, my brother, surely would have taken the guns. He had once worked in a gun shop; he would know the rules, laws, culture . . . whatever it was that applied. Though I could see how he and my dad might have found it funny to leave the guns for me to deal with if transporting them was illegal. I was the straitlaced one in the family—the one least likely to cause trouble or break the law (because I was "fine"—I couldn't be "fine" and also in jail). That and the fact that guns made me uncomfortable would be an irresistible comedic setup from my dad and brother's points of view.

But surely, they took the guns. They probably couldn't see driving halfway across the country without guns in any event.

Chris put the pretty little bullet boxes in his car, along with the vintage metal bar signs Dad had texted we could keep.

Two minutes after the movers left, my dad's dogsitter came by with a box of things she had thought he would want. She had removed them from the house so no one would steal them. The box had silverware, an "as seen on TV" food chopper, some mail, shelf lining, and a handful of keys to who only knew what. I did not think this was anything anyone would steal, but I thanked her nonetheless. I put all that in Chris's car too.

"What are we going to do with this?" Chris said.

"No idea. But be gentle. That may be my inheritance."

We drove away from the empty house in the rain.

Usually I can sleep in a car easily. Not that morning. Once back at home in Riverside, I again unsuccessfully tried to nap but gave up. I freshened up a bit, but there was no reason to do much more than that just to stand in the rain with a dozen smelly, wet beagles. There was no reason to continue pacing either, since there was no telling if the sixty-mile drive would take one hour or three. I looked around the house for the things I'd need for Poppy.

This was a good distraction, I thought. I could focus on the dog and not on the fact that my dad no longer lived nearby. The moving van had pulled away and that was that. Roe had been a distraction from the loss of Daphne, and now Poppy would be a distraction from the loss of my dad. Well, loss of proximity anyway. I mean, he was still alive. (*Note to self: check with therapist on all this distraction. Is this unhealthy avoidance? Second note to self: find a therapist.*)

But this wasn't a distraction. This was a dog. A traumatized dog who needed my help, my attention, my focus.

I had to focus.

I grabbed a leash, one of Percival's harnesses, a blanket, and some treats, trying to cover the basics, worried our new Poppy might be stuck in the car for hours on end. With a quick kiss to Chris, Roe, and Percival (maybe not in that order), I headed out at 2:30 in the afternoon, hoping to arrive by the designated 5:00 P.M. start time.

My emotions, like my thoughts, were all over the place, pinging and dashing and darting faster than the raindrops on my windshield. *My dad is officially gone from California. Daphne died. I wasn't there with her when she died. I let her down. I am on my way to pick up a new, frightened dog. It's too soon. I already have another new dog who now will be with Chris for two weeks. I am so tired. I'm cold. My dad is gone. Chris and Percival and Roe are going back to Paso Robles. I shouldn't be getting this other dog. How will my dad do in Missouri? I can't picture him in Missouri. I am excited to see these newly rescued dogs though. If only it wasn't so cold. If only I wasn't so tired. I miss Daphne.*

The drive, and my brain leaps and swirls, reminded me of driving Daphne from Paso Robles to Orange County for one of her chemo treatments while having a conference call about the merger of my law firm. I couldn't focus then either.

Driving to LA with no idea what to expect. Maybe this is all too much. Maybe this is an unhealthy response to Daphne's unexpected death. Or to my dad leaving. Or maybe this is exactly what I need. Or none of the above. Maybe it's just nuts.

And none of that mattered. I had made a commitment, and now I was on my way to pick up a beagle who was likely just being unloaded from an airplane after a long, stressful flight from China. I had to pull it together. It was fair to say the dog would have had a more difficult day than I by the time we finally met.

An hour and a half later—one full hour early—I arrived at the address I had been given for the great beagle pickup. I stepped through the front gate and a young, bearded man carrying a box nodded to me and then jerked his head in what I took was a motion for me to head to the backyard. I made my way around the house, through the side gate, and into the backyard.

The rain had drenched the lawn area where the dogs would be brought in and released, so the staff and volunteers were working to set up the garage-turned-event-space into a welcoming, celebratory room for the dogs' much-anticipated arrival and ceremonial cage release. Public relations don't get much better than videos showing the rescue and release of these dogs. A rainbow-colored banner strung across the back wall read "Ringo's Rockin' Rescue," which I learned later was because someone had sponsored the cost of this rescue and named it after his beloved late dog Ringo. There were tall narrow banners on either side of the rainbow one, both with the BFP logo; one read "Rescue. Rehab. Repeat." and featured Chi Chi, a golden retriever rescued from the Chinese dog meat trade. Chi Chi had lost the bottom half of all four legs (they had been tied together too tightly for too long), but she had been a joyful soul, able to walk with the help of prosthetics and vigorous therapy. She had passed away recently from cancer, leaving her adopters bereft. I had never met her, but I knew her story. She was beloved not just among the BFP adopters and fosters but also by the larger dog-adoring world. She had been given the American Humane Hero Dog Award for her work as a therapy dog and her example of perseverance and courage.

The second banner read "Rescue. Protect. Love." (Cool concepts, right? And maybe a summary of my day.) I was pretty certain the dog featured was Rocket, one of the early rescues when BFP first started. Yep. That was what this was all about. Rescue. Protect. Love. *That's a good reminder. That's what I was doing here.*

I stood around wondering how to make myself useful. I chatted with a few staff people (all different since the days when we adopted Percival; BFP had been a much smaller organization back then) and helped string some twinkle lights down the pathway the dogs would be coming down. That's when I noticed through the windows that there seemed to be several people in the house itself. Maybe I was supposed to go inside? Maybe the guy had jerked his head toward the house and not the backyard? Just like that, the worries were back. Nothing about this felt right. The weather was depressing. I was out of place, useless, in the way. And we already had two dogs. *I shouldn't have volunteered. I shouldn't be here.*

Give me twenty-three unknown dogs on a Thanksgiving weekend over even a half-dozen humans (known or unknown) anytime. Chris has a running joke about producing a reality television show called *Terrorizing Teresa*, that would involve sending me to places and events known for their crowds of people—Times Square on New Year's Eve, Vegas on Halloween, Carnival in Rio, Burning Man somewhere in the desert, those sorts of things. He's kidding, of course, but such is my discomfort with groups of people, especially if there are no rules, no assigned seats, no "program." And here was a situation where I could not determine the program nor create a plan.

The back door to the house opened and as two people stepped out, I could see that there were indeed several people milling about inside the warm and cozy house. I was supposed to have gone through the front door like a human, not around the back like a stray animal.

I made my way inside and found coffee, snacks, and excited people talking. There was a registration table near the front door where I should have checked in and received the fosters' bag of supplies and goodies. I could have been warm and dry for the past hour by simply going to the front door. Everyone—men, women, and children—had on a BFP T-shirt or sweatshirt. I pulled a T-shirt out of the bag I had been given and quickly realized it was at least two sizes too small. I would not be dressed like the rest of the group either. *Of course I wouldn't.* That's also when I noticed everyone had come in pairs or entire family units. Maybe Chris should have come with me. But what would we have done with Percival and Roe? *Why was this all feeling so uncomfortable? Why was I getting everything wrong? Why didn't I back out when I had the chance?*

I get this kind of thing wrong—these meaningful family moments—a lot. They sneak up on me and I think, "Oh, this. This is what families do. Huh." I remembered when I passed the bar exam and went to the swearing-in ceremony at the Disneyland Hotel (yeah, imagine a bunch of lawyers at the happiest place on earth; irony had not yet died). I went with my then boyfriend (later husband, later still ex-husband), who was also there to be sworn in. He was an only child, an immigrant from what was then Yugoslavia, whose parents' wildest dream was to see him become a lawyer in America. I had plenty of family (truly, more than was necessary; at that point the count would have been four parents, three siblings, a grandfather, perhaps a step-grandmother), and still neither of us had thought to invite any family members. Everyone else in the room had swarming relatives, friends, flowers, photographers, champagne, and general celebratory things going on. They also seemed to know about the free passes to the amusement park that day for all inductees. We got sworn in and returned to work . . . in separate cars. I seem then, now, always, unable to recognize family moments until they are upon me. Or I'm just too determined to do things on my own—or maybe these are the same thing.

At any rate, I was alone.

I hung back, sipping coffee and snacking on the vegan cookies on offer until eventually I saw a BFP board member named Valerie I had met before, though I couldn't for the life of me tell you when. Good enough! I approached her and reintroduced myself.

"Yes, of course. The author!"

Okay, well that's a nice way to be known. "Yes. Percival's mom," I said, because that's also a nice way to be known.

Then I saw a couple come through the front door. Deia and Aaron had adopted Percival's brother, now known as River, and I knew them from a couple of rescue group reunions and of course, from Facebook. They would be fostering from this same rescue as well, which was a wonderful coincidence. *Okay, things were getting better.*

Finally, Shannon Keith, the founder of Beagle Freedom Project, welcomed everyone, gave a quick speech, and explained that the dogs were on their way from the Los Angeles airport. The moment we had all been waiting for was almost upon us—soon we'd see the first steps of freedom.

I, like thousands of others, had seen the videos of the beagles BFP had rescued from laboratories as they were released from their crates and able to walk on grass for the first time, freely. I had watched Percival's rescue video countless times: twelve beagles rescued from a laboratory in northern California on December 11, 2012, released from their crates, free to set foot on grass, move about unrestrained, and begin to trust. That video, like all the BFP rescue videos, was a sentimental tear-jerker. The volunteers all wore Santa hats and the dogs were all given reindeer and holiday names (Percival had been Comet . . . he's much more of a Percival). Some of the dogs had adjusted quickly, stepping gingerly onto the lawn then running and playing, while others were too frightened to move.

The most recent rescue video I had seen had been the last China rescue—the one that launched me on this quest for a female lemon beagle. I had never seen a freedom celebration live, however. I had never witnessed a dog rescued from a laboratory or the dog meat trade get its first taste of freedom, of its new life. This was the part I had been looking forward to. I decided to put my apprehensions aside and enjoy this moment. This was a special occasion for some very lucky dogs. And soon I'd meet our Poppy girl.

We all shuffled into the backyard. The air was dank and the ground muddy, but the rain had stopped, at least temporarily. The sky was dark, but the yard was well lit, and the twinkle lights added a touch of cheerful whimsy to offset the weather. Shannon asked for some couples to help carry the crates of dogs in and announced that the van was due to arrive any minute. Again, I wished Chris was with me so we could volunteer to carry their crates in, never mind that I probably couldn't lift my share of the weight.

I got out my phone and tried to find a place to stand so I could see the dogs as they came in and take a few photos. The rest of the excited foster families did the same.

I wasn't sure how this would work. I didn't know if we picked a dog or if they had been assigned to us. Megan had told me she put me down for a female lemon beagle, but I was uncertain what that meant. One of the emails had mentioned we should spend time with the dogs and see if there was one in particular we felt a connection with. I had never met a beagle I didn't con-nect with, so that wasn't a helpful instruction. I tried to tell myself it didn't matter. I was going to foster, not adopt. Chris and I had decided that. We were keeping Roe and fostering Poppy, whoever she might be. I would just take whatever dog needed me. I'd give in to the universe this time (honestly, she's a bitch to be battling all the time).

A couple came walking through the yard carrying a crate with a large tri-colored beagle. Then another couple with another crate. Then Curtis and his wife, Melody, a couple I had known for years through BFP, came through carrying a crate with two small beagles inside. I could see these were lemon beagles: tiny, huddled together in matching turquoise sweaters. They looked so small and so vulnerable, sticking close by each other in the back of the cage. Curtis and I had worked together on a few rescues—the kind where someone posts on Facebook about a dog needing help, and a ragtag rescue village steps up to pull the dog from the shelter (often Curtis), transport the dog (again, often Curtis, sometimes me), and get them to a safe environment (one of the many rescues I dealt with). Curtis and Melody were also regular volunteers with BFP and had several rescue dogs of their own, including Rocket, the dog on the "Rescue. Rehab. Repeat." banner, a sixteen-year old BFP rescue with Cushing's disease they had lovingly cared for and often brought to events. Those two tiny lemon beagles were in good hands being carried to freedom by Curtis and Melody.

The parade of crates kept coming. They were set down inside the converted garage in front of the big welcome banner, side by side. Eight crates total. Eleven adult dogs and some puppies with their mother.

The doors to the crates all faced toward us and we humans, desperate for a glimpse, so wanting to reach out and console these frightened pups, all gathered in front of them, phone cameras trained on them, recording every moment. The small room quickly filled with warmth, beagle noises, and the familiar musty smell of wet dog. Wisely, Shannon asked us all to back up and explained that they would open the crates one at a time and let the dogs come out on their own schedule. We were not to make loud noises or quick motions, and we should know that after a long flight and the time at the airport, it was likely they would all be going "potty" very soon after they were released.

As she talked, one of the beagles began to howl rambunctiously. *AR-AR-AR-AROOOOOO!* It was the one adult male in the group, a big tri-colored boy. He stood, wagging his tail and urging someone, anyone, to open the crate.

I loved him instantly.

That demanding howl and spirited personality were deeply reminiscent of Seamus, the diabolically cute beagle we'd had before Daphne—the one who saw me through my cancer battle and showed me how to do it. I laughed at the howling beagle's antics.

That one. I'll take that one. How fun would that be?

Wait. Fun for me, not fun for my neighbors at the condo. And the neighbor on one side already complained about anything he could and was constantly shooting disapproving looks at us, our gardener, and anyone who came within glaring distance (the poor mailman!).

So, no. Not the howler. Not even when he howled again and had the whole crowd laughing. *Just like Seamus. No. Don't. Bad. Oh, this was going to be hard.* I'd long ago gotten over a young girl's penchant for bad boys, but misbehaving dogs will always have my heart.

Kevin, the adoption and foster coordinator for BFP, first opened the crate of everyone's favorite howler (after Seamus of course). The beagle came out willingly, walked, sniffed around, and in a matter of seconds peed and pooped nonchalantly and voluminously. Kevin began to open the rest of the crates and we humans tried as best we could not to crowd forward, while the beagles all worked up the courage to leave their crates.

It was frenzied and joyful, with the dogs and humans scrambling about, exploring, trying to figure things out—the beagles restrained by fear and their new strange circumstances, and the humans restrained (barely) by politeness and respect for these pups. But truly, all humans were vibrating with the urgent need to pet and comfort one of these beautiful creatures who'd come from such horrific circumstances. I was no different. I leaned forward, willing one of them to come to me so I could shower it in love.

Near me was a crate that held the mama beagle and two of her pups, though the pups were nearly as large as she was. Mama did not come out of her crate. She would walk to the edge, look out, and return to the safety of the far back of the crate, hiding, hoping not to be seen and that her babies would do the same. Soon the male beagle, the howler, trotted over to check on them and boldly walked into the crate. He looked as though he was encouraging her, telling her it was okay, come on out and play! Mama allowed him in but wanted nothing to do with leaving the crate. *Thanks, but no thanks, buddy. Do you see all those people?* She hunkered down.

I quickly spotted another bigger, tri-colored female stepping out of her crate. When I saw her face I caught my breath. I immediately moved toward her. She had those big brown "root beer candy" eyes of my Daphne! *That one. Come see me, please!* I knelt, hoping she would come to me, making our bond instant and clear to all. I did not want to step in front of everyone or move forward too quickly, possibly scaring her, but my Daphne doppelganger did not seem to notice me in the crowd, and I needed her to. *How does she not know of our connection?* She moved toward someone else far to my right.

It's okay. It would be a bad idea to get a dog who looked so much like Daphne. I would cry every time I saw her. I'm crying now! I turned my attention away from her, for my sake and hers.

Kevin was opening the crate with the two little lemon beagle girls. They came out slowly, very shyly, and almost immediately ran behind the row of crates. With all the dogs now loose—all but mama and her pups outside their crates and exploring—it was hard to track any one dog. They seemed to be everywhere at once. And true to what we were told, they were peeing and pooping all over the place. BFP, a true PR machine, wisely edits the freedom videos to not show the massive amounts of urine and feces involved in these releases. *Maybe best Chris didn't come. I think he's had enough dog shit and piss for a while. He's temperamental like that.*

Humans and beagles were all ushered into the yard, where it was colder and damper but smelled decidedly better. People began to trail after their favored beagles and very soon I saw that my Daphne look-alike had an ardent fan. A couple in their thirties had followed her around, and eventually the man picked her up and held her. For the rest of the evening he stayed by her, petting her, talking to her, and very clearly falling in love. *Okay, so, good. She has a home. I won't make that mistake.* I fervently hoped they would post regular updates of her to the BFP adopters and fosters Facebook page.

The Seamus sound-alike also had a fan. A mom and her young son seemed to have attached themselves to him, and while mom may have been trying to redirect her son to a less rambunctious dog, the boy knew what he wanted.

I couldn't blame him. If you get a beagle, you must have a very good sense of humor. Mom was going to learn that soon. Her son had picked out quite a character.

Slowly I realized that we were indeed supposed to be choosing which dog we wanted. They weren't matching us up so much as letting us pick. I reminded myself, for the hundredth time that day, that I wasn't adopting, I was fostering, so I may as well let the others choose. I'd take the one that was left. They're all beagles. They're all fabulous. I couldn't lose. No one could.

As beagles and people paired off, I saw there were a few dogs still in the yard, unattached. One of them, staying as far away from people as she could, was one of the little lemon girls. I walked toward her. She cowered, but she did not run. I bent down to her and held my hand out. She stepped backward a few feet and then stopped, looking at me. She was tiny, by beagle standards. Her head was about half the size Daphne's had been. She was mostly white, with tan patches around her dark little eyes, staring back quizzically. I could see she was trying to overcome her fear, trying to figure out just what exactly had happened to her these last twenty-four hours. Her ears, floppy but not as long as an average beagle's, moved forward and just as quickly twitched back.

"It's okay, baby. I'm okay. You'll be fine, sweetie. It's all good from here on out," I said. I stayed put, squatted down, hand out, talking gently to her until she slowly stretched her head forward, sniffing at my hand, her back legs firmly planted. I petted the top of her head. But her bravery evaporated, and she bolted away. She moved farther into the backyard, skulking along the bushes.

I walked around a bit more, watching as families chose their dogs and posed for photos. I petted a few more beagles, talked to the happy couple who chose my root beer candy–eyed girl. Eventually I spotted my shy lemon girl again, still far in the back of the yard, up against a brick planter but no longer behind the bushes. I approached her slowly and sat on the damp brick wall beside her. She watched my every move, primed to bolt. I understood. There were plenty of people in my life I was primed to bolt from; heck, how many times had I wanted to bolt from this very event? I was able to pet her head, stroking down her back. Even with the protection of the little sweater she wore, I could feel her shaking. I bent down and scooped her up, bringing her up onto my lap in a quick but gentle motion. She struggled for a bit, but I held her closer, brought her in against my sweatshirt and held her firmly. I talked softly to her, promising it would all get better. I promised her a warm bed, treats, and some really good food before I realized I had picked my dog.

I was holding Poppy.

This was the dog that needed me. A female lemon beagle, just as planned.

I carried her around a bit, holding her close and talking quietly to her. When I saw Melody and Curtis, I asked if they could take a photo of us. Our first "freedom photo."

"Is that the one?" Curtis said.

"I think so. She's super frightened."

"Percival will show her around and get her all fixed up. She's so lucky! Look how cute that little thing is!" he said.

"I'm feeling pretty lucky, too. Thanks."

I found Megan and told her this was the dog I wanted to foster. Much to my surprise, she showed me a list of names I was to choose from. Where Percival's rescue buddies had been given reindeer and holiday names to coordinate with their December rescue, these dogs would all have "rock star" names. I should have realized there would be a list of names, but I had not thought that through (yeah, add that to the list of "things not thought through"). She was, and had been for a month in my mind, Poppy. But, I recalled then, as Megan held the clipboard with the list in front of me, generally, fosters kept the assigned name, but adopters were free to change the name if they'd like. I was fostering.

I perused the list of names still available, quickly noting that Pink was on the list. I love Pink. Pink's *Funhouse* album and that title track specifically was my anthem through cancer treatment. (*"This used to be a funhouse, but now it's full of evil clowns. It's time to start the countdown, I'm gonna burn it down"*—come on, how is that not about my cancerous breast?) Pink is a badass, and this dog was going to need to become a badass to get over her fears and rough beginning. Plus, Pink started with a P and so did Poppy, so the names would be easy to switch if . . . *if what?*

"Pink. I love Pink." I said.

"I do too! I put that name on the list so I'm glad someone chose it." Megan wrote down Pink's information next to her name, along with my name. We were now a matched pair.

I headed across the yard to have our official rescue day photo taken and to talk to the videographer. Deia and Aaron—the parents of Percival's brother River—were also there, holding Pink's little lemon sister.

"No way! Are you guys fostering that one?" I said.

"Yes," Aaron said. "She's so scared. She's like the most frightened one here, so we have to help her."

I lifted Pink up. "I have her sister! We're going to share a set of brothers and sisters now."

We all laughed. River and Percival looked a lot alike. Pink and her sister, now named Miley, were nearly identical. We set them down to be with each other a bit longer, before it was time for photos and the organized chaos of departure (or maybe it had simply become a more tolerable chaos since it was now all about the dogs). We almost couldn't tell Miley and Pink apart when we picked them up again. Deia and Aaron didn't live far from me, so I was hopeful we could get all four dogs together for a playdate.

I gathered my things, the bag of supplies from BFP, and of course Pink. She was carried out to my car by Matt, one of the BFP employees, since walking on a leash was not yet in her skill set and carrying that many supplies and a nervous beagle was not in mine.

Matt set Pink down gently in my back seat, and I hooked her harness to the seat belt attachment. She lay down immediately.

How strange this all must be to her. I had never really thought of it from the dog's point of view. It's always a bit of a mystery bringing a new dog into one's life with so much unknown. But what must it be like for the dog? So utterly confused and dependent on humans. She wouldn't have any idea what her life would be like in five minutes, let alone weeks from now. This assuredly was one of those times where a dog's nature to live in the moment was a gift. She was safe, she was warm, and she was already loved, though she may not have known that last part yet.

"We're headed home, my little Pink Poppy. I promise you; you'll be fine."

She looked at me with those little dark eyes, so quizzical. She was just so cute. And so, so tiny. As she watched me with her head tilted sideways, I noticed her mouth had a little brown smudge on the right side that made her look like she was smiling. Her muzzle was mostly white, but this tan patch near her mouth looked like smeared lipstick—like the smeared lipstick after a drunken make-out session, I thought, because I was tired, and it had been a long day.

"You've been making out, Poppy? . . . Pink? . . . Pretty girl?" I cooed.

She looked at me, head tilted to the other side now, dark eyes staring. Was I a friend or foe?

The tan mouth smudge also gave her a bit of an Elvis smirk, I thought. Given my dad's Elvis fandom, I had seen plenty of that playful smirk. I made a mental note to text my dad a photo of Poppy's smirk. Then I headed home with my new little girl, the start of a whole new life for her.

I had no more clue as to what the next few days and weeks would bring us than Pink Poppy did.

6

ADJUSTMENTS

Poppy, I mean Pink, was having none of it.

We arrived home just after 9:00 p.m., and I soon realized that although I was exhausted and needed sleep, Pink Poppy did not. My routine of sleeping downstairs with new dogs so I could easily get them outside to the yard as needed also meant nothing to her. She was too anxious to stay on the couch with me and utterly unfamiliar with dog beds. She pulsated with nervous energy. She zoomed around the house, staying close to the walls, until eventually she found the stairs and darted up them. I followed her upstairs but not quickly enough to see where she'd gone. I looked in the bedroom, then my office, then the library and both bathrooms.

She was nowhere to be found.

Could she have gone back downstairs without me knowing? No. Not possible. Was it? I searched the rooms again and ridiculously began calling out her names—both of which had been her names for all of two or three hours by then as I seemed to flip between them. Though I was aware of the futility of my pleas of "Poppy? Pink? Baby girl? Sweetie? Pink Poppy?" I was also trying to calm my own panic. How could I have lost a dog within fifteen minutes of getting her home?

Back downstairs, I searched the rooms and then went into the front courtyard to search for her. There was a good reason I searched the courtyard. When we'd first got Daphne, she had "disappeared" for a frightening ten minutes or so until we found her, lying down in the bushes in the courtyard. It broke my heart to see her needing the safety of a spot like that, something I was certain she'd done while a stray on the streets. I had petted her and given her a treat and she quickly followed me back into the house. She hid in the bushes a few more times though before she came to think of her safe spot as the couch or our bed, or anywhere we were. Maybe Poppy was doing the same thing. Maybe she was hiding in the bushes to feel safe. Only it was still raining and cold; how safe could she feel?

I searched the bushes and even went back into the garage to make sure she hadn't somehow slipped into the garage when I was unloading the car.

Nope. No Poppy.

I returned upstairs, hurrying, calling her name, and in general, panicking.

As I entered the bedroom, I spied two little white paws sticking out from under my bed. I exhaled breath I had not known I was holding. *Oh, thank Buddha.* She'd found a safe spot all right. I knelt and looked under the bed. Though she looked back at me quizzically, she soon shrunk further back to the middle under the king-sized bed. I couldn't reach her, but I didn't need to. I'd let her stay until she felt comfortable enough to come out on her own, though I hoped it wouldn't take long. I really needed to sleep.

She stayed under the bed as I moved about the bedroom; occasionally I could hear movement and what I thought—hoped—was a soft *thump thump* of her tail. I washed my face, changed into pajamas, and settled into bed with a book.

I was exhausted, but also wanted to make sure she was as comfortable as possible for a first night. If staying under the bed gave her comfort, so be it. Her comfort was more important than my need to hold her. Experts say it takes at least three weeks for a dog to settle into a new environment and routine. I knew that to be true from my experiences with Seamus, Daphne, Percival, and even Roe recently (he now barked regularly, something not on display in the weeks before). I wondered what Pink Poppy's true personality might become. Adorable, that much I knew. I slipped into sleep.

When I awoke after midnight, the bedroom light was still on, my book was on my chest, and Poppy was curled up at the foot of my bed. *Okay, good, brave girl. I guess we'll sleep upstairs.* I turned out the light and quickly fell back asleep.

❖

I was awoken with a small jolt—the force of four little paws running across my midsection. Poppy leapt from the bed and zoomed about the bedroom as I turned and looked at the clock: 4:00 A.M.

Poppy ran in circles, leaping up onto, across, and then off the bed. Rounding the corner, grabbing toys from the dog bed, and flinging them into the air, springing onto the bed again, across my legs, back down to the floor, where she grabbed one of my slippers and raced out of the room with it. (*Okay, so maybe her true personality would be "adorable but devious"—which is your basic beagle personality.*) I could hear her bound down the stairs. I had no choice but to get out of bed and follow her or lose a slipper, which I briefly considered—it wasn't an expensive slipper, and sleep was a prized commodity in my life.

Once downstairs I realized I must have missed some earlier activity. She'd had a bout of diarrhea in the family room, luckily on the hardwood floor, but unluckily she'd also just run through it. So much for getting her outside in time.

Nonetheless, I opened the French doors both to encourage her to head outside and to air out the stench. She raced around jubilantly, inside and outside of the house, while I cleaned up. 4:00 A.M. clean-ups of messes like that is part and parcel of having a new dog, whether it's a foster, a rescue, or a new puppy, but that didn't make it enjoyable. Watching Poppy run and play with toys was, however, thoroughly enjoyable, even in the predawn hours.

I tried to approach her to pet her and maybe get her to head back upstairs with me, but she shied away again. I noticed that she was watching me, though, evaluating, trying to figure this new situation out. Her inquisitive little face melted me. I yearned to hold her and comfort her, but knew I had to let that happen on her terms, in her time.

I lay down on the couch, figuring we'd give the downstairs sleeping one more try under the digestive circumstances, but she quickly ran past me and bolted up the stairs again. This time when I followed her up, I found her not under the bed but on it, curled up on Chris's pillow next to mine. I quietly, as calmly as I could, crawled into bed and turned out the light.

When I next awoke, at 7:00 A.M., she was asleep on my pillow, her head resting on my shoulder, and one paw on my arm. She was breathing deeply and evenly, her little smeared lipstick mark on display. She was so precious that, were it possible, I'd stay there immobilized for days if that's what she needed. But of course, I couldn't.

Our magical love spell had to be broken by my need to earn a living; dog beds, toys, and food do not buy themselves. Pink Poppy would be coming with me, somehow. My office had all the necessary supplies, including a stack of pee pads, but that was as far ahead as I had thought. What I had not thought through was getting this skittish pup from my home to my office. She was not accustomed to a leash or a harness and found them both terrifying. Whatever ground I may have gained in the first night and with our morning cuddles, I feared I would lose in my efforts to get her harness on and walk her on a leash.

I went through my morning routine while Poppy stayed on my bed, watching me. She came downstairs for her breakfast, then quickly returned upstairs to her perch on my pillow. Soon, it was time to head to the office. I picked her up, struggled to get her in her harness, and carried her to the car, talking to her and again trying to assure her things will get better. I wished I could take the day off work, but I'd already missed so much work through Daphne's illness and dealing with my father's house sale, I needed to be in my office. It was a Friday; we just had to get through this one day and we'd have a weekend to get to know each other. This was one time I couldn't just let her adjust on her own. The constraints of earning a living compete with the desires and realities of rescuing dogs—something everyone in dog rescue knows to be true.

I carried her into my office, and though she was smaller than any of my other beagles, my back was screaming at me that carrying her everywhere was not going to be an option. We'd work on walking on a leash over the weekend, definitely.

Once inside, she immediately dropped down and froze in the reception area, her belly on the floor and ears pulled back. I had hooked the leash to the harness by then, but I wasn't going to drag her.

"Oh, that poor thing. She's terrified," my assistant said. And when she stood to approach Poppy, Poppy jumped and ran behind me, shaking. I once again picked her up, this time carrying her to my office down the hallway. I put her down in the dog bed in the corner, near a window, with several toys. She touched none of the toys and remained exactly as she was, unmoving, while I got my coffee and returned to my desk. After ten minutes of me working quietly, she came over and crawled under my desk, choosing to curl up and sleep at my feet.

I had only two client appointments that day, and I hoped Poppy would stay in my office, under my desk or on the dog bed. To be safe, I asked my paralegal, Jessica, to check in on her from time to time. I needn't have worried. Poppy stayed hunkered under my desk, and each time Jessica went to check on her she shrunk further into the corner.

"I feel bad for her," Jessica said.

"I know. She's a bit traumatized. These dogs take work, but she's doing pretty amazing considering twenty-four hours ago she was on a plane flying in from China," I said.

"True. Yeah, poor thing."

People always said "poor thing" about Percival too, when they heard his background. I suppose I also think "poor thing," initially when meeting a rescue dog with a sad backstory. But dogs are my one area of optimism—I focus on the positives and try not to let the dog's background influence the rest of their life. They're no longer victims. They're now safe and loved and forever will be. And dogs, unlike people, are much better at forgetting and moving on. (Despite all my time with dogs, this was not a lesson I'd been able to learn from them. I hold my grudges like . . . well, like a dog with a bone. This makes "grudges" my "bones." Again, let's not dwell here.)

After my second client meeting, Jessica may have felt a little less bad for her as Poppy had had another diarrhea explosion. Jessica, kindly, was in my office trying to clean it up when I came out of the conference room.

"Some of it hit the pee pads, but this is kind of a disaster."

She was not exaggerating. The smell was nearly as shocking as the visual. "I see that. We'll add getting the carpets cleaned to our 'must do soon' list. Thanks for taking care of that." Truly, not in her job description, I promise. Jessica loved dogs too, and she and her fiancé had recently moved into an apartment that allowed small dogs; they hoped to adopt one soon. Maybe this was good training?

Luckily, most of my clients were "dog people" and very familiar with and supportive of my dog rescue efforts, but this disaster in my office was taking "supportive" to a different level. I sincerely hoped this was just a nervous tummy and Pink Poppy would be fine soon. Nonetheless, I made a vet appointment for the next day. She needed a thorough exam anyway.

When I finished up work, it was after 7:00 P.M. Poppy had mostly slept under my desk, but I noticed after 5:00 P.M. when everyone else had gone, if I got up and got a glass of water or put something in someone else's inbox, she would come out and check to see where I was, then quickly run back to her hiding spot. If I ventured further to grab a file from the file room, she'd follow ten feet behind, but as I turned to head back to my office, she'd race ahead of me. *Okay, good. She's getting to know me. She wants to be around me, she's just nervous. Not bad for twenty-four hours.*

But the moment I picked up her leash, she scurried out from under my desk, just as she had earlier in the day when I tried to take her outside for a potty break. I followed her around and around in my office—she was quick and agile and wanted nothing to do with the leash. I sat back down in my chair and pretended to work until eventually she returned to her spot at my feet. Slowly, I reached down and clipped her leash on to her harness. I left her there, leash attached but loose, for a short while as I petted her. Then I bent down and scooped her up. Thank goodness this was a small dog or my back could not take it.

Let me pause to explain that back thing since I've probably whined about it a few times. Also, I don't want you to start thinking I'm 103 years old. I'm not. But I am falling apart. Sort of.

In May 2017, I'd fallen breaking up a fight between Daphne and Percival. I fell backward and hit my spine on the corner of the door jamb, then fell to the floor. It was so painful that the first thing I did after I hit the ground was to check to make sure I could move my arms and legs. I could, so eventually I got up, took some ibuprofen, and went to bed, turning down Chris's offer to take me to urgent care. Three weeks later my two-year-old car broke down, and I had to get myself and Percival and Daphne both out of the car and into a tow truck by lifting each of their thirty-pound bodies, because that's outside the job description of a tow truck driver. It had been hard enough to convince him to let the dogs in his truck with us. A month after that I went to Europe with Chris, shuffling down cobblestone streets, searching for cafés with padded seat chairs, and lying down in parks when I couldn't climb the stairs to our room. Three months later, I was still shuffling rather than walking, and couldn't stand for long periods of time, so I finally went to urgent care.

After X-rays and a quick review of the results, the doctor turned to me and said, "You have a very high tolerance for pain. Your back is broken."

I'd been told about my pain tolerance before, but this was surprising, to say the least. Also, I felt much better about Chris having to carry our luggage on our trip. "Broken? I feel like if you break your back, you'd know it."

He pointed to my T12 vertebra on the X-ray. "It's a compression fracture. See the collapse there? You probably lost a half inch or an inch of height."

"Will I get it back?"

I have no idea why this was my first thought. Maybe I just don't like things being taken away from me. I am, or I was, five feet ten inches tall. I could afford some shrinkage, but it still seems like I should have some say so.

"No," he said, as unequivocally as the oncologist had said "Yes" when I asked if I'd lose my hair in chemo. At least my hair had grown back.

Now that you know I'm not ancient-old, perhaps you are thinking I'm incredibly stubborn or stupid. Let me just tell you I come by that honestly. (You can decide which of "stubborn" or "stupid" I mean after you read this next part.)

When I was ten years old my parents took us all on a family cross-country motorhome trip in celebration of their remarriage, I think ("celebration" is the wrong word . . . you'll see). We drove from California up through Oregon and Washington, across to Minnesota, and then made a diagonal route back. In

South Dakota I fell off a ladder in the motor home and my right arm broke. Or, it didn't. That was the argument my parents had. My mother distinctly heard the bone snap. My father thought my mother was hysterical and I could not have broken my arm in that fall, right there in front of them. They yelled. They screamed. They put ice and an Ace bandage on my arm. The sides that my parents had carefully arranged in their household put me firmly on my dad's team. So on cue, when asked, I sided with my dad and said no, my arm was not broken—at ten years old I was capable of this diagnosis, of course. Thus, I broke the tie. We are all going to have to assume that in 1973 South Dakota had no hospitals available to break the tie, thus it fell to a ten-year-old.

Broken, not broken: time would tell. And time did tell. Because when we got to Las Vegas (right, you will also have to assume no hospitals in Wyoming or Utah were available for tie-breaking; I know I do) my parents took us all to Circus Circus. I'm certain they would have taken us to a better gambling establishment, but this was before Vegas became so ridiculously family-friendly. Their only option with three kids in tow was Circus Circus, where some man, no doubt desperate to escape the hordes of small children, ran smack into me and rebroke my arm. But, good news! He also broke the tie (or my screaming did). My parents whisked me off to a hospital—the one back in California where my father worked.

What have we learned? My bones are as loosely knit as my family? Broken bones do not need to interfere with a vacation? Judges will accept both answers.

Shortly after I set aside my lifetime of learning and went to urgent care to learn my back was broken, I also learned I had osteoporosis, likely caused by the chemotherapy I'd been through when I had breast cancer nine years earlier (you'll be happy to know I went to the doctor for that), and thus another factor in how my vertebra broke with the fall. And so began six months of physical therapy, a lifetime of bone-strengthening medication, and three months of wearing a back brace—this monstrous piece of equipment that included a bar coming up my front with a padded shield across my chest to keep me from slouching or looking remotely normal. I also wasn't supposed to lift anything over five pounds. As I explained to the doctor, I have client files that weigh more than five pounds, and I'm sure my purse does as well (I did not mention lifting the thirty-pound beagles). Nonetheless, since I didn't want surgery, I tried to be somewhat mindful. Somewhat.

But enough about me—let's get back to the dog; that's what we're all here for.

Eighteen months after I broke my back, when I was in my office alone on that Friday night, I didn't have any other options but to pick Poppy up. She wasn't going to walk out on her own, and I wasn't going to sleep in my office. I picked her up, over the strenuous objections of my T12 vertebra, or what remained of it. I held her as I turned out the lights in the office, set the alarm, and locked the door. Then I shuffled, still carrying her, still ignoring crumbly, grumbly T12, who'd upped its protestations, out to my car, where I struggled to get the keys out of my purse without dropping the dog, who'd turned into dead weight of, I'd conservatively guess, 328 pounds. But that's just a guess.

I set Poppy down in the back seat and she slunk into the far corner. I snapped the seat belt restraint on, petted her head, and again told her it would all be okay. And I made a mental note to stock up on ibuprofen.

Also, tequila.

On Saturday I had only one errand and could then spend the day at home with Poppy, helping her adjust to the house, to me, and almost as importantly, to a leash. But first, I'd have to get her to the vet—another potentially traumatic interaction, with stranger danger, and new space, and the dreaded leash. Beagle Freedom Project asked us to take the new fosters to the vet right away for general health exams. With this group of dogs there seemed to be confusion over whether they were spayed or not, so that also needed to be checked out, along with her tummy issues (sounds so much better than "exploding diarrhea," right?).

After a night that went much like the previous one—including a 4:00 A.M. wake up and a fecal detonation—I headed downstairs for my much-needed coffee. Poppy stayed on the bed, where she'd once again slept on my pillow, often with her head on my shoulder, which was so adorable it easily allowed me to forget all the rest. As I turned to head back upstairs with my coffee cup (I'd selected the cup from the Wired Puppy café in Provincetown; you decide why I made that selection), I could see her little face peeking between the bannister railings, looking down, making sure I was still nearby and hadn't left her. When she saw me, she ran back to the bed. I had to scoot her over so I could sit in bed, sipping my coffee and planning the logistics of my day, as I usually did. She snuggled in under my arm.

"Wouldn't it be nice to stay here all day like this, baby girl?"

Her face, that darling little white face with brown patches over both eyes, and those dark inquisitive eyes, seemed to answer "Absolutely! Let's do it." Or maybe it was "No idea what you're saying, but I like your tone of voice!" Or maybe it was just her face. I had RBF, resting bitch face; Pink Poppy had resting adorable, enthusiastic face.

When it came time to take her to the vet, though, it became clear that what was on her Saturday agenda was in fact snuggles in bed and nothing else. *Nothing*. The moment she saw the leash, she darted under the bed. It took me ten minutes to lure her out with treats, and I felt like Judas when I grabbed her by the collar and snapped the harness and leash on to her. Her expression was one of betrayal. The terror in her eyes was heart-stopping.

What was she thinking? What did she fear? Humans in general? Or had a leash meant something different where she'd been?

This was the most difficult part of fostering these dogs—we knew so little about their backgrounds, just enough of an idea of horrific circumstances to let one's imagination go wild. For years a beeping noise of any kind (alarm, oven timer, smoke alarm, a truck backing up) would send Percival racing to the farthest place he could reach to hide, shaking and drooling. We assumed there was a beeping noise in the laboratory he was in that signaled the start or progress of whatever testing was being done on him. He eventually got over it, but it was heartbreaking to see. I still remember his fear when I hear a beeping noise, and I often will move quickly to stop the noise or comfort Percy-pie—my own acquired Pavlovian response.

But a leash was not something Poppy and I could avoid. I'd have to show her it was nothing to fear. I'd have to convince her a leash meant walks, it meant going places with me, sunshine, fresh air, big adventures! Unfortunately, this time it meant she was going to the vet.

The dogs had been checked by a vet in China before they were permitted on a flight to the United States, so she'd had a little experience with vets. At this point in her life, though, I was certain all she wanted was a little comfort, quiet, and routine. Time to figure things out.

"Come on baby girl, just one quick visit to the vet, and I'll bring you back home and we can stay home all day. You can rest, stay in bed, whatever you want," I told her as I carried her downstairs, through the hall, into the courtyard, up the stairs, into the garage, and out to my car. Well, I told her that when I could catch a breath. It was more like "You . . . [huff] . . . can . . . [puff] . . . stay in . . . [gasp] . . . bed."

Once at the vet, I again had to pick her up and carry her in. Since the vet's office is on a busy avenue, this was not the time to start her leash training. It may have been the time to consider going back to strength training with the physical therapist, but why would I do that? I had dogs to carry.

For all Pink Poppy had been through, she was a healthy dog. An ear infection and the upset stomach were our only issues. Ear drops would fix one problem, and skipping a meal and then a diet of rice and bland foods would fix the other. The vet determined that she had been spayed and that she was probably only eighteen months old at the most, not the two to three years we'd been told. All in all, a very good visit.

Back at home I opened the back door to my car and opened her crate, encouraging her to come out on her own. She hesitated but soon, to my surprise, she hopped out of the car. She moved about the garage, sniffing, and wagging her tail. She moved her whole body with her tail, curving so that her nose nearly touched her butt on the right and then swinging around and doing the same thing on the left. I could see she was happy, excited even, to be back home.

"You're certainly a little wiggle butt, aren't you?"

My Daphne had had a swagger to her walk. When she first came to us, she was very overweight, so the swagger, when viewed from behind as she walked, gave her the nickname Doodlebutt. I had a feeling Wigglebutt would stick for Poppy, and I liked that connection. Even if her eventual adopter changed her very adorable name. (Ouch. On so many levels.)

Poppy followed me out of the garage and back into the house. I was as excited as she was to have a long stretch of time with just us in the house. No noises, no distractions, nothing to be afraid of. Poppy immediately settled in on the couch. I grabbed my laptop and did the same.

Throughout the day I put her leash on her and just let her sit with the leash, getting used to it. I left her harness on as well. At one point I thought about going to my office to pick up some files so I could work at home all day the following day as well. But I didn't want to push things by taking her with me. Instead, once Poppy was asleep on my bed, I snuck out of the house to head to my office. I was gone a total of forty-five minutes.

I walked back into the house and set my purse down on the kitchen counter. "Poppy? Pink?"

She did not greet me. I didn't expect that she would, necessarily. We hadn't been apart enough to know what her routine might become when we were reunited. But I do enjoy being greeted by an enthusiastic dog when I come home.

"Poppy?" I headed upstairs.

The hallway was strewn with evidence of a crime. A beagle crime.

One of my shoes, shredded, lay next to my pajamas, also shredded, in the doorway to the bedroom. As I walked into the bedroom, the scene worsened. She'd torn everything down off my nightstand, toppled a glass of water, ripped the covers off two books, chewed the pages of the books, and left them for dead. Magazines had not survived the carnage, nor had my reading glasses.

I bent down to pick up the mess.

"Oh, Poppy!" The shredded shoe was from my favorite pair of black flats—one of the last leather pairs I owned. I'd stopped buying leather when I'd chosen a vegan lifestyle, but I kept what I already had. And now I had one less leather shoe. She'd ripped out the inside and chewed the back down to the sole.

Poppy heard my tone of voice, my disappointment, and in what seemed one swift motion, hopped down off her perch on my pillow and scrambled under the bed.

So Poppy is a chewer. Good to know.

Percival had gone through a similar adjustment period. We called him "Shredder" for about the first year we had him—and books were a favorite of his too. As I cleaned up the mess, I tried to think how long that behavior lasted in Percival. He was two years old when we adopted him. Was it for another two years? Longer? Maybe less? What I really wanted to know was how many more pairs of shoes I was likely to lose.

In what became a familiar habit, I began to Poppy-proof the house, to avoid leading her into temptation. Shoes were rounded up and put in the closet. The closet door, almost always open because it's installed wrong and is difficult to open and close, was closed. Books were moved off the night-stand and onto the much higher dresser, as was my journal. Magazines were removed from the coffee table in the den. It was an amateur move to not have done all that before I left, so I could hardly be upset with her. And I may have been a tiny bit proud she had missed me when I was gone.

🐾

For the next thirty-six hours or so, my Pink Poppy girl and I were home alone getting used to each other. I kept the leash out, occasionally putting it on her and offering her a treat. *Leash is good. Good girl!* She had the usual two gears of a puppy—deep sleep and zoom. She preferred sleeping next to me, whether on the couch or on my pillow, and I did not object to this. When I was roaming about the house, doing dishes or laundry, or putting things away, she chose to go into the large crate in my den. There was a cushion and a blanket, and she dragged several toys in with her, creating a den of her own.

Toys and treats were new to her, but she quickly adapted to both. I had bought her a squeak toy in the form of a latte with a fabric foam topping that she proudly carried around with her and sometimes used as a pillow until, apparently in need of caffeine, she disemboweled it. Since all the beagles I've ever had in my life engaged in the same behavior with squeak toys, I took this as a good sign. She was getting in touch with her beagle self.

I texted Chris photos. Lots of photos. Mostly with the caption *"Isn't she cute?"*

I sent him a video of Poppy playing as I encouraged her, in dog baby talk, of course.

"You're calling her Poppy," he said.

"Yes, that's her name."

"I thought her name was Pink? You told me you chose that name."

"I did. But I don't think it matters. Occasionally I say Pink Poppy."

"I feel like that's a sign. You're calling her the name we meant to call our next dog, but we have Roe. Pink is a foster dog."

Was it a sign? I'd been calling her Poppy in my head for so long it was hard to make the switch. Pink wasn't a bad name for her. She had a little pink underbelly, and a pink spot on the tip of her nose, and she was certainly little and "girly" (not that Pink the rock star is, particularly).

"She's answering to my voice, but I don't think she knows her name. I'll call her Pink Poppy," I texted back.

"That's a little better but I'm already worried."

I wasn't worried because I wasn't allowing myself to think about fostering versus adopting. I was instead convincing myself that for the next few weeks the labels didn't matter. My job was to get her accustomed to a life of freedom and build her confidence, along with her "dog-ness." I was throwing myself into that job.

I texted a photo of Pink Poppy looking up into the camera with her dainty face and those dark almond eyes, so curious, so irresistible.

"I'm screwed," he texted back.

Later I gave Poppy a quick bath and put her new collar on. She'd come to me with a Beagle Freedom Project collar, but it was too big. When I bought the latte squeak toy I also bought her a collar—both were red. All of my beagles had what I called their "signature colors." My first beagle, Raz, had hot pink; Rabu had blue, Richelieu was red, Roxy yellow, Seamus had green of course, Daphne's was purple, Percival's was orange (the anti-cruelty to animals ribbon color), and Roe's was turquoise. I'd decided to go back to red for Poppy, because, well, poppies. It occurred to me that if Chris saw the color theme happening it might have been another "sign," but I brushed that thought aside. *She is mine for now and for the foreseeable future, and that is all that matters.*

Over the next ten days, Poppy settled into a routine of sorts. Unfortunately, the routine still involved the 4:00 A.M. wake ups. I'd then take her downstairs and outside, waiting for her to do her business, which she did sometimes. Other times she'd look at me as though I'd lost my mind and run back into the warmth of the house. She learned the doggie door very quickly; a few treats in my hand beckoning her to one side or the other and she got it. She seemed fascinated that she could come and go as she pleased, but that didn't mean she instantly grasped that she should go outside to potty. I had to encourage that, especially since it was cold out. Then we'd return to bed until later in the morning, when she'd wake me again, no alarm needed. I'd feed her and grab my coffee, and we'd cuddle for a bit. All was well and cozy. Until I started to dress for work.

As soon as I walked toward my dresser, she leapt from the top of the bed, where she'd been curled up and peaceful as I did my hair and makeup, and belly-crawled under the bed. Always to the middle, always out of reach. I'd have to bribe her with more treats and then drag her out and carry her downstairs with me. She could not be left home alone yet, or I was certain I'd have no home to return to. Chewing drywall was not unimaginable. I worked long hours, so crating wasn't an option. And I had to get her used to other people—my office, with a staff of two and a few clients a day, was a good place to do that, especially since there were plenty of doors to close off escape routes and a lawn with a pond right out front. Pink Poppy, however, did not see the genius of my plan. She saw only how nice our weekend girltime was and questioned why anybody would change that. It's always difficult to explain to a dog that the human needs to make a living.

At my office, Jessica, easily forgiving Poppy for her "messes," tried hard to get Pink Poppy comfortable around her, bringing her treats, sitting on the floor with her, petting her when she could. My administrative assistant, who sat up front at the reception desk with a door closed behind her to keep Poppy in the back offices, had far less contact with the dog. Poppy showed signs of warming to Jessica but remained distrustful of my assistant. (Poppy was obviously prescient; a few months later that same assistant walked out at lunch never to return, with no notice given. And she left a mess behind that took far longer to clean up than Poppy's messes had taken.)

With clients, Poppy would poke her head into the conference room, checking to see where I was, but the moment she was acknowledged in any way (usually with squeals or movements to pet her) she raced back to my office and under the desk. I let her explore and figure things out in her own time. Eventually, with certain clients—though I could never discern what characteristics made it so—she would come all the way into the conference room, sometimes even approaching and sniffing, but never staying long. You could see in her expression and her consistent efforts just how hard she was trying and just how much trauma she had to overcome.

Which meant that everyone fell in love with her.

I could see small progress just in the first two weeks. I could put a leash on her, and I could get her to follow me outside to the lawn. Eventually, Jessica could do the same. But we could not get her to walk around the lawn. Instead she either hunkered down on all fours, immobile, or took a few steps and then quickly began scrambling to return to my office. When she did walk, she pulled to stay along the side of the building, right up against it, rather than out in the lawn area.

I got in the habit of singing Sara Bareilles's "Brave," to Poppy, though I can't sing, and I don't know the words other than "I wanna see you be brave." Poppy didn't mind, which is another great thing about dogs.

She was making progress on the leash, but our walks could hardly be considered exercise. And now that she'd had plenty of sleep and a good diet, her energy was strong . . . too strong. When I left her home while grocery shopping, I lost another shoe, several more magazines, and a coffee table book. A second pair of reading glasses also did not fare well, though I could still use them if I didn't mind the chewed-up arm catching in my hair when I took the glasses on and off. I continued to offer her toys, but she insisted my belongings were more fun. The 4:00 A.M. zoomies were another tradition I could not break her of. I was increasingly exhausted and cranky (with humans, not with Poppy). Thus, I decided to take her to doggie day care for a day of exercise and socialization, two things she desperately needed.

Over the past decade, all my dogs have gone to Ruff House Pet Resort, a place good for a dog's socialization, exercise needs, and group playtime. Seamus was their very first customer when it opened (under previous ownership). Seamus, like Poppy, did not care for being home alone and needed more energy burned off than I could accomplish. Doggie daycare was a lifesaver for us and for Seamus (for my neighbors as well, since Seamus howled incessantly when left alone).

But how would Poppy do with strangers and other dogs? I thought she'd likely be fine with other dogs. She'd been packed in with a lot of them in China, had come over to the United States with eleven others, and hadn't seemed bothered by the one or two dogs we'd encountered on our "walks." Ruff House assured me they would test her, and if she was too frightened or aggressive, they'd let me know and I could come get her. Plus, they had a webcam, so I'd be able to see for myself.

She was, understandably, a bit nervous, as was I, but watching on my computer at work I could see her tail tucked but wagging, and she was doing her wigglebutt thing as she approached the staff people. She stuck mostly to the perimeter of the play area, and spent time napping in the little tents they had in the corners of the room. But by the afternoon she was climbing the ramps and it looked like she'd made at least one little doggie friend, a fluffy black terrier. I'd like to say I took advantage of her absence to get more work done, but I may have spent a fair amount of time watching the Ruff House webcam. Thankfully they close from noon to 2:00 P.M. while the dogs nap, which gave me no choice but to get some legal work done and earn the money to pay for things like doggie-daycare.

When I picked her up after work, Poppy ran to me squealing in excitement. She yipped and yapped and jumped and twirled. I could barely catch her to pet her. The staff told me she had done well. They'd been worried since they had a dog not long ago who had been rescued from the Korean dog meat trade. That dog had been frightened and growling and snapping at the other dogs and staff, so, sadly, he could not stay. I felt bad for him and his human and was that much more relieved Poppy had done fine. Truth be told, I had needed this break from my little whirling dervish.

I was less nervous when I picked her up than I had been when I dropped her off, so I only then noticed that Ruff House had a Christmas backdrop set up in the lobby, complete with large, brightly wrapped fake presents in front of it, where customers could take holiday photos with their dogs. Although

Christmas is my least favorite holiday—given that death, cancer, and comas were the usual ornaments on my holiday tree—I still could not resist.

I texted the photo to Chris with my usual caption: "Isn't Poppy cute?"

He texted back, "Pink is adorable." And then, "Christmas, really?"

Even with my Christmas aversion, Poppy looked adorable sniffing at the beribboned box that was bigger than she was. A couple of merry photos couldn't jinx the holidays. Could it?

A few days and several shredded items later, it was at long last time for Poppy and me to head up to Paso Robles. Time for Poppy to meet Chris, and Percival and Roe. And despite my holiday history, I was excited to spend the holidays with three dogs in the house. I'd loaded up on dog toys and treats and even remembered to order a few gifts for Chris online, since Poppy was not allowing me shopping time outside the house. I can be festive and celebrate dogs; I'd just ignore the holiday of which we do not speak. Maybe if I called it "Dog-mas" my luck would change.

Fortunately, a few days before my arrival, Chris had remembered we needed to ask our landlord's permission to keep a third dog on the premises, even temporarily. Our landlord's granddaughter and her husband and daughter lived in the house next door to us, so it wasn't like we could hide the number of dogs, nor are beagles known for their silence. The houses were close together—their house was the guest house to our larger house—and the area we'd fenced off for the dogs was right under their bedroom window. When Chris asked permission to bring Poppy home, I was sure he had emphasized that she was a foster dog. They had happily agreed. I don't know what we would have done if they hadn't. The thought never even crossed my mind.

With the landlord's permission, we were set. Poppy, my nervous little shredding machine, with her exuberance and energy, and I, with my dread of the holidays but excitement over these new pups, would be in Paso Robles for two weeks, with lots of time off and the Beagle Boys to show Poppy the ropes. Perfect. I thought it would be much like our recent wonderful Rescue Ranch Thanksgiving—short on family, but long on dog cuddles. Assuming everyone got along, which was, of course, my plan.

7

LOGISTICS

❧

As soon as I pulled into the parking lot, I realized my predicament. Poppy was not likely to just hop out of the crate and merrily trot into the wine tasting room where Chris was working, especially since it was located on the corner of 13th and Pine Street, one of the busiest intersections in Paso Robles. I needed to pick her up and carry her in. After a four-hour drive, I was tired and would have preferred she hop out and trot in at the end of her leash. But we were not there yet in her leash training. Not at all. I knew I'd have to pick her up, vertebra be damned.

She shrunk to the back of her crate the moment I opened the car door. The traffic and perhaps the drizzle of rain were overwhelming her. I reached in and pulled her to me, then carried her in to meet Chris, soothing her and coaxing her to be brave. She calmed in my arms, but was immediately nervous again when we walked into the wine tasting room, a brightly colored, gorgeous space that at that time, luckily, had only two guests along with Chris and Nicki, the young woman working with him.

I quickly settled on the couch, where there were plenty of jewel-toned pillows, up against a royal blue wall, and where dogs were as welcome as humans.

Poppy stayed pressed up against me as the humans *oohed* and *awwed* over her from a distance. Chris, all six-foot-two of him, approached and Poppy quickly moved behind me, then around me and up into my lap.

"Just sit down next to me and let her smell you and get used to you," I said.

"Hi, Pink. Hi, little girl. You are very cute," Chris said. He offered his hand to her to sniff, but she pulled away.

"She'll get used to you. She's still a little overwhelmed and people are scary."

Nicki offered to take our photo, so I put Poppy on my lap and Chris handed her his phone.

"Our first family photo," I said.

"Our first *foster* photo," Chris said. "And aren't we missing two important family members?"

I kissed the top of Poppy's head. "Right. I just meant our first photo together with Poppy."

"Pink." He was smiling, leaning toward me, eyebrows raised.

"Pink Poppy," I compromised. (That *was* a compromise. She was a foster dog, but at the same time, she *was* Poppy.)

I had arrived Saturday afternoon instead of my usual near-midnight Friday night trip so that Chris could take his lunch break and be home with me to introduce the dogs to each other in daylight, with plenty of hours for them to get used to one another before we all settled down to sleep. Since Percival mostly slept on our bed (again, sometimes he just needed to be alone and would choose his own bed) and Roe always slept on our bed, mashed up against one or the other of us, and now Poppy had declared my pillow her pillow, it was important they get used to each other before we attempted the five-to-a-bed feat, which I knew was coming even if Chris didn't.

As we sat in the wine tasting room, I worked out the logistics of the introduction in my mind. With the soggy weather, taking the three of them for a walk as we had done when introducing Roe to Percival was a less appealing option. Poppy was also still too fearful of the leash and too likely to attempt to bolt. I figured out a way to make an indoor introduction easier—a way that I hoped would be less overwhelming for Poppy.

In our Paso Robles home, Chris had installed a baby gate at the top of the stairs. That allowed us to contain the dogs upstairs, where they had access to our bedroom, the laundry room, and the doggie door to head outside to the fenced yard. Because our home was built into a hill it had separate yards off both the upstairs area and the downstairs. The gate also prevented them from charging the front door when we came home. We could use that to our advantage when we brought Poppy in. Chris agreed with my plan and we headed home.

We brought her in, let her off the leash, and let her roam about the house for a bit, with Roe and Percival at the gate singing the song of their people. Soon, Poppy ran up the stairs and the howling stopped as they all vigorously sniffed at each other through the baby gate. Tails wagged crazily. When Poppy ran back downstairs, excitedly racing about, we opened the gate and let Roe and Percival join her.

There was frantic sniffing, as dogs will do, and Poppy stood very still, occasionally looking to me, but just as often sniffing at Roe. Percival was more interested in Chris, but soon, Poppy did a play bow and they were all off and running.

"They seem fine," Chris said with his usual wry understatement, as three furry blurs whizzed by.

"Looks that way," I said. "She will finally burn some energy off. I think they'll all be good for each other."

It was also doing my heart a lot of good to see them all playing. It was December 21, I was trying to focus on the dogs and ignore the holiday (except for the many dog toys I'd bought), but I was also missing Daphne. I missed her particularly in Paso Robles because she had loved being a country dog so thoroughly and just didn't get enough time there.

The five of us settled in the living room—Chris in his armchair and Percival on his lap, Roe and Poppy and me on the couch. Poppy seemed to have an early preference for Roe. It was easy to see she was already following his lead, which is why when he jumped on the couch, she followed. As Chris and I talked, Poppy and Roe wrestled a bit on the couch. Then they'd leap off, chase each other around and leap back on to the couch. Poppy often took a shortcut and instead of running circles around the couch, she leapt up on to the back of the couch then flung herself down toward Roe in a surprise aerial attack as he raced around the couch. Eventually, Roe jumped back onto the couch and began to settle in with his favorite blanket, declaring an end to play time. Poppy sprung toward him, bouncing back and forth begging him to continue their antics, and very much getting in his face. Roe let out one sharp, assertive bark and put his paw on top of her head. His message was clear: "Enough."

Message received; Poppy sprung up onto the other end of the couch, curled up and went to sleep. She was a quick study when she wanted to be.

Chris returned to work while I stayed home, unpacking, settling in and enjoying the exuberant joy of these three dogs. Roe showed Poppy the ropes—she followed him in and out of the doggie door within the first hour of being there. Whatever he did, she trailed after him and mimicked. And when she got up on our bed for a nap, it wasn't my pillow she went for, but rather she made Roe her pillow, curling up right next to him. At first she was in a tight round ball up against him, but soon after her head was on his haunches. He didn't seem to mind at all. As for Percival, well, he ran and played with Poppy a bit but as was his way he also needed his space. During their naptime he retreated to the dog bed, away from both Poppy and Roe. They seemed to quickly figure out a routine and a relationship.

Or so I thought.

When Chris arrived home that evening, I was reading on the couch, with Poppy and Roe beside me. Percival was curled up in Chris's armchair—well, curled up until the moment he heard the crunch of Chris's car tires on our dirt and gravel drive, then he sprung from the chair and dashed to the front door. Percival's life revolves around Chris, and he has a certain routine that must be adhered to. Each evening when Chris comes home, he sits in the armchair (the very one Percival waits in) and Percival climbs into his lap, fastidiously licking Chris's face while simultaneously demanding back scratches, head pets, behind-the-ear scratches, for a general party-of-two love-fest. This must not be interfered with. And if Chris doesn't sit down soon enough, Percival pouts, or he runs to him and begins pawing at his leg, softly at first but quickly accelerating to violently. Percival demands the same routine in the morning as well, though then it's in bed. As soon as Chris is awake (sometimes sooner), Percival is standing on his chest wanting kisses and scratches. I don't even exist for either of them until this routine is over.

On that night, Percival's frantic behavior, and Chris's entrance to our quiet home, startled Poppy. Roe had also run to the door, as he too was happy when Chris came home, so Poppy followed him as she'd been doing all afternoon. Once she saw Chris, though, she was no longer willing to take Roe's lead. She stopped abruptly, her eyes wide. She turned and raced up the stairs, tail tucked.

I followed her up to reassure her, but she'd scurried under the bed. She looked determined to stay there, and no amount of soothing baby talk from me was going to change that. I let her be. I'd learned a while ago that coddling a dog engaged in undesired behavior would only reinforce that behavior. I'd let her learn to be brave. And I hoped Roe would communicate to her that Chris was not to be feared.

Poppy stayed upstairs under the bed the rest of the night. As we got ready for bed, I tried briefly to encourage her to come out, again without success.

"Are we going to have all three on the bed?" Chris said.

Not an unfair question, just not one I had the answer to. I often let the dogs decide important questions like that. "She's been sleeping on my pillow, right next to my head. So if she does come up on the bed, she won't likely get in the way."

"I'm worried about Percival and his night thing."

That was a legitimate concern. One I'd worried about as well. When we first adopted Percival he would frequently have night terrors (PTSD from his time in a laboratory). He'd wake abruptly, growling, snarling, and snapping at anything nearby. Often it was Daphne nearby, and she would instinctively respond to his first growls or whimpers by putting her face in his to see what was going on and he'd react by snapping at her. A brawl would break out in the middle of the night, terrifying all concerned. Over the years this mellowed and happened less frequently, but the thing was we never knew when or why it would happen. We just knew it was heartbreaking when it did.

Percival insisted on sleeping under the covers, burrowing down no matter the weather. We could sometimes hear the low growl and shake him awake, snapping him out of it. But we didn't always hear the warning, if there was one. So far, Roe had been able to sleep next to Percival with no issues. The two of them tangled their limbs, used each other as pillows, and even stepped on or over each other without Percival ever going off. Roe clearly had good, nonthreatening energy. But how would Percival be with Poppy? Could he adjust to yet another new dog?

We had our answer soon enough. Somewhere in the middle of the night, Poppy hopped up on the bed and assumed her favored position, sharing my pillow, with her head resting on my shoulder. I knew she was there, but I hadn't realized Percival had burrowed down under the blankets and was pressed tight up against Chris, about a foot below Poppy.

If I had realized that I might have known what would soon happen.

At daybreak, Poppy stood and moved down toward Roe at the foot of the bed. In doing so she stepped on Percival, and Percival promptly lost his mind. He flipped over and came up out from under the covers snarling and snapping. Poppy leapt off the bed and, in what was becoming her signature move, scurried under the bed.

Roe, however, was not to be scared off. He went at Percival. Chris and I each grabbed a dog. I got Roe's collar and was able to restrain him, awkward angle and all, and Chris picked up Percival and stood.

"Jesus Christ," Chris said.

"Yeah, I guess my little fantasy of a simple, instantly adjusted pack was maybe a little too soon."

"You think? This is going to be a problem."

"It's not even been twenty-four hours. There's bound to be an adjustment period." I said this, believing it, while holding back a snarling dog in a stare-off with another snarling dog, while the third dog shivered under the bed.

I'm a true believer in the goodness of animals. Sometimes blindingly so.

"Three dogs is going to be a problem. Roe and Percival were getting along fine."

I wanted to make a joke about a woman always being to blame for men's issues, but Chris didn't seem to be in a joking mood and, on second thought,

I didn't want to draw attention to the fact that in this circumstance he was probably right.

"They were, and they will. It was just Percival's little freak-out thing," I tried.

"I hope you're right. You're the one who will be home with them all day today."

"Well, let's take them for a walk together. That always helps." With the half day together and Roe's obvious effect on Poppy, I was feeling brave about taking her out on a walk. The alternative—leaving Roe and Percival and their sudden male hostilities alone in the house circling each other—was not appealing.

"I'm going to take him out to the backyard, then you can let Roe go." He was still holding thirty-pound Percival, but at least the snarling had stopped. With any luck the Beagle Boys had both moved on to "Where's breakfast?" mode.

Chris carried Percival down the hall toward the laundry room, while Roe strained at his collar, firmly in my grasp. The laundry room had their leashes (*walks!!!*) and their food and bowls (*breakfast!!*), so I chose to think Roe wanted to go after those two things and not his new nemesis. Poppy remained silent.

Fortunately, I was right, because I needed a win at that point. Chris deferred to me in most things dog (not wine, though, just to be clear—we each have our passions), but it seemed I was not seeing this situation clearly. Perhaps willfully not seeing it clearly (added to therapy list). Once Chris grabbed the harnesses and leashes, I released Roe and all he or Percival cared about was their harnesses—though for different reasons. Roe danced about and raced around, excited at the prospect of a walk. Percival, on the other hand, took the sight of the harness as his cue to hide, usually by returning to the bedroom and pretending to be asleep. Thus far, this was something he and Poppy had in common.

That morning in Paso, though, I needed her to go on the walk and follow Roe's lead, not Percival's. Walks tend to bond dogs and get them all focused on the same things, the common enemies of beagles—squirrels, rabbits, any other dog, and of course, the neighbor's cats.

Chris was naturally the one to get Percival's harness on him. But even Chris had trouble getting Percival ready for a walk (this was a trait I shared with Percival, as I too am exercise-adverse). The routine involved first finding Percival under the sheets, picking up his dead weight, holding him upright with one hand, and slipping the harness over his head with the other hand before he could twist away and again collapse with a dramatic sigh. Chris, or sometimes I, would then roll him from side to side so we could snap the various snaps until he was properly harnessed. Percival did not so much as lift a paw in assistance during the process and always managed to make the harness look like a straitjacket. Often, he ran to me, as though the exercise-less one would understand his determination not to move and protect him. (On the rare occasion Chris did leave him behind, Percival would howl and whine the entire hour Chris was gone. He didn't want to go, but that didn't mean he wanted Chris spending time with another dog.)

Roe, though, Roe practically danced his way into his harness. He couldn't get it on fast enough. Usually when Chris sat at the edge of the bed putting his own shoes on for the walk, Roe would crawl into Chris's lap in anticipation, ready to go-go-go-go-go. Nothing could convince Roe that his positioning, standing on Chris's thighs, slowed down the process. He did the same that morning.

Since Roe was so obviously excited about what was happening next, Poppy eventually came out from under the bed. But she did not stand still for me to put the harness on her. I had to follow her around, sit on the couch, wait for her to approach me, and attempt a variety of trickery, while she evaded, wagged her tail, looked cute, and basically made a mockery of my need for control.

Finally, with an impatient Roe tap dancing at the front door, Poppy stood still long enough to be harnessed. I was exhausted before the walk even began. And, no surprise here, the maneuvering was irritating my crumbly ol' T12 vertebra, which also was going to be subjected to a steep hill down our driveway.

My plan was to put Roe and Poppy on the dual leash. I hoped she'd get his positive energy and a bit of the "full speed ahead" walk mentality. But Chris would need to walk them—the risk of me being pulled in different directions and falling again seemed high. I'd walk Percival. We called Percival Ferdinand on walks, since he, like the bull from the story, needed to stop and smell all the flowers. This was not a trait we wanted to teach Poppy, though truth be told, I didn't mind a rose-smelling walk.

Everyone harnessed and leashed and mostly raring to go, tallyho and all that, we were off.

And then we weren't.

Poppy was initially swept up in Roe's exuberance as the two of them rushed out the door side by side. But whether it was the bracing cool air, the welcome mat, or a whiff of the neighbor's cat, something made her slam on the brakes and hunker down. Roe continued ahead with all his might, which meant Chris was jerked forward by one part of the leash and anchored in place by the other. Percival and I, bringing up the rear, had to jump to the right to avoiding stepping on Poppy or running up Chris's back. The ensuing physical reactions and entanglement of legs, leashes, and desires would have been some excellent slapstick, had it not been for the one terrified little beagle, who had, in her attempts to get away from it all, wrapped Chris up like a leash mummy. Any attempt by Chris to lift his leg and untangle it from the leash caused Poppy to pull away, further immobilizing Chris. Were she any bigger or he any smaller, he would have gone down hard.

"Hold on, hold on. Let me get her," I said. I tried to move toward Poppy, but then Percival decided he also didn't want to go on a walk and had dropped into his patented four-paw stop—all four legs locked, with the full weight of himself thrown backward in defiance, refusing to be swept up in our clown circus. "Can you take Percival's leash?"

"Can I handle one more dog? Sure. Yes. Why not? Obviously I have these two under control," said the leash mummy.

Humor in the face of looming disaster is one of the reasons I love him.

"So I can grab Poppy. Then you can unhook her leash."

The dual leash that Roe and Poppy were on was one of my favorite dog inventions. Each had a separate leash, but they hooked together on a large swiveling D-ring that then just had one strap with the handle that Chris was holding. Thanks to the swiveling motion the two leashes rarely got tangled. Naturally, this was one of those rare times it did tangle, however, since Poppy had run around Chris's legs a few times. But it meant he was only holding one handle and did have a free hand (though it was attached to his only free limb). The mummy obediently took Percival's leash from me.

I picked up Poppy, holding her close so I could unhook her leash from her harness. Chris was able to hold the leash for both Roe, pulling forward, and Percival, pulling backward, long enough to untangle Poppy's leash from his legs.

I snapped Poppy's leash back on her harness and she sprung forward, now headed in the same direction as Roe. I'd like to think she simply quickly got the hang of walking, but it was hard to ignore that she was running from Chris on the other end of the leash.

"This will be fun," Chris said, no longer mummified but walking quickly and leaning backward to counteract the force of the two dogs headed with all their might down our dirt and gravel driveway hill.

Percival must have thought it looked like fun, or, more likely, he was not going to tolerate Poppy and Roe running off with his man-crush Chris. He hopped up and raced after them, dragging me along.

"Yep. Good times!" I yelled after Chris. I was being sarcastic, and I wasn't. We hadn't gotten off to a great start, but I was thrilled to see Poppy walking on the leash, thrilled to be back in Paso, and thrilled to be walking three beagles with Chris.

Despite our comedic start, my plan worked. Though she kept her tail tucked and her body low to the ground for the first ten minutes of the walk, Poppy soon picked up Roe's energy. She glanced at him frequently and did as he did—running, smelling, scouting for rabbits. Over the hour we were out her tail came up, though never quite at full mast, and her face relaxed. She stayed close by Roe, occasionally joined by Percival-Ferdinand if they happened to be smelling a blade of grass or a weed he was interested in. Anytime she noticed Chris, however, Poppy pulled away or crouched down.

"She's still not used to the leash or you; it will take some time," I said.

"She's doing better than I thought she would," he said.

"And much better than she was doing in Riverside with just me. Roe is really helping her."

"Roe is the perfect dog!"

"Roe-Roe *is* perfect," I said.

Roe howled his big, hunting dog howl, deep and loud, in agreement. I jumped. I was not yet used to just how loud his howl was. *Not the perfect dog to come back and forth to Riverside with me, not with that loud howl. My neighbor would have the National Guard out.*

Poppy did not join in the howl; we had yet to hear her make a noise at all. A small, quiet dog. *Hmmmm.*

After only a few more walks with Roe over the next few days, Poppy was fine on a leash. She still balked at the sight of her harness, though. As soon as she saw her harness, or even Percival's or Roe's, she hid under the bed or ran in zoomie circles around the house, but eventually I could catch her and we'd all head out without much of the entanglements of the first walk.

Chris also soon figured out that if he was sitting on the couch, Poppy was less frightened. And if he was lying down, she was not afraid at all. She continued to sleep on my pillow, with Chris on the pillow next to her, and even began to imitate Percival by climbing on top of Chris for serious morning petting. But once he stood, she fled. She'd be under the bed before he was even fully upright. If we were downstairs and Chris got off the couch to head to the bathroom or the kitchen, Poppy raced behind the armchair in the corner—a place we came to call her "cave"—and disappeared. She wouldn't emerge until ten, fifteen, even twenty minutes after Chris sat back down.

While I could see she still had fears, I was impressed—proud, even—of how far she had come. She was at her core, it seemed, a very happy dog. That, in turn, made me happy.

"It kind of breaks my heart to see her so afraid of me," Chris said.

"I know. She got used to me pretty quickly, but she kind of had to. It will get better," I said. I wanted Chris to love this little dog like I did. She was trying so hard—I could see that in her face, in her intense little eyes. She wanted to be brave.

Once I get to the actual Christmas day, I generally can relax and even say the "C" word. The tragedies of holidays past all occurred between Thanksgiving and December 24. Though it was ridiculous to then think I'd entered some bubble of safety, and not rational at all (I mean *at all*—wasn't I just taunting the universe again?), I tended to settle in and enjoy the actual day. No doubt because for many years now Christmas morning was a morning of coffee, food, books, dogs, Chris and I reading or playing board games, and eventually sharing a bottle of wine. What's not to like?

This Christmas morning was a bit more rambunctious—it was a sonata of squeaks, paper shredding, and Roe's hearty howls of joy. I began to wonder if that's where his name came from—when he howled it sounded like "ROE-ROE-ROE-ROE-ROE."

We *may* have overdone it with the presents for the dogs. They each had far more gifts than we did, but that's what made it fun. Percival had always loved toys and gleefully grabbed and squeaked each toy, running around with it before settling down to the serious business of disemboweling the moose, the hedgehog, and Santa. It was clear neither Roe nor Poppy had ever had any toys, but for Roe the hunting instinct must have kicked in. He took to the disemboweling game instantly. He and Percival even played tug-of-war for a bit. Poppy's technique was different. She carried the toys around, sometimes using them for a pillow, sometimes racing upstairs to hide them under our bed.

"Great, our shoes and books she shreds, but the toys are precious," Chris said.

"Well, the toys are hers, the shoes were ours," I said.

"So she's selfish?"

"She's a beagle!" I said this happily, as though the "it's my world, you're just living in it" attitude of a beagle was a good thing, because to me it was. I simply love their attitudes, and I loved Poppy getting more beagle-y.

"Is she, though?" Chris said.

Fair point. Poppy did not look like a pure beagle. She was too small, for one. And her head was much smaller than a beagle's. I thought she might be mixed with Jack Russell terrier—especially the way she jumped and leaped and seemed to have springs for legs. Beagles are high-energy dogs (when they're not couch potatoes), but their energy seems to always be in a forward motion, led by their nose to the ground in the constant search for food. Poppy's energy moved vertically as much as horizontally. She could spring from standing still to the top of a table in a flash. Often that was our dining room table.

"She's definitely part beagle. But she's all cute."

"She is pretty cute."

Poppy hopped up into my lap and leaned into me. I kissed the top of her head and stroked her back. "I love her."

Silence.

Uncomfortable silence.

"I know you do. That's what I'm worried about," he said. "You're fostering her, but I can already see you want to keep her."

"Of course I want to keep her, I want to keep all dogs. But I know I'm fostering." (I did not know that, but I was trying to know that.)

"Do you, though?" (I'm not fooling him? Shocking.)

"I do. But I'm fostering her for a while. It's been less than three weeks. She has a long way to go. She's not ready to be adopted yet." (Translation: can't I just foster her forever?)

"She's shredding everything we own and peeing everywhere, and you don't even seem to notice."

"She's a puppy. And Percival did all of that too. She was getting the hang of things in Riverside, and then I changed her routine. She'll get it. At least she's going on the pee pads. She just needs time." (*Like, forever. That amount of time.*)

"I'm just worried the longer you have her, the harder it's going to be to let her go."

"Well, of course it is. That's the nature of fostering. But I love Roe too, and we can only have two dogs. I know that." To my surprise I began to tear up. "Can we not talk about this on Christmas?"

"Okay, okay. Don't cry. We can talk about it later."

Chris came over to comfort me, or maybe to pet Poppy or both, but Poppy vaulted from my lap and slunk back behind my chair to her cave. *Not helping, Poppy. Not helping.*

8

TRIALS

Again, I was on the road, wind in my hair, NPR on my radio, cruising past the happy cows on Highway 46, on my way back to Riverside, with a dog in my back seat. (Okay, still no wind in my hair; I just like that image, if not the reality). I still had the confusion about where home was, but Poppy was with me, and a canine traveling companion always makes the drive better. With a dog, I can be headed home.

Unfortunately, when we returned to Riverside, we returned to step one in Poppy's housetraining process. Whatever routine Poppy had picked up in her first two weeks in Riverside, she'd forgotten about in Paso Robles. She did at least remember how to use the doggie door, but she preferred I open the French doors to the patio for her, and she preferred this once again at 4:00 A.M. If I hesitated too long, she preferred the living room floor. Sometimes the hallway. I put pee pads down in both spots as well as in the bedroom. Then she chose the bathroom rug, which I could at least easily throw in the wash. She also took a shine to trash as a favorite toy, even though to the best of my knowledge nothing in the trash cans squeaked. Did she need a big beagle brother more than she needed me?

None of that could dampen my happiness to have her with me (pun intended; no, really). The Riverside house was no longer without a dog. I now had an abundantly energetic and happy canine companion. I needed that. Despite her fears, her nervousness, and all she'd been through, she was a joyful and playful dog. That fascinated me. *Show me your ways, Poppy.*

For her part, Poppy enjoyed being home with me, but she did not enjoy going to work with me. I couldn't figure out what it was about going to my office that she disliked; after all, it wasn't like she had any actual work to do or a boss to answer to, or even clients to keep happy. Was it the car? The people coming and going from the office? Was it boring? Oddly, the thing she seemed to hate most was when I'd put the leash on her and walk her around the pond in our building's courtyard. It was a nice grassy area with a tree, some bushes, and a small rock waterfall at one end of the pond. The pond even had turtles, and the tree often had squirrels. What more could a dog want?

She hated it. Even if she was up, prancing around my office and looking like she could use a walk, the moment my hand went toward the leash, she flew under my desk and wedged herself into the far corner. I would lure her out with treats or sometimes just drag her out. More often, I just tried to explain the joys of outdoors to her and carried her outside, where, once on the ground, she'd drop to the grass and freeze. Hardly the best position for her to do the dirty business I wanted her to be doing on the lawn. Pee pads in my executive office wasn't really the professional look I was going for, but as you know, my office had seen far worse. Luckily, I can close my office door and meet with clients in the conference room, but still, Poppy needed to get comfortable going outside.

Jessica frequently offered to take Poppy outside if I was in a meeting (kindness, yes; she may have also been hoping to avoid any more Poppy poopy incidents—though that issue had been resolved in Poppy, I'm sure the memory lived on in Jessica). She had no better luck than I did encouraging Poppy to think of the lawn and the walk around the pond as a good thing. Between us we did at least get the little beagle to the point of hurrying around the pond, still crouched low to the ground, and racing back into the office to her safe zone. That was something like a walk, though she looked like a baby alligator running on a leash.

Poppy even started voluntarily going into Jessica's office as well. She wouldn't stay long, and usually she was sniffing around at Jessica's lunch, but I could see that even the quick visit was making Jessica happy.

Still, I was surprised when Jessica came into my office one afternoon.

"I know you said you're fostering Poppy, so if she's going to be available for adoption, I just wanted to tell you that Austin and I would be interested in adopting her."

Instantly my mind raced ahead to all the positives: *I'd know where Poppy was. I could keep tabs on her. I could maybe visit her, or dog-sit if they needed me to. Poppy could come to the office regularly! The perfect solution! I would not fail at fostering, but I'd still get time with this dog I'd come to adore. This was fabulous!*

My brain then shifted to the other obvious facts: Poppy would be a difficult first dog. Jessica and Austin live in an apartment; if Poppy ever learns to howl like most beagles, this might be an issue. Poppy wasn't yet ready to be adopted—another change in circumstances might set her back in her training.

Mostly what I thought was *Poppy could keep coming to my office!* (At this point, I may seem like that pathetic girl who thinks she can *make* her bad boyfriend love her, but I'm only trying to make a beagle love a law office, so let's pretend it's totally different.)

"Oh! That would be good. You'll have to apply through Beagle Freedom Project. And I'm not sure how they'll respond because you're in an apartment, but it's worth a try," I said.

"I didn't mean right away. I know she's not ready. But maybe after a little while?"

Like after she's house trained and no longer hiding under beds and desks? Smart!

"Yeah, I think she needs to stay with me for a little while longer. But I'll send you the information to apply."

Jessica left, happy. I looked down at Poppy, curled up on the dog bed I'd moved under the desk. She was looking up at me, thumping her tail, content in her little space.

"How would that be, Popstar? Would you like to live with Jessica and Austin?"

Poppy's tail continued to thump away, and then she rose up, doing her wigglebutt thing from side to side. When I reached down to pet her, she licked my hand.

A few days later, Jessica sent in her application, and I asked BFP if it was okay for Jessica and Austin to have some trial visits. They agreed.

I had not been able to leave Poppy home alone for longer than an hour without suffering dire consequences, and I couldn't afford to lose any more shoes or books. No matter how high up I placed things—and by now every surface above three feet was covered with items that used to be placed below three feet—Poppy found a way to drag items down to shredding level. Underneath my bed was a book and shoe wasteland. I needed a few hours off Poppy duty to get some errands done. A trial visit would be a good thing for everyone. We chose a Saturday afternoon.

I brought Poppy, some of her favorite toys (which were not my shoes), her crate, some treats, and several pee pads over to Jessica and Austin's apartment. I needn't have bothered. Jessica had loaded up on treats, toys, and, based on her office experiences with Poppy, plenty of pee pads and carpet cleaner. Poppy would be fine. They were taking this seriously.

"Okay, so as you know, she's likely to hide in the corner of your couch or stay in her crate. But just give her space and let her come out when she's ready. She's a little bit used to you," I said, looking at Jessica, "but sorry, Austin, she's probably not going to be coming over to you just yet."

"Jessica told me. It's okay. She's really cute. Littler than I was thinking," Austin said.

"Yeah, she's tiny for a beagle."

Poppy had begun to explore their living room a bit, so I decided to head out while she was distracted.

I dropped off my dry cleaning, got my car washed, and went grocery shopping, I also continually checked my phone for messages.

How was she doing? Was she okay? Did she miss me? Do they like her? No messages is probably a good thing—it had only been a few hours—I had to remind myself. After having Poppy with me nearly 24/7 for the last five weeks, it was disconcerting to be without her. I'd gotten so used to that little inquisitive face looking at me for guidance, that springy body of hers doing her gymnastics over the furniture, and, mostly, her cuddled in next to me. None of those things could happen while I was out running errands of course, but I missed her. There was a void, and I felt it in just a few hours without her. Being dogless is not my thing.

When I picked Poppy up, Jessica told me Poppy had spent most of her time on the floor but leaning up against the couch, near Jessica. Jessica had been able to pet her a little and give her a treat and Poppy did head to the pee pad in the hallway when needed, so all in all a good visit. As predicted, Austin was not able to approach her. Austin, like Chris, is a tall and large man. Poppy preferred everyone be seated, but even that wasn't enough for her to approach Austin. Such familiarity would take some time. But they seemed happy to have had her—a dog of their own on a tryout basis.

On Sunday I took Poppy over to my friend Michelle's house to continue Poppy's socializing and run off a little of that manic energy of hers. Michelle has a beautiful home and yard that looked like a slice of Provence, right there in River City. Over the years, Chris and I had brought all our dogs over to play in this vast, beautiful, wild yard. We called it—based on our dogs' exuberance when there—Doggie Disneyland.

Michelle was also a serious dog lover and had two rescue dogs, Rex, a little terrier mix who was all attitude, and Alex, a big, loveable ottoman of a Rottweiler/shepherd mix of sorts. Poppy didn't seem to be afraid of other dogs, and Rex was about her size. I thought some running around time would be good for her, and I could use some time in Michelle's relaxing backyard with a cup of coffee and some conversation. The day was gorgeous, sunny, clear, and crisp.

Poppy took to the yard and the concept of free roaming easily—running around the lawn, trying to get Rex to play with her, and then tearing down the steps to the back fence. That part made me a little nervous. Michelle's house backed up to a slice of Sycamore Canyon Wilderness Park—a finger of the park that came up between two rows of houses and stretched to the Canyon Crest golf course on the other end. That part of her yard always made me nervous. The wilderness park was home to coyotes, the occasional mountain lion, and snakes. Looming danger, with a simple chain link fence between it and a pleasant vegetable garden.

"It's well fenced," Michelle said, as I stared at the back fence. "If Rex hasn't gotten out, Poppy won't."

"True. And Seamus was the master of escape, and he never got out of your yard."

Roe had also spent an afternoon there, in the first week he was with me. And Roe was a retired hunting dog. If there was a way out, he certainly would have found it. I relaxed.

Michelle and I sat in the sunshine, sipping coffee and talking while the dogs played.

"She's really cute. She's so small, though," Michelle said. "Are you keeping her?"

Michelle knew me well enough that she probably meant the question as a rhetorical one. But I had a plan! A plan about which I was still trying to convince myself, so why not try it out on Michelle?

"No. I think my paralegal will be adopting her. Which will be perfect because I'll still get to see her a lot," I said.

Michelle's face told me my plan was not foolproof. Or I was a fool. Something having to do with foolish . . . "Have they had a dog before?" she asked.

"No, but Jessica has been around Poppy a lot in the office. And she won't be adopting her until Poppy is housebroken, and a bit more . . . well, normal. She's still terrified of things."

"A beagle as a first dog?" Michelle's face was definitely telling me this was not a good plan. (Imagine—me with a plan that was no good. Impossible.)

I understood her point. Beagles are smart, stubborn dogs. Beagles take a lot of patience. And a good sense of humor about all the trouble they get in stealing your food, shredding your belongings, howling, and generally not listening to you unless they felt like it (which they did if you had food, and usually only then). And Poppy certainly had her own issues. Getting a harness and leash on her was still a bit tricky, and if she didn't want to be caught, she was wickedly fast and slippery. But Jessica knew these things and loved Poppy anyway. And other people have been known to train beagles. So I've been told (mostly by readers of my first book).

"I know. But they're young. They have energy."

I stood to take a photo. Poppy had jumped up onto the two-foot retaining wall, painted bright Provence blue and capped with red-orange bricks, with the wild green hillside behind her, and she was smelling the flowering yellow kangaroo paw bush—a peaceful, colorful little scene my camera could not resist. She looked happy, and I was happy to see her exploring and being just a bit braver. She turned and looked at me just as I took the photo.

🐾

Poppy was progressing quickly.

Jessica and Austin were game to try another visit with Poppy—this time for an overnight stay. We agreed they would watch her on the Tuesday night following their Saturday visit, which was going to work out well for me. A client had long ago given me tickets to a Lakers game. Not just any tickets, season tickets on the floor. The only people sitting in front of us would be the Lakers themselves. I'm not a huge sports fan, but as a kid my dad had been a Lakers fan, and we saw a few games in the Jerry West/Wilt Chamberlain era, so I had a bit of a fondness for the team. I also knew Chris would enjoy the game, especially in these seats, which would have been hard (and rude) to pass up. Plus, there was also the chance we'd be seated near some celebrities—the seats were that good, and Lakers games were usually peopled with celebrities like Jay-Z, Beyoncé, Jack Nicholson, and a Kardashian or two.

The plan was that Chris would drive down to Riverside Tuesday morning, bringing Roe and Percival with him, and then head back up early Thursday morning to be back at the winery tasting room for his 3:00 P.M. shift. A lot of driving in a short time, but he thought it was worth it. Plus, I'd get to see my boys (including Chris) midweek in Riverside, a nice treat. We considered leaving Poppy home with Percival and Roe while we went to the game but decided that she was far more likely to influence them than the other way around. Which is to say, we were far more likely to come home to a shredded couch than a couch with three beagles curled up sleeping soundly. Jessica and

Austin gave us a nice option—Poppy could stay with them while we went to the game, and we'd pick her up in the morning. We were all set. (Hear the universe, anyone?)

On Tuesday evening, Chris and I raced across the intersection outside Staples Center in downtown Los Angeles in a torrential downpour. We had left Riverside early, expecting the usual LA traffic to move in one more circle of hell due to the rain. But the drive was surprisingly quick and easy. The parking attendant told us umbrellas weren't allowed in Staples Center (why? And why would I have asked him? And why would I have believed him? I have no answers). We were drenched by the time we got to the door—the wrong door, as it turned out. It was only 5:00 P.M. and the security guard told us they didn't start letting people in until 6:00 P.M., at any door but the one we raced over to. He also told us that of course we could have brought our umbrellas with us.

"There's a Starbucks over there, want to make a run for it?" Chris pointed down and across the street, where there was a movie theater and shopping center.

"No. I just want to stay out of the rain." We had huddled under a ledge and were watching the rain slicing down.

"For an hour?"

"Fair point. Maybe if we move down to the main entrance there will be more cover."

And we did just that, hurrying along the side of the building to get to the main entrance to stand along with a hundred or so other unfashionably early, but not nearly as wet, folks. There was more cover and we quickly found a spot to wait. No matter the weather or our soggy outsides, we were happy to be out on a date. We hadn't been able to do much of that in the months before. Daphne had been ill and in need of a lot of expensive health care, and after she passed, even if we'd had extra money for dates I was in no mood. There'd also been my dad's move and the emotional drain of that (his and mine), and then Roe and then Poppy, and well . . . there just hadn't been a lot of Chris and Teresa time.

"Something's bound to go wrong," I said.

"Oh, nice. What? Maybe lightning will strike?"

"I'll slip and fall on the wet ground? Another back injury seems reasonable."

"Active shooter?"

"Wow. Going all out. The balcony collapses?"

"Meteor strikes?"

"People are going to move far away from us," I said. We were perhaps a bit bad-luck prone, but at least we still had our sense of humor.

"As well they should."

One person, however, was not moving away from us—the guy selling all the counterfeit Lakers gear. Chris waved him away with a polite but firm "No, thank you."

"I don't know. I'm thinking about the gold and purple beanie hat. My hair is kind of a mess," I said.

"Do not make eye contact!" Chris stressed this point because he knew that if I made eye contact the guy would approach us and I would inevitably buy something at the first price he tossed out. I hate bargaining and tend to feel sorry for people hustling for a living like that. Even if they're hustling me.

"I know. I know. I won't. But really, how much could it be?" I said.

"Earthquake?"

"Oh, back to that game. So much more fun than me buying cheap, counterfeit Lakers gear. Okay, tsunami!"

"It is raining a lot. That one has real possibility."

We amused one another with potential tragedies unfolding until the doors finally opened and we merged, holding hands, into the throng of humanity.

We were greeted with shaking pom-poms, behind which were young girls . . . no . . . young women. (I'm at that age where everyone below the age of forty looks like a teenager, and everyone above forty looks older than me. The age of lost perspective.) They were dressed in purple and gold spandex shorts and crop tops that moved their breasts beyond the realm of gravity, and they flashed huge smiles that exposed ridiculously white teeth. We moved toward them because they were handing out something, and who doesn't like a freebie, right?

We each took what they handed us, which turned out to be rain ponchos. Well, that's a bit of an overstatement. More like gold-colored plastic trash bags, with hoods and a Lakers logo.

"Were those Laker Girls? The actual cheerleaders, dancers, whatevers?" I said.

"I would assume so from the outfits," Chris said.

"They look like they're fifteen years old. I thought maybe they were in training. Like Explorer Laker Girls or something."

"I don't think that's a thing."

"On to food. Find me a cocktail and some yummy vegan junk food."

We had read somewhere that there was vegan food available at Staples Center, so we set out on our search. A full loop around the arena later, we still had not discovered any vegan food. But Chris, who is not vegan, found a fried chicken and honey biscuit stand and was all-in. I grabbed a small bag of potato chips in case the vegan food never materialized.

Then we had the fun of making our way to our seats. Down, down, down, the stairs past several checkpoints where, we joked, they weeded out the riffraff (like us, had we had to purchase tickets ourselves), until finally we were standing on the court. This was not unlike boarding a plane when you have to walk past all the lucky folks in first class sipping on champagne, while you make your way to your tiny little seat in the back of the plane where you're lucky if they toss you a miniature bag of pretzels. Only in reverse. This time, we were the champagne sippers walking past the pretzel people.

The attendant pointed to our seats and the menus where we could order food and drinks. Our seats were on the court. I guessed that service was pretty good.

"Oooooh, that's probably how I get vegan food," I said, perusing the courtside menu.

Chris was too busy enjoying his greasy fried chicken to worry that we could have done better. We sat and looked around. The floors were glossy, everything seemed lit up beyond daylight, music blared, while the arena began to fill. The young couple next to us took about 162 selfies.

"I'm going to make you do that too, you realize, right?" I said, nudging Chris out of his fried chicken spell.

"Oh, I'm aware. Just wait until the players are out."

Directly in front of us, with only a couple of feet separating us, was another row of chairs—the players' chairs. The odds were good the people seated in front of us, on the same level as us, were going to be tall. And probably standing up a lot. These were spectacular seats for feeling part of the game, almost part of the team, but maybe less so for viewing the actual game. That point was driven home when a Lakers employee wheeled out a large container of Gatorade on a cart and stopped directly in front of us. Then a petite female security guard took her position next to the Gatorade. The theft of Gatorade must be a serious concern.

"So here's the silver lining. Every time a player gets a cup of Gatorade he will literally be facing me. I should be able to get a lot of portrait shots!" I said.

"If only you knew who any of the players are," Chris said.

"Sadly, I only recognize the coach—Luke Walton, right? And I think that's more because I remember his dad. Though I can't remember his dad's name."

"Bill Walton. Right, that would make sense."

The fact that I remembered Bill Walton could only mean he played on the Lakers or some other team around the same time Jerry West and Wilt Chamberlain played. (Chris would not have been born yet, but thankfully he didn't mention that.) And so ends the tour of my professional basketball knowledge. (Wait, I also know Paula Abdul was a Laker Girl; I feel like that should count as sports knowledge. The fact that I also know she was married to Emilio Estevez probably doesn't count as sports knowledge, though. So, yep. That's it—the end of my sports knowledge.)

Chris returned to his meal while I tried to find someone I could ask about getting vegan food. Soon, the loud music and spinning, brightly colored lights cranked up to another level and the Laker Girls ran out onto the court.

"I can't even tell if those are the same Laker Girls that handed us the trash bag ponchos. Maybe that *was* the second string?" I said.

"I'm fine with all of them," Chris said. He was the stereotypical picture of male happiness—a cocktail, fried food, front row seats to a sportsing thing, and cheerleaders nearby.

"This is not a bad way to spend an evening," I said.

"Not bad at all." He leaned over and kissed me, and we took a moment to just enjoy each other, smiling face-to-face. "This is a great date night," he said.

"Time for the selfie!" I grabbed my phone and handed it to him.

"Let's do selfie," he said in the vocal-fry of a twenty-something So Cal girl that had become a running joke with us years ago. Neither of us remembers why anymore, but I'm thankful for it because we now have years and years of selfie memories.

When the announcements of the players started I took my phone back. I noticed I had two missed calls and several text messages. All from Jessica.

I didn't panic. I was too happy in the moment. (I should know better.) I thought perhaps Poppy was hiding from her or wasn't eating. Or maybe she had a question about the food—how much to give, when to give it—things I had told her but maybe not written down.

I didn't listen to the messages, I just called, Lakers warm-up music blaring in the background, lights swirling, people cheering.

"Poppy got loose . . . She's gone . . . She ran away. We're trying to catch her. Oh my god. I'm sorry. She's running," Jessica was uncharacteristically panicked and near tears.

"Wait, what? I'm at the game, I can barely hear you. Hang on." I thought she was telling me Poppy had escaped, but my brain was rejecting that and I was standing in a crowded arena minutes before tip-off and sixty miles away. So that just can't be. It can't.

I grabbed Chris's arm and leaned toward him. "It's Jessica. I can't hear her. I'm going to find a quieter place."

I snatched my ticket from my purse and moved away from the floor seats, heading upstairs.

"We took her for a walk. It started raining. I don't know. The thunder scared her and she just bolted and twisted and she got out from the harness.

She ran . . . she just ran . . . and um, under a fence and we've been chasing her. But we lost her. I'm so sorry. Oh god."

"Okay, okay. Um. She has a GPS tracker on her collar. Let me look at that and tell you where she is. Is it still raining?"

"Yes, it's raining hard."

"I'll call you back. Please keep looking."

I checked the GPS tracker app on my phone. What I saw was terrifying. Poppy had run out from their apartment complex, across Central Avenue to the shopping center, raced around the shopping center, crossed back over Central Avenue, then across an equally busy Canyon Crest Drive, into a neighborhood. She'd crossed two very busy streets during a very busy time in the midst of a rainstorm.

I called Jessica with the directions and told her we were on our way back, then returned to our valuable, and now useless, seats.

"Poppy got away from Jessica and Austin. She's now running loose through the Canyon Crest area. We have to go."

"Now?" Chris looked from me back to the court, where the Lakers were finishing their warm-up. "We can't get there for an hour or two. Don't you think they'll catch her?" Chris said, his disappointment nearly as strong as my fear.

"No, I don't. She's fast, and she's scared. And I won't enjoy any part of this worrying about her."

Chris looked back to the court. The players were returning to their seats in front of us. "Can we watch the tip-off? It's about four minutes away."

I checked the GPS one more time. Poppy has stayed in the neighborhood, with quieter streets and, please Buddha, less traffic, but was moving around. Would four minutes make a difference? It would to Chris, but there was no way to know about Poppy. "Okay. And then we have to go. We have to. I'm sorry."

"Okay. No, I get it. I'm hoping they catch her."

I took a screen shot of the GPS map and texted it to Jessica.

She texted back, "We almost had her, but she slipped away. We can see her, we just can't catch her."

Okay, good. At least they knew where she was, and she was no longer in the busy intersection.

The tip-off happened, along with about thirty seconds of play that felt like hours, and we bolted from our seats, running up the flights of stairs it had been so fun to walk down.

On our way out of Staples Center, I thought about trying to find someone to hand our tickets to—give someone better seats. Why let them go to waste? A father and son out for a night? A young couple? It didn't matter; I couldn't focus. I briefly wondered if the client who gave me the tickets would watch the game on television and see the empty seats. Well, I'd have a good excuse.

Chris drove while I texted with Jessica, sending her screenshots of the GPS map. Each refresh of the tracker terrified me more. Poppy ran back across the busy streets, around the shopping center again, and then back to the neighborhood. But this time, she headed up a green belt and into a wilderness park. Jessica texted that they were following her, but she'd slipped under a fence. It was dark and pouring rain, and they needed to go get a flashlight.

For one of the longest hours of my life this went on: I checked my GPS app, took a screenshot, and texted it to Jessica, while Chris drove in the rain and tried to tell me comforting, hopeful things. Poppy moved farther into the wilderness park, making my screenshots nearly useless to Jessica and Austin. There are not a lot of distinguishing features on a GPS map of a wilderness park, just the occasional trail name.

"This was not on either of our tragedy bingo cards tonight," I said.

"It was not," Chris said.

I checked the GPS tracker again. Poppy was still in the wilderness park, but she had moved again.

Jessica and Austin had been trailing the dog for over two hours by then, and they were not familiar with the wilderness park, let alone at night in a storm. They needed help. I needed help. Poppy needed help.

I suddenly remembered my friend Michelle, whose home backed up to the Sycamore Canyon Wilderness Park. I knew she walked her dogs there regularly and knew the park. Maybe Poppy would make her way to Michelle's house, a place she'd been before, with dogs she knew. Maybe Michelle could help Jessica and Austin.

Michelle did not hesitate. She grabbed a raincoat, a leash, and a heavy-duty flashlight and instructed Jessica and Austin on where to meet her—a trailhead that could take them into the area it seemed Poppy had settled down. She texted me the same information, and Chris drove us to that park entrance.

As Chris and I exited the car I realized we were not dressed for the occasion. Not at all. We were dressed for an indoor basketball game. While I had boots and jeans on, the boots were more for fashion and less for hiking, the jeans were thin, and over my shirt I had only a crocheted poncho, which when soaked would weigh ten pounds or so.

Poncho!

"Chris, grab our Lakers poncho trash bag things!"

"You're kidding."

"It will keep us dry for a little while longer. And for the record, I should have bought the black-market beanie hat."

When Michelle, Jessica, and Austin came over a hill and toward us, we were unraveling the gold plastic ponchos and trying to put them over our clothes.

"Is that all you have?" Michelle said. She was an expert traveler and had appropriate clothing for just about any weather or occasion. She was clad in a heavy raincoat and hood, carrying a flashlight that looked like it could light up a significant portion of the park.

"I wasn't planning on hiking tonight," I said.

Jessica and Austin were in sweatshirts and jeans, and they were drenched. They had not planned on hiking that night either. They looked miserable and tired. It occurred to me then, seeing Jessica's anguished face, that she had not just lost a dog, but her boss' dog. I wasn't angry with her—I felt bad for her. And for Poppy. And for me. For all of us, standing in the rain at the edge of a wilderness park.

Austin began to explain everywhere they'd followed her and how fast she was and where he thought she might be.

Michelle cut him off. "Check the GPS. Where is she right now?"

I checked and showed Michelle the screen. I was unfamiliar with Sycamore Canyon Wilderness Park and unable to tell much even from the GPS screen. We were standing at a city park—the kind with swings, and a climbing tower, and sand where kids play. That park was adjacent to the wilderness park, but there seemed to be more tract homes than wilderness in front of me. I assumed, based on the signage and my phone screen, that those homes abutted the wilderness park.

"I don't know if there is an entrance over there, but our best bet is that neighborhood." Michelle pointed to a development of large homes. "Maybe we can find a greenbelt between houses or someplace where we can enter the canyon."

"Let's go." I couldn't stand still. We needed to move. Time was wasting.

We all returned to our cars and followed Michelle through the neighborhood. She stopped at the end of a street with a high gate, behind which was a canyon.

I checked the GPS. Poppy was still moving, but we seemed to have moved closer. The five of us piled out of our cars.

"Let's spread out and walk the neighborhood—see if there is any opening we can get through," Chris said.

"We already looked. We couldn't find one," Austin said.

"Okay, let's find a neighbor who will let us in to their backyard," I said. I was met with four incredulous stares. Incredulous enough that I turned to look at the homes. They were large, imposing, and well gated—no doubt to keep out the creatures living in the wilderness behind them, and, well, the humans chasing them.

"Call out to her. She probably wants to come home by now," Chris said.

We walked to the end of the street and stood at the tall fence. "POPPY! POPPY! POPPY POPSTAR!" I shouted.

Chris joined in calling to her and we all stood watching for any movement at all.

"I can't really figure out where we are. Where is this in relation to where she entered the park? It seems so far," I said.

"It's east and maybe a little south," Chris said.

"Not helpful." I am, to put it mildly, directionally challenged.

"It's far, but she could definitely travel this far."

I kept yelling to her, with the others chiming in from distances of ten yards or so from me. There still was no movement, except from the house nearest us.

The lights came on, flooding the driveway to our right and a man walked out the front door of a large home. "What is going on?" he shouted down to us.

Michelle, who was closest to him, walked closer. "Sorry, sir. They've lost a dog and she ran into the canyon. That's who we're calling to."

"There's a lot of coyotes out there," he said. Which was hardly the invitation to his backyard I was hoping for.

"Yes, we know. We're trying not to think about that part."

"Well, good luck." He turned and disappeared back into his mini-manse, without issuing a backyard invite.

I checked the GPS app again. Poppy was moving away from us. Or from him. Headed back the direction she had come.

I showed Chris.

"Back in the car. Back to the park entrance we just came from."

Again, like a bad episode of slapstick minus the comedy, the five of us climbed back into our three cars and sped through the neighborhood back to where we'd come from.

"Okay, so if you follow this trail and just keep heading that way, that's going to be your best bet." Michelle pointed to a trail along the side of the family park. "It will take you past this neighborhood and then into the heart of the wilderness park."

"Okay, let's go." I started to walk in the direction she pointed.

"Hold up. Here," Michelle took off her raincoat and handed it to me, along with her gloves. "And take this." She gave me the flashlight. "And there's a smaller flashlight in the pocket of the raincoat. The battery isn't fully charged in the big one, so it won't last all night. I've got to get home to my own dogs."

"Okay, thanks." I put the raincoat on over the wet plastic Lakers poncho, which was over my wet crocheted poncho, and handed Chris the larger flashlight.

"Okay, let's go," Chris said.

"Thanks, Michelle," I said.

"I can come back tomorrow and help if you need me. I hope you don't, but if you do, let me know."

Tomorrow. I couldn't think about the possibility we wouldn't find Poppy that night. It was cold, and dark, and wet, and I kept picturing that sweet little face of hers, the fear she must be feeling. We had to find her tonight.

"God, I hope not. But thanks," I said. And then, as I started up the trail, "Okay let's go."

Austin and Chris quickly took the lead, with me, and then Jessica, trailing behind. Jessica got farther and farther behind as we moved deeper into the canyon. The farther we moved from the park and the houses, the darker it got. With the flashlights we could see maybe ten feet in front of us—dirt, boulders, occasional trees.

Eventually Austin stopped and waited for Jessica, while Chris and I moved ahead. By the time Austin again caught up with us, Jessica was no longer with him.

"Jessica had to go back to the car. She's not feeling good and can't keep hiking."

It was now after 10:00 P.M. They'd been following the dog for five hours or so. "Okay, I understand," I said. Jessica had not told me she wasn't feeling well; she hadn't even said she was tired, but then, she wouldn't. She'd been working for me by then for about two years. She'd started as an intern and was so quiet, so uncommunicative it almost masked how smart she was. Almost. I'd hired her full time and as she got more comfortable, she spoke up more often and even, on occasion, joked with me. But she was most content in her quiet office alone. It was not a surprise then that having lost her boss's dog in a wilderness park on a rainy night she was not prepared to walk up to that same boss and complain about not feeling good. Thankfully, she at least let Austin know that.

I checked the GPS app again and showed Austin and Chris the screen. "She hasn't moved from this spot."

The many scenarios why she hadn't moved from that spot played out in my head. I tried to focus on the scenario where she'd crawled under a rock formation—there were plenty of them—and was curled up dry and sleeping. But my mind would quickly flip to coyote packs attacking her and the GPS monitor attached to her collar being all that was left. The alternative between the hopeful and the horror was simply that she'd gotten out of the collar and the GPS monitor lay useless on the ground, no longer attached to the dog, in the spot we were desperately trying to reach.

While those scenes played out in my mind, Chris and Austin discussed how best to get to that spot based on the trails the map showed. Poppy, or at least the GPS tracker, was between two trails—one called Farside and another called Slip and Slide Trail. Had I not lost all sense of humor by then, those names would have made me laugh, given our predicament. Instead we all tried to figure out when and where we'd have to veer off a trail. Chris had pulled up Google Maps and was using that as a guide. It gave the trails, and the names, but not the topography. It was hard to know if Poppy was in the middle of a canyon, standing on or under a rock formation, or simply out on grassy flatland. From what I could see, any of that was possible. Chris and Austin chose a path and headed out, I followed behind as quickly as I could.

After five minutes of walking, I checked the battery on my phone— 20 percent—and the GPS app one more time. Poppy hadn't moved, but this time I noted that the battery on her monitor was also at 20 percent. I'd been worried my phone would die, but it had not occurred to me that the battery on her tracker would die. Especially not this soon. *Shit.*

And then *Shit!* Again. I slipped on a wet rock and nearly dropped straight down onto my tailbone. I reached out to steady myself on the rocks to my right. I felt the jolt of the near fall through my entire body, but it remained pulsating in crumbly, grumpy T12, which was signaling it had had enough. I found a large boulder, covered overhead a bit by the branches of a nearby tree, and I sat, hoping to give my back some relief and catch my breath.

I tried to figure out some options. I didn't want Chris and Austin waiting for me, nor did I want to be alone in a wilderness park. The whole endeavor seemed futile and dangerous for all of us. At the same time, I could not imagine going home without this dog. I could not imagine giving up. The rain had lightened up a bit, but the wind had stepped in for a turn. I was cold, but not freezing. Maybe I could keep going, keep looking, but just follow behind them on the trail. If I could still see them, it would be okay.

I stood, ready to move forward and with the first step onto slick ground, slipped again. This time my tailbone hit the boulder I'd just been sitting on and pain shot up my spine. I used the flashlight on my phone (Chris had Michelle's large one) to examine the path in front of me, using more of the depleting battery. The trail was muddy and dotted with wet rocks. From what I could see, I was in a rock crevice of sorts and about to head down a slippery trail where my shoe choice would work against me.

The boots I was wearing had a slick bottom and a one-inch heel. And since I'd long ago stopped buying leather, they were faux leather, and they had already soaked through. As Chris and Austin moved farther ahead of me and out of my sight, I knew I couldn't keep up. Falling and rebreaking my back was a real possibility, and not one that would help Poppy. All I could do was find high ground and sit, keeping watch for her while they continued the search. At least if I stayed out in the park, and if we saw her, I could call to her, something, anything, I wasn't even sure what we'd do. But I was likely the only one she would come to.

Chris did not hear me call out to him; they marched ahead. I texted him that I would stay put at the top of the hill they'd just gone down. He texted back "Good idea."

I sat on another boulder, under what I could only assume was a sycamore tree, getting colder and soggier, from the rain and my tears both. I kept thinking of that '70s song "Wildfire" where the girl goes searching for her lost pony in a blizzard and dies. I did not want that song stuck in my head, but there it was. *She ran calling Wiiiiiiiiiiiiiildfire, She ran calling Wi-i-i-i-ildfire . . .*

I'd lost a dog once before. I was a teenager—sixteen, maybe seventeen—and my parents had divorced a couple of years before (the second time—are you still trying to keep track? Don't). For reasons I can no longer recall, my mother decided she did not want my childhood dog, Tippy, living at her house, even though I was living there. My mother and I were at war with each other then, and Tippy was collateral damage. So Tippy went to stay with my father and his new girlfriend in their home a few cities away, where I also lived every other weekend. In no time at all (in my mind, it was immediately after the first weekend I was at my father's home and then had to leave Tippy behind), Tippy slipped out the front door and was gone. He was missing for a few miserable days of searching, yelling, and blaming, before I found him at the pound in yet another city. I had walked right by the kennel he was in, not recognizing him until he barked and jumped and flung himself against the chain link fencing to get my attention. I turned and saw a skinny, dirty, matted version of my little Tippy, a twelve year-old black cockapoo just as disoriented by his new living situation as I was. I understood his running away. Nothing felt like home then. But that dog was my home. I sprung him from the pound and my mother agreed to let him come back to her house.

That was forty years ago, and Tippy lived until my second year of law school, so a happy ending of sorts. But on this night, in this storm, sitting on a boulder alone in the middle of a wilderness park, my back throbbing, I cried for Tippy, and for Daphne, and for Poppy.

In response, the sky cracked open and cried too. The rain began pouring down, now sideways in the wind. No tree covering would help me. I looked at my phone, holding it inside my raincoat.

11:14 P.M. Eleven percent battery.

I checked Poppy's GPS. She had 14 percent battery and had not moved. *Please be hunkered down, safe for the night, baby girl. Please.* I tried to picture her curled up, nose tucked up under her tail as she often did, warm, dry, under one of these many rock formations. *It could happen.*

I thought I saw a brief bolt of lightning and seconds later thunder rolled.

I texted Chris, "I'm going back to the car. Battery dying. You guys should come back."

The odds of us finding Poppy, out in this weather, were nil. I knew that. Endangering our own lives was not going to help her. The coyotes likely weren't out in this weather either.

Chris responded, "Going a little farther. We found a trail. Low battery for me too."

I headed back down the trail I was on, toward the car. The wind was at my back, which meant it was in Chris and Austin's faces. We weren't catching any breaks.

As I came up the last hill, on the trail leading back to the family park area and where our cars were, I realized another piece of bad luck. Chris had the car keys. And I had my phone with the GPS app. We should have traded. But we hadn't thought of that, and he had been too far ahead of me.

I remembered, though, that Jessica was in their car, waiting for Austin.

I knocked on her window and opened the door.

"Anything?" She said.

"No, she hasn't moved from that same spot in a while. I told Chris and Austin to come back, there's nothing else we can do tonight. But they're going a little farther."

"I'm so sorry."

I could hear the pain in Jessica's voice and see the torment on her face. "I know. It's not your fault," I said. And indeed, I had rattled through a million reasons why it was all my fault.

"I'm just so sorry."

We sat, not talking, for another thirty minutes before Chris and Austin came up over the hill toward the cars.

"I'm sorry, baby. Nothing." Chris said.

"We can come back in the morning," Austin said.

"We have to. As soon as it's daylight." I said.

"Okay, we'll text you in the morning."

The battery on Poppy's GPS monitor died at 1:30 A.M. I know because I was still awake. I thought about all she'd been through in China, though I could only guess. I thought about her propensity to hide under the bed or my desk and hoped that would serve her well out in the wilderness. I thought about her innocent face and that little smudge by her mouth. I listened to the rain and the rolling thunder.

When I woke, it was still dark out, but it had stopped raining. I looked at the clock. It was 4:00 A.M. Poppy's favorite time to rise and want to play.

9

REINFORCEMENTS

Roe had slept pressed up against my legs, as though he knew the comfort I needed. And of course, he did—he's a dog. Percival had slept next to Chris, because Percival always needed the comfort of Chris, but this time perhaps Chris needed comfort, too. I slipped out of bed, trying not to disturb any of them, and went downstairs. I stood in the kitchen sipping hot black coffee and checking my phone to see what time sunrise would be.

Chris awoke soon after and came downstairs too, both dogs following him and looking more than a little confused. Though it was still dark out, we decided to get dressed and head to Sycamore Canyon. There was nothing else to do. I finished my cup of coffee and ate a banana before throwing on yoga pants—I don't own sweatpants, or sturdy jeans, or anything properly worn for hiking—a T-shirt, a sweatshirt, and all of Michelle's rain gear. Roe and Percival were interested in us while we were in the kitchen, but less so when we got dressed. Both dogs returned to bed.

"Should we take them with us?" I said. "Maybe she'd come to them?"

"Or they'd smell her and head to her?" Chris said.

"Maybe."

"But if it rains again, Percival won't keep going."

"Roe would." Both things were true—Percival was far too prissy to walk in the rain, and there was nothing we were aware of that would stop Roe from exploring the outdoors. It was probably also true that we watched too much television. Contrary to our Animal Planet–influenced imaginings, these dogs were not search and rescue dogs, and the three dogs had not had enough time together to be so bonded they would come running to each other on first sniff.

"You're right, though. We should leave them here so we can concentrate on Poppy," I said.

We arrived at the main wilderness park entrance. Jessica and Austin had agreed to go back to the area we'd been in the night before, near the playground, and head in on those trails. We'd meet up somewhere in the middle. Perhaps.

"Look at that sign." I pointed to the large trail map on the information board at the head of the trail. "1,492 acres. I had no idea this park was this big. Oh my god." Nearly fifteen hundred acres and we were searching for a terrified nineteen-pound beagle. We had come in from Central Avenue—a busy thoroughfare that led to the 215 freeway. I'd driven by it many times and noted the parking lot, the little nature center, and a few trails visible from the street. But I'd never stopped. Never walked the trails. I had no idea the park was nearly fifteen hundred acres; I never imagined it could be.

"I didn't know that either. But at least we know where she went," Chris said.

"Well, we know where she went last night. But we're going to need more people to cover this area."

The night before, I had called the Beagle Freedom Project emergency line. And I'd both called and emailed in the morning before we headed out. I remembered a couple of years back when a BFP dog had gotten lost when a gardener had left a gate open. The dog, Davey, was part of a twosome of very bonded beagles who'd been particularly traumatized in a lab. They were much loved by the BFP family. The two men who adopted them had put out a plea for help in finding them and BFP had responded, flooding the neighborhood with flyers, sending teams of people out searching, and creating two large banners that hung across freeway overpasses. Davey had been found in under twenty-four hours. I hoped we'd be so lucky.

Only a hundred yards into the trail I heard running water.

"Is that a waterfall?" I said.

"Sounds like it," Chris said, not sounding nearly as surprised as I was.

We turned a corner and followed the sound down a thin trail. Water rushed down a creek, six or seven feet wide, running rapid from last night's downpour. I followed it up and saw the waterfall, about eight, maybe ten feet tall. We'd had an unusually wet winter—enough to end California's drought and then some. A waterfall had never looked so violent to me. I wanted to think, "Well, she'll have fresh water," but instead my brain screamed, "*She could drown.*" Much like Poppy herself did, I now saw everything as potential danger.

Chis and I met each other's eyes, seeing the same fears. "I never realized all this was out here," I said.

We continued down what seemed to be the main trail with Chris mapping out our path using Google Maps. I also had an AllTrails app, which gave walking routes for this park, as well as thousands of others. I'd bought the app when doctors told me the best thing I could do for my back was to walk. We started taking Daphne and Percival on long walks, using the app to find gorgeous nature trails and interesting seaside walks so I could distract myself from the pain and the knowledge that I was exercising. But the app was less useful for finding a lost dog. Poppy was not likely to stick to a trail, let alone one that nicely looped back to the same starting point. So, relying on Chris and his map, I followed a few steps behind him as the sun rose.

We passed what both the AllTrails app and Google Maps pinpointed as the Cougar Rock formation. And I told myself it must be named that because of its shape, and not a gathering of mountain lions. For Poppy's sake and mine, I didn't want to think about cougars. Even Chris—never one to pass up the opportunity for a joke—said nothing (with our twelve-year age difference, there was a time when my "cougar" status was a regular joke).

That part of the park, perhaps because it was nearly daylight, seemed less ominous than where we'd been the night before. The hills were smaller and there were large swaths of semi-flat earth, with only rocks and desert brush, where it seemed we were skimming the top of a mountain, giving us a vantage point to watch for a small white dog zipping across the landscape.

The rain stopped. The earth was damp, the sky misty, and the air had a chill. As we walked the sky changed colors, with a show of peach, pink, and streaks of lavender.

"In any other circumstance, this would be beautiful," I said.

"There is no other circumstance where we'd be out hiking at sunrise," Chris said. "But I know what you mean."

We walked, with me calling out to Poppy. "Poppy! Poppy Popstar! Come on baby, come on girl. Come on out. Paaaaaaaaaaa-peeeeeeeeeeee!"

We climbed higher and higher and made our way farther into the expansive park. After two hours, I had to rest. Again I found a boulder to serve as a chair and sat, drinking water.

I looked across the wilderness. Hard to imagine this vast wilderness existed amid a city of over 300,000 people, much less the same one I'd lived in for most of the last twenty years. After only a couple hours' hiking, we were now far enough in that we could not see any of the homes bordering the park to the west or the east, and we'd long ago stopped hearing the traffic on Central Avenue. The only sign that we were still near the city was the cell phone reception. Not only could we still use the maps and apps, but I could text Jessica.

"Anything?

"Nothing. But we saw a coyote, so we changed trails."

I did not want to think about coyotes. I could not think about coyotes. "Do you know where you are?"

"Austin says we're near where he and Chris walked to last night."

I *really* did not want to think about coyotes near where we last knew Poppy, or at least her GPS tracker, to be. "Okay. We're heading your way."

We continued walking until we met up with them. I thought we had covered one end to the other, but when I looked at the map on my phone, sized to show the entire park, I realized that what we'd covered was only the northern section—maybe one-fourth of the total area. We'd need a better plan. More people. More signs.

And more coffee.

Jessica could no longer hike. Her back and leg were hurting. And I couldn't think of a plan other than "No one leaves this wilderness park until we find

Poppy," which seemed like an imperfect plan at best. Instead, we hiked back out to Jessica and Austin's car, and they drove us around to ours. They headed to my office, where they would make flyers and hang them throughout the surrounding neighborhoods and the shopping center where Poppy had dashed in and out. I emailed Jessica the photo of Poppy standing on Michelle's bright blue wall. It was a beautiful photo, and soon it would be prominently featured in thousands of "LOST" flyers. How fortuitous that I had taken the photo only days before, though I never imagined this was how the photo would be used.

Chris and I returned home to feed Roe and Percival, get some breakfast, and figure out a plan. I posted a plea on Facebook, asking for volunteers to search or hang flyers and begging anyone in the area to keep an eye out. I left a message with my assistant to cancel all my appointments that day. Chris called work to arrange for someone to cover his shift that evening. He'd never make it back to Paso Robles in time even if we found her that morning. And neither of us had more than a couple of hours of sleep, so driving four hours was not wise. Jessica, who usually would open the office at 8:00 A.M., seemed to understand, without us discussing it, that her job now was to find Poppy. Austin took the day off from work as well.

But it was still only four of us, a wilderness park the size of 150 football fields, and one very fast, very frightened beagle.

Just before 9:00 A.M., I got a call from Kevin, the head of Fosters and Adoptions for BFP. Reinforcements were coming. Kevin posted to the Fosters and Adopters Facebook page to see if anyone else in the vicinity could come help with the search. A team of BFP staff people would be out in a few hours; we'd meet at the entrance to the park.

The responses to my pleas and Kevin's Facebook post came in quickly from volunteers who could help search or hang flyers. Some could come immediately, some in an hour, some later that afternoon or evening. I was quickly overwhelmed trying to keep track. Chris printed out a map of the park—which was helpful in both giving me a sense of where we'd been and allowing me to make notes on the back as to who was coming when. I printed out several of the flyers Jessica had made up and emailed to me. We headed back to the park.

By then it was probably ten in the morning—Poppy had been missing for sixteen or seventeen hours (eternity, if you asked me).

Aaron was the first to meet us. Aaron may have had a special attachment to Poppy, since he and his wife had fostered Poppy's look-alike sister, Miley. But also, Aaron was a good guy. Chris directed him to a section of the park, and he headed out quickly. I received a text from a stranger, Justine, who saw my post on Facebook, shared within an hour by over twenty friends, and offered to come help. I said yes and told her to meet me at the entrance to the park. Chris took a few flyers to hand out to any hikers he saw in the canyon and headed back out on the trail we'd been hiking. I stayed in the parking lot to meet the arriving volunteers and hand flyers to anyone who came to the trailhead—joggers, dog walkers, and even a mountain biker. Everyone gave me the same look. It was a look I recognized from my cancer days. A look of pity. A look that said, "This is hopeless, and you poor thing, you don't even realize that."

I ignored the looks, just as I had ten years ago. Then and now, I had to believe there was hope. There *was* hope because people were coming out to help—*strangers*—were coming out to help. People I barely knew, people I knew a little, people who simply loved dogs—they were all coming to help. Knowing that was as comforting as the mug of coffee I clung to as I sat in my car in the nature center parking lot waiting for volunteers and responding to messages.

Laurie, the friend who had hosted Geraldine and the twenty-three rescue dogs at her ranch over Thanksgiving, texted me:

"Contact Mike Noon. He's an expert at this. Do whatever he says—he can help."

I didn't know who Mike Noon was, and there was no contact information, but if Laurie said Mike knew what to do, I was going to contact Mike.

A car pulled in the parking lot and parked right next to mine in an otherwise empty parking lot. A young, tall, blond woman in a sweatshirt and exercise pants hopped out, dog leash and water bottle in hand.

I got out of my car. "Are you Justine?"

"Yes, Teresa? Hi. I'm so sorry about your dog. I've done this a lot. We'll find her. Where do you need me?"

She sounded so confident. She had none of the "you poor thing" tone—straight to the business at hand. Exactly what we needed.

I showed Justine the map. "Poppy entered the park here. GPS last showed her here. We've got people out on this trail and this one," I pointed to the various spots on the north end of the wilderness park.

She pointed at a trail, leading down to where Poppy had entered the park. "I'll head out here."

"Okay, thanks." I handed her a few flyers. "If you see any hikers, please hand them one."

"I will."

And she was off, moving quickly, determined to find a dog she'd never even met. *Thank you.*

Laurie called me. "I called Mike. Unfortunately, he can't help right now. His dad just came home on hospice and he's got to stay with him. But he said to concentrate on flyers. Get flyers up everywhere. And don't let anybody chase her. Don't be out walking around the canyon. Just put out flyers everywhere around the park."

"Okay. I've got my paralegal getting a bunch printed, and she's out putting them up."

"I'm going to come out. I just don't know how long it will take."

Laurie lived in Manhattan Beach—the west side of Los Angeles. It could take hours to get to Riverside, but I was not going to say no to more help. "Thank you. Call me when you're close, and I'll give you the update."

"I hope when I call you don't even need me anymore and your sweet girl is home safe."

"Me too." The concern in Laurie's voice was such that I blinked back tears.

Kevin and the BFP crew—Megan and Angela—arrived just after noon. Again, I showed the map, the trails others were on, and where we had last seen Poppy. Kevin quickly picked a trail, and the three of them headed out as well. I did not understand Mike's comment to Laurie that we should not be out walking the trails. I didn't know what else to do. How else would we find her?

Most of the day there had been only a light mist. The rain had let up. But the skies were changing. The clouds were darkening, and the wind picked up.

From my phone I posted to Nextdoor, Lost Dogs of Riverside, and PawBoost, all suggestions made by people on social media. I noted another Facebook comment made on the page of yet another friend who had shared my post:

"Call Mike Noon or Babs Fry. They can help." Phone numbers were included.

Clearly, Mike was The One. I didn't know who Babs was or how she could help, but I knew Mike wasn't available, and I knew I needed to do more. I called Babs.

As the phone rang, I wondered how I could ask for help, how I could not sound like a child who lost her puppy, how I could not cry when I said anything at all.

"Hi, my name is Teresa and my dog is lost. I was told you might be able to help."

"I can definitely help," she said without hesitation. She spoke with confidence and enthusiasm. "Tell me what happened. Tell me about the dog."

I told her, with as much detail as I could, about Poppy—where she came from, how long we'd had her, how she escaped, and where we last knew she was.

"Okay, only last night. That's good."

Only last night? We were coming up on an unbearable twenty-four hours this poor dog had been coyote bait in fifteen hundred acres of wilderness! In a storm! "It feels like forever."

"I know," she said. Her voice was calm, sympathetic, and at the same time all business. She had done this before, that was obvious. "But finding a lost dog, especially one this frightened, is a long game. It could be days or weeks. Sometimes longer. Tell me what you've done so far."

I pushed the "weeks" and "sometimes longer" out of my mind. It could *not* be weeks or months. I would lose my mind—the stress, the worry, the guilt, the *not knowing*. I told Babs what I'd done—the people out searching, the flyers, the social media posts, the hiking until midnight.

"Okay, we're going to need to regroup. I need you to call everyone back in. They can't be out there walking the trails. And we're going to need to talk about those flyers too."

She was definitive. I liked that. And I noted the "we" in her speech. But call everyone back in? How would we ever find Poppy if no one was out looking. "Call them back?"

"To your dog, to Poppy, everyone is a predator. She's frightened and she does not trust humans. A human—a stranger—out there walking around presents as much danger to her, in her mind, as a coyote. And she's going to see and smell you guys long before you will ever see her. And she'll hide. Her instincts are strong. All those people on the trails—spreading scent—they'll keep her in hiding or send her off in another direction."

Instantly I could see the logic to this. And wasn't this what Mike had told Laurie, too? But I was already feeling hopeless and useless—just *less* in general—and now I needed to pull back on what we had been able to do. My logic, usually so firmly in control, fought hard with my emotions.

"So what do we do?" I said.

"What you want are sightings. Not anybody chasing her or trying to catch her. Not now. We want to get flyers in the surrounding area. Make hundreds of flyers and hand them out to every Tom, Dick, and Harry around. That's what you want your volunteers doing—plastering the neighborhood in flyers."

"We've been doing that. We have flyers out."

"And we need to talk about those flyers."

Babs had seen the one on Facebook where she'd been tagged. She patiently and methodically explained what needed to be on the flyer, and more importantly, what shouldn't be. I'd gotten most of it wrong.

"Photo of the dog, clear, from the side if possible—you did great with that. Then just a simple 'Lost Dog' and 'Do Not Chase.' Under no circumstances should you put 'reward' on the flyer," she said. "That just encourages people to chase her. You just want people to call and tell you when and where they saw the dog and, if possible, what direction the dog was headed. That's the goal. Rewards will bring out the kooks and the bad actors—people just wanting a reward. You'll even get people giving you bad information. They'll make up things."

I wanted to be horrified that people would do such things, but I knew she was right. I settled on being horrified that I'd done so much wrong. "I've wasted the last twenty-four hours."

"No, no, you haven't. It's what a lot of people do. It's human instinct. But we've got to approach this from the dog's instincts. She's frightened and on the run. Her instinct is to avoid people at all costs."

"I get it. That all makes sense." I was the only human being Poppy had begun to trust, and she still hid from me at times. She would be hiding from all these strangers out looking for her. *Of course, she would.* I should have realized that.

"I will text you a sample of what the flyer should look like. Use one phone number and one only—it should probably be yours. And make sure your voice mail isn't full. You need to be able to accept messages. And answer calls even when you don't recognize the number. Strangers will be calling you."

"Okay. Okay. Thanks."

"Bring everyone back in. Get everyone walking the neighborhoods, any nearby shopping center, everywhere but in that canyon. What we want are sightings so we can figure out her pattern. If anyone is out in the canyon, they need to just find a high vantage point and sit and watch for her. No chasing, no scaring the dog. No spreading scent through the park. And especially you—you might be the one person she'll eventually come to, but if your scent is all over that park she may be chasing all over."

"I did walk all over the park last night and this morning."

"It was raining. But don't do it anymore. Get the people back in, get the signs out, and then let's talk some more."

I appreciated her directness. She had a sense of calm and control, and I needed that. But waves of exhaustion and embarrassment took turns washing over me. *I'd done everything wrong.*

My wallowing in pity was cut short with a stream of texts, sent using the group text I had started earlier.

Justine: Walking along creek area received a tip from a hiker that Poppy may be near water by 2 homeless encampments. Where the power lines meet the creek.

Oh my god! Someone saw her! She's still alive! My adrenaline soared. The texts pinged.

Chris: I'll turn around and try to meet you.

Aaron: I'll head that way. I see power lines.

Aaron would be coming from the east side of the park, clear across to the west. Could he make it across the entire wilderness park?

Kevin: Where does the creek meet the powerlines?

And that was a good question. This was some really messed up version of Professor Plum in the library with a wrench.

Chris answered, telling Kevin he thought the creek was in the southwest area of the wilderness park. Kevin and his group had gone east, I thought. I wasn't certain. Maybe it was south? I am terrible with directions—north is always straight in front of me, even if I'm looking at a sunset. And what if there was more than one creek? Justine and Chris seemed to understand where they were, and Justine knew the direction the hiker had come from. But could anyone else find that spot? And should they? Babs had told me to call them in. That was before the sighting though.

The texts kept flying.

Aaron: Not sure how long this will take. I've got about another hour I can stay.

Chris: I've got to hike back to the main entrance and pick up a new trail.

Teresa: Chris I can show you the trail Justine went down.

Chris: Coming your way.

Another car pulled in and parked beside me. I had no way of knowing if this was another volunteer or just someone coming out to enjoy the park. Given the weather, though, I assumed it was a volunteer and got out of my car.

"Are you Teresa?" The young woman said as she got out of her car.

"I am, yes."

"I thought so from the Beagle Freedom Project bumper sticker," she said, grinning.

"Ah yes, we're like a cult."

"I'm Cecilia. I'm Dexter's mom." Like any good dog person, she knew I'd more likely recognize her dog's name than hers, and she was right. Cecilia was active on the BFP Fosters and Adopters page, posting photos of her dog crew and often helping others. She'd recently helped Deia and Aaron with Poppy's sister, Miley, by loaning them a crate to contain Miley's, uh, well, her enthusiasm. Miley, like Poppy, was a destructive chewer and couldn't be left alone unconstrained for too long.

I gave her the quick rundown, and by the time I finished Chris had popped up from the trail. I introduced them.

"I'm about to head in that way. I think I know where the creek meets the power lines. I'm going to try to follow the power lines in," Chris said.

"I can go with you," Cecilia said.

And they were off before I had time to think that I was supposed to be calling everyone in, not sending them off on the trails. *But Poppy was out there.*

I returned to my car and responded to a few emails and Facebook posts from people wanting to help and people hoping we'd already found her.

Chris and Cecilia quickly reappeared.

"We're on the wrong side of the creek, and we can't cross it here," Chris said. And as he said it, I remembered the fast running creek and waterfall we'd encountered early that morning.

"And I didn't realize how steep the trails are. I can't hike that. I'm not built for hiking," Cecilia said. "I'm slowing him down already."

Cecilia was short and voluptuous. Not built for speed, no. Chris was a big guy himself, but he was in good shape and had been hiking and walking with our dogs for years. I had only been able to keep up that morning from adrenaline.

"I understand, believe me," I said.

"I'm going to drive around to the entrance on the west and see if I can get in that way," she said.

"Take me with you. I'll head in where we know Poppy slipped into the park last night. You can drop me on Via La Paloma," Chris said.

"Be careful," I said (because useless platitudes were all I had at that point, it seemed).

"I will."

Chris and Cecilia headed out in her car.

I'd been stationed at the main entrance to the park for hours—texting, calling, trying my best to coordinate a rescue effort. My brain fought itself over the "right" thing to do. Should I be out hiking too? Babs said no, but she had also said to bring everyone back in. I was getting some traction on social media to get volunteers to go out with flyers. Some volunteered for that evening and some for the next day. Jessica and Austin had been dispatched to make the new flyers—luckily the one thing I'd gotten right on the flyer before was the photo. Babs had said to use a photo with a side view of the dog, since that's how people would likely sight her. The photo I had from our time in Michelle's backyard paradise was a side view. Poppy was standing on the royal blue wall, in front of the very canyon wherein she was now lost. Jessica and Austin were printing those flyers.

Justine texted a map of the park, on which she'd drawn an arrow pointing to a creek. "Trying to get to this creek. I believe that is the one the hiker means."

Aaron: Just found a part of the creek. I'm following it.

Chris: I'm at the power lines & the creek. Think I see an encampment. Trying to get there.

Justine: Coming from opposite side hear water and see the power lines almost there and have seen semi fresh pup poops so hoping we're close gang!!! Be safe walking thru this very soft dirt and sliding rocks.

Chris texted a photo of where he was. A rocky creek was visible in the crevice between two hills and power lines stretched along the top of one of the hills.

Justine: We're near each other I believe. At creek going to walk downstream as I haven't seen an encampment yet.

A few minutes passed. No word from Aaron. I thought about calling Babs back and asking *what now?* It was a sighting. Or a possible sighting. Justine had the flyer with her, she could have shown it to the hiker, so maybe it was an actual sighting. Or maybe he was just suggesting that's where dogs hang out.

Chris texted again: It wasn't an encampment. It's a bunch of planter boxes.

Then moments later, Chris: Not planters. Beekeeper boxes! Bees!

I could picture him running as he texted.

I texted Babs, letting her know of the sighting.

Kevin texted: We're coming out. We've got to head back. We'll be back tomorrow morning and we'll rally more troops.

I couldn't blame them. This was an expansive chunk of wilderness, and the weather remained cool, windy, and damp with intermittent showers. They'd already been out hiking for hours and they were not dressed for wet weather. Most Southern Californians don't own proper rain gear—sweatshirts and yoga pants or jeans is the standard winter attire. While I understood they'd need to leave, I felt a bit of panic. We hadn't found Poppy yet. We couldn't give up. I didn't want anyone leaving. Somehow that seemed like a defeat.

After twenty minutes, Kevin, Megan, and Angela walked out of the trail, looking disheartened. I'd been sitting in my car, which had become my command central, trying to coordinate volunteers and gather information while maintaining hope. I recognized Kevin's expression, because it was one I'd been trying to avoid myself. It said, "*This is hopeless.*"

"I had no idea the park was this vast. It's huge," he said.

"I know. That's why we need more people."

"We have to go back to LA, but we'll send more people tomorrow. Let's figure out a meet-up place and get folks sent out with flyers and signs. And as many people out hiking as possible."

I explained to him what Babs had said.

"That makes sense," he said. "A lot of sense. Plus, that's a lot of ground to try and cover. The odds of us . . ."

He didn't finish the thought. We cannot think about not finding her. *Not finding her is not an option.*

They got into their car, each of them giving me a look meant to convey both sympathy and encouragement, with an attempt at hiding the hopelessness. The Beagle Freedom Project community—family, many say—is a tight one. Once you've met one of these dogs rescued from a laboratory or, more recently, the Chinese or Korean dog meat trade, you're committed to the dogs and the work of the organization. The dogs all have varying degrees of trauma, and it takes a support team to help see them through. When one of the dogs is sick, is having a difficult adjustment time, or gets lost, we all feel it. The BFP Adopters and Fosters Facebook page is filled with posts from people sharing and asking for advice on the particular issues these dogs have, whether it's night terrors, carsickness to an extreme, cancers, or learning to walk on a leash. I knew Kevin, Megan, and Angela were feeling my pain. And I hoped they'd be back with many more people tomorrow.

Tomorrow? Would we have to be out here again tomorrow?

Justine texted: Chris, how far upstream are you? The man said it was about 2 miles up.

Chris: Looks like I'm close to the mouth of the stream. Where it flows to.

Justine: Ok I am towards the top heading downstream to you.

They again exchanged map photos with pinpoints of where they each were. They were however each using different maps. Justine's was the Google default map—basically a drawing. Chris's was the satellite map.

Chris: Gully on the left side is the creek. I'm now where Three Bridges trail meets the creek. There is no bridge here and no upstream trail.

There were no emojis and texts are terrible for conveying emotion, but it seemed certain Chris was frustrated. He'd been hiking most of the day. He had to be exhausted, and this search for a homeless encampment "where the creek meets the powerlines" seemed like some dystopian version of hide-and-seek.

I wanted to call everyone back. I wanted a lead. I wanted to find Poppy.

Justine: Ok I'm directly next to the heavily flowing creek and see what looks to be clothing hanging in the distance I am trying to get there.

Chris: Can you use Google satellite maps to show your location? It's more topographically accurate.

(And yes, Chris would and did use "topographically accurate" in a text—more reason to love him.)

Justine quickly switched to a satellite map and texted a screenshot. I could not tell if they were anywhere near each other. It all looked like greenery and rocks to me.

I was so intensely following the texts I almost dropped the phone when it rang.

"A sighting is great news," Babs said. "That's fantastic. When you have a sighting call me. Don't text. I always answer my phone, but I don't always see the texts right away. Sightings and new information deserve a phone call."

"Okay. I will remember that. I'm not sure if it's a sighting. The hiker said he thought he saw her near a homeless encampment. By the creek."

"He probably did see her. She probably smelled their food. The homeless can be a great resource. They know everything that goes on in their area."

"Justine—the woman who talked to the hiker—is headed there now. So is Chris and one other person, but we're not entirely sure where this place is."

"That's too many people. You need to call everyone back. You just want one person to find the encampment and talk to the people there. Give them a flyer. Tell them not to chase her if they see her."

"Okay. Chris and Justine are the two likely to get there. I think it might be safer if it's Chris."

"They're probably not dangerous, but you never know."

Babs knew what she was doing, I could feel that. I needed a plan and she had the experience. She was steady, consistent, sympathetic, but also adamant in what we should do. I would follow her instructions. I sent the group a text.

Justine was the first to respond: "Okay I'm not far from where the encampment should be and then I will head back."

Chris: "Will head back."

After twenty minutes or so Aaron texted a map and a note: "Good luck everyone. I was looking out from the park this morning between about 11 and 1230ish where I could see inside the gray area from the elevation. I then hiked the green path." He'd highlighted a long trail across the park, east to west. "Looking for you guys but was a bit further back. Met Cecilia at the cul-de-sac where she gave me a ride back to the park. Wish I could help longer but had to get back. We'll find her!"

Aaron had covered a lot of ground. He'd been out searching for over four hours. I'd forgotten Cecilia was even still out there. Thank goodness she'd found Aaron and at least saved him from having to hike clear across the wilderness canyon again.

No sooner had I thought that than Cecilia pulled up next to me. Chris and Cecilia both got out of her car.

"I found Aaron and drove him back to his car and then I found Chris, so I brought him back," Cecilia said.

"I came out the trail into the neighborhood fully prepared to get an Uber back here, but Cecilia came along at just the right time," Chris said.

Cecilia laughed. "At least I was good for something today!"

"You were great. I appreciate everybody coming out," I said.

I was confused as to where everybody was and how, in all the vast wilderness and surrounding neighborhoods any of them could find each other, but they all seemed to have their bearings. I did not. I definitely did not.

"I've got to get home to my dogs, but I'll come back tomorrow if you still need people," she said.

"I hope we don't. But if we do, I will text."

Cecilia drove away and Chris turned to me, "I'm worried about Justine being out there."

"Me too."

"She was determined to get to the homeless encampment, but it's not likely Poppy is there."

"She can talk to them, though. Find out if they've seen her?"

"Yeah, I'm just not sure how safe it is."

"True. And the sky looks threatening."

He texted Justine: Are you okay? On your way back?

Justine: Yes on my way back slowly but surely. Sorry for the wait I was deep into the area.

Chris: Just wanted to make sure you were safe.

Justine: Yes I definitely am just feeling the aftermath of 3 knee surgeries and a few months out of the gym sadly.

"Oh my god," Chris said.

"What?"

"She's had knee surgeries and she's out there hiking this crazy canyon. That's insane!"

"And a total stranger. That's amazing."

"You dog ladies are nuts."

"We are."

Justine texted again: I'm near Sycamore Highlands Park but heading toward Central.

She also texted a photo that to me looked like all the photos that had been texted that day. It was just rocks, and trails, and hills, and canyons, and greenery, and dark, angry clouds. It was nowhere for a nineteen-pound skittish beagle pup to be.

Justine texted another photo of a boulder onto which someone had spray painted "Parila Creek" and an arrow pointing left. There was also a grouping of palm trees in the photo. Still, I couldn't tell where in the fifteen hundred acres she was.

While we waited for Justine, I caught up with Laurie, still on the freeway for over two hours now. She had texted hoping we found Poppy.

I called her. "No such luck. But we had a sighting."

"Oh my god. That's wonderful!"

"If it was her. At least there is hope she survived the night."

"Okay, I'm going to keep driving in. I think I'm close. The next exit is Van Buren Boulevard."

She was close. Chris and I had not eaten all day, so we made plans to be at the local Carl's Jr. since they now had the vegan Beyond Burger (hold the cheese and mayo). It would be easier for her to find us at a fast-food restaurant anyway.

Justine made it out of the wilderness park safely. She was young and in shape, but that would not be an easy hike even without knee surgery, so I was not surprised she was breathing heavily. We gave her a moment to catch her breath.

"I didn't find them," she said.

"It's okay. It may have been dangerous," I said.

"Oh no, it wasn't that. I wasn't worried about that. I just couldn't find an encampment anywhere. I'll come back at daybreak tomorrow. I'll bring my dog. He's been helpful finding lost dogs in the past."

"Thank you, really. It's very kind of you to do all of this for a total stranger."

"I love dogs. When I hear about a lost dog, I just have to help. I've just got to go home to my own pack now and get them fed."

"Thank you again."

Chris and I returned to my car as Justine drove off.

"I guess it's just us now," Chris said.

"No. Jessica and Austin have been making and posting flyers all day. They'll meet us at Carl's Jr. to give us more flyers. The correct flyers. And Laurie Gentry drove all the way in from west LA. She's meeting us at Carl's too."

"Great. I'm starving."

Chris was sweaty and dirty from the hike, and I knew he hadn't slept much more than I did the night before. I hated to leave the wilderness park, and at the same time felt useless.

I reviewed our circumstances: Babs had said not to walk around and spread scent. We had the one possible sighting but hadn't confirmed anything. We likely had only another hour or so of daylight. There was probably nothing more to do than to hand out more and more flyers. Flyers to every "Tom, Dick, and Harry," as Babs had said. But we needed to eat. Chris needed to sit and rest. I would hand out flyers at Carl's Jr. and around the shopping center there, too.

We pulled into the parking lot at Carl's Jr. and my phone rang. I looked at the screen. It was Mike Noon—the rescue expert Laurie had talked to for us. There was no reason for this feeling, but I was certain the cavalry had just arrived.

10

ELEMENTS

❖

"I heard you had a sighting."

Babs's voice had been warm and slightly high-pitched, but with some grit—like honey poured on gravel. Mike's voice was all gravel.

"Yeah, maybe. Nothing definite. A hiker said he may have seen her by a homeless encampment."

"That's likely. That's a good thing. What are you doing now?"

"Meeting Laurie at Carl's Jr. We need to eat."

"This is a good time for that."

It was? It was not quite 4:00 P.M. Not lunch and not dinner, not that we had anything like a normal schedule. I didn't feel right about stopping and eating at all.

"She's not likely to be out anywhere you could see her right now," Mike continued. "Get some food. Get some rest. Then keep walking the neighborhoods with flyers. Bring flyers into Carl's Jr. with you. Hand them to everyone. Homeless folk often hang out at fast-food joints, hand them the flyers too."

"That's what Babs said too."

"Listen to Babs. She knows what she's doing, and I don't say that about too many people."

Mike and Babs know each other? I suppose that makes sense—everyone in the dog rescue world seems to know each other, so why not in the dog . . . huh, what do we call this? Dog search and rescue? At any rate, Babs knew what she was doing, and Mike knew what he was doing. I knew that much. I'm not usually one to follow orders without questioning. I am firmly in the "question authority" camp. But not now. Not with these two. I was out of my element and distraught. These two voices on the phone were my lifeline. I would listen. I would do what they said. They would help me find Poppy.

"I am. I'm trying to. I guess I did everything wrong in the beginning so I'm trying to correct things. The flyers, not having people out walking the wilderness park."

"The search can be as much about controlling the people as anything else. That includes yourself."

"I can see that."

"Where was the sighting? Was it anywhere near where she went in the park?"

I had to think about that. And then I had to ask Chris. I still didn't quite know where the creek met the power lines.

"Chris says yes. Not far. Maybe a half mile."

"That's nothing for a dog. What you want to do tonight is go back to the spot she went into the park and sit. Bring some rotisserie chicken, a sock of yours, things with familiar smells. And just sit, see if she'll show herself. Often a dog will try to find its way out the same way it went in."

"That makes sense."

"Dogs who get loose and run after a car accident will return to the scene of the accident. Maybe not right away, but eventually. They're looking for their human, and that's the last place they saw them."

"That's not the last place she saw me. She was with someone else. A potential adopter. My paralegal, Jessica. Not close to my house."

"The spot she went in is still the best chance for a sighting tonight. Did Babs tell you to set up a warming box?"

Babs had. And I had forgotten that. The warming box was something else I hadn't really understood or registered at first in my continuing worry and agitation.

"Get some food. Some rest. Get more flyers out. At sundown go sit somewhere near where she went in and just wait. You're not searching. You're waiting for her to find you. When you can't sit anymore, set up the warming box."

Direct. To the point. These were my instructions. This is what I would do. Except the resting part. I couldn't rest.

🐾

Chris and I placed our Beyond Burgers order, filled our large iced teas, and sat in a booth. Jessica and Austin arrived with the flyers and left quickly, still covering neighborhoods. I filled Chris in on Mike's directions and the fact that I'd be spending the evening sitting at the end of the Via La Paloma cul-de-sac.

"What's a warming box?" he said.

"I need to get a box, something she could crawl into, and put things with familiar smells in it—a worn sock of mine, one of her toys—and then some roasted chicken. Things to lure her out. Dogs can smell from a great distance, especially beagles."

"So can coyotes."

"Yeah, I know. I guess we're hoping she comes back to the same spot in the neighborhood, but the coyotes don't? Or she'd be more likely to hunker down in the box with the familiar smells, but the coyote would either grab the chicken and run, or be warned off by the human scent?"

"That makes sense."

"Oh good, my logic hasn't completely failed me."

I was going on faith in Mike and Babs, and I needed to do something, so I'd do this, without fully understanding why, but as always it helped to work out the logic.

"Do you want me to go get the roasted chicken?"

Chris was asking not just to save me an errand but because he knew buying roasted chicken would be hard for me. I'd been a vegan for seven years. I'd long ago lost the ability to disassociate "food" from "an animal that didn't want to die." And I love chickens—the living, clucking kind. I knew the point of the chicken was the smell to lure Poppy in. The vegan chick'un strips in the frozen food section were not going to do the trick. I tried to think of something vegan that would still have an enticing smell. Toast was all I could come up with—all my dogs loved toast, no doubt because I regularly shared the crust. But toast would not maintain its toasty smell. Especially not in the rain, and it had begun raining again.

"Yes. Thank you. Get the chicken."

"Okay. Then can you go home and feed Roe and Percival? And find something to use as the warming box?"

Oh, right. Our dogs. They needed attention too. But if I went all the way home and fed the dogs, by the time I came back it would be nearly dark out. I needed to be sitting at the edge of the park with the chicken smells, and the me smells.

"That won't work. I'll have to get the chicken and get out there. You go home and feed Roe and Percival, and see what you can find for a box."

"You sure?"

"Yeah. I have to get out there."

Laurie arrived and we updated her. Chris showed her a map of the park on his phone.

"What do you want me to do? I'm sorry it took me so long to get here. This is really far out here."

Everyone from LA considered Riverside to be far, far away. I often joked with my LA friends that LA to Riverside was no farther than Riverside to LA, but they never saw it that way. And Laurie had been stuck on the freeway for a very long time; she'd been driving in rush hour(s) traffic. Too many people who work in Orange County or Los Angeles can't also afford to live there, so they live east in Riverside County. Which means the time between 3:00 P.M. and 7:00 P.M. the freeways heading east are always bumper-to-bumper traffic.

"I know. I'm sorry. Thank you for coming out," I said.

"I'm going to go home to feed our dogs. But I'll drive you by the neighborhood she was running around in last night and show you where she escaped into the park. Maybe walk around with flyers and plaster that neighborhood," Chris said.

"Okay, I can do that."

I pointed out the window, across Central Avenue to the large Bunker Hill apartment complex. "That's where she got loose. She ran across to this shopping center and back again, and then across that intersection."

"Oh my god. She ran across this busy street?" Laurie said.

"Several times. And in even more traffic, since it was about 5:30 last night," I said. I realized then that it had been not quite twenty-four hours since Poppy went missing. It felt like days.

"Oh that poor, sweet, terrified thing!"

Chris headed home. Laurie headed to Via La Paloma. I walked across the parking lot of the Canyon Crest Shopping Center to pick up rotisserie chicken at the grocery store. As I did, I saw the veterinarian's office and quickly decided to go in and post a flyer. This was a vet office we'd been in many times, as it was owned by our long-term vet, Dr. Davis, though we usually saw him in his downtown office.

I walked in and waved the flyer at the receptionist. "Okay to put this on the bulletin board?"

"Sure, no problem."

I walked across the lobby to the community bulletin board on the far wall. A woman with a small, fluffy poodle on her lap watched me as I hung the flyer. When I turned and caught her glance, she said, "I'm so sorry."

Oh no. No no no no no. No sympathy! I can't handle sympathy. I had been trying so hard to remain hopeful, and strong, and organized, and all the things I was supposed to be. I had pushed down the knot of fear and hopelessness, but this woman's face showed it all and that knot just untangled, whipped up, and smacked me in the face. "Thank you," I said. My voice cracked.

I hurried out of the office and worked on pulling myself together, stopping the tears, before heading into the grocery store. Suddenly I preferred the looks that told me I was crazy to think the dog would survive. I find it much easier to be angry at people than to be sad, hopeless, or heartbroken (more notes for the future therapist).

I knew where the rotisserie chicken was in the grocery store. It's hard to avoid, sitting as it is in a heated island in the middle of the path through the deli and on to the produce section. I was used to avoiding both the deli and the chicken and marching straight on to the fruits and vegetables. Or sometimes the potato chips (hey, they're vegan). This time I had to stop at the chicken. I could smell it from the moment I walked in the door, so I understood Babs and Mike's point about using it to lure a hungry, lost dog. But wasn't there something—anything—that had a potent smell that didn't involve a dead animal? Garlic? That was not likely to get her attention. Stinky cheese? No, that's dairy and involves a lot of animal suffering too. And I didn't think Poppy's gastronomic tendencies were refined enough to be lured in by a smelly Limburger. I paced around the store a bit, away from the chicken, racking my sleep-deprived and very stressed brain.

Nothing.

And I was wasting time.

I grabbed a bag of chicken, silently thanking the chicken for its sacrifice. I'm trying to save a life, and though this isn't what is meant by the "circle of life," I told myself it was. I was doing what I had to do to save my dog. I pushed the hypocrisy I felt back down with where I'd sequestered the hopelessness and fear. I can unpack all of those later. (I think we all know that will be at two in the morning.)

I drove to Via La Paloma and parked at the end of the street, at the edge of the wilderness park. The west side of the street was lined with houses. The east side was as well, and those houses backed up to the Sycamore Canyon. Poppy had run between two houses on the east side, under a fence, and then on into the Wilderness Park. It seemed unlikely we would see her come back out exactly the same way, but at the far south end of the street the east side houses stopped and the rocky hillside was exposed. At the end of the cul-de-sac was a large expanse of hillside dotted with trees and rocks. The slope up into the park had a natural opening and visible trail. I could easily picture a little white dog trotting down the hill, headed my way.

I got out of the car and put on Michelle's raincoat. I grabbed a flashlight, a blanket, and my bag of rotisserie chicken and walked toward the opening. That's when I saw Laurie, sitting on a large boulder watching the same trail.

"Seems like a logical entry or exit, doesn't it?" I said.

ABOVE: Roe Roe and his gorgeous eyes. BELOW: Our Percy-Pie, the sweetest little flirt.

The beagle boys, Roe (left) and Percival (right).

ABOVE: A few of the beagles eagerly awaiting dinner at Rescue Ranch. BELOW: The living room of Rescue Ranch in Lompoc.

ABOVE: Lucky dogs out enjoying Rescue Ranch. BELOW: What it looks like when one is feeding twenty-three dogs.

ABOVE: The picture of bliss. BELOW: That time I learned to love early mornings, "Rescue Ranch" November 2018.

LEFT: The Gratitude rock after the Malibu fire. BELOW: Chris and Geraldine, with just a few of the dogs at Rescue Ranch over Thanksgiving.

ABOVE: The arrival of the beagles from China. BELOW: My Daphne doppleganger. Such a sweet face.

ABOVE LEFT: The night the pups all arrived from China. ABOVE RIGHT: Poppy one week after her arrival in the U.S. BELOW: Poppy loves her big brother Roe.

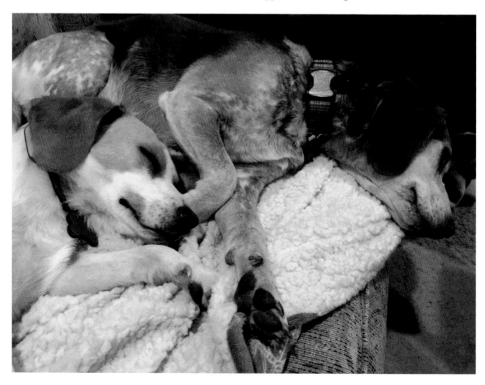

ABOVE LEFT: Poppy's first Christmas photo at Ruff House Pet Resort. ABOVE RIGHT: Poppy during her first visit to Paso Robles (December 2018). BELOW: Poppy and Roe enjoying Christmas 2018. (We may have spoiled them.)

ABOVE: The moment before we learned Poppy was lost. Lakers game, floor seats. BELOW LEFT: The GPS tracker when Poppy was first lost in the wilderness park. BELOW RIGHT: The GPS tracker showing one frightened dog on the run.

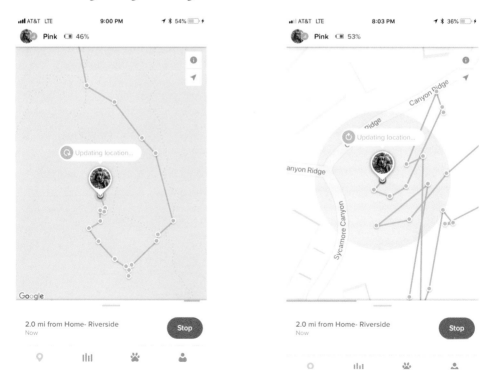

LEFT: The fabulous, steady, and determined Mike Noon, pet recovery specialist. BELOW: Poppy posing for what would become her "Lost Dog" poster.

Now that's a lost dog sign! Matt Rossell's handiwork (which was taken down after only a few hours). It had my phone number big and bold below Poppy's photo (now omitted).

ABOVE LEFT: Conor Parker, one of Poppy's biggest heroes. ABOVE RIGHT: Poppy after I picked her up from Conor's. BELOW: Poppy Popstar, home at last.

ABOVE: Hero to hero, Mike Noon and Conor Parker meeting and greeting. BELOW: Nicole, Mike, Wendy, Laurie, Jeanne K., Conor, me, Babs, Deia, and Mike K. (left to right) at the thank-you party.

ABOVE: Poppy returns to Sycamore Canyon Wilderness Park under much better circumstances.
BELOW: Me with Pickle—a short-term but successful foster.

ABOVE: Poppy comes back home, accompanied by Pickle the puggle (March 2019). BELOW LEFT: Poppy and me hiking in Sycamore Canyon Wilderness Park just for fun this time. BELOW RIGHT: Poppy enjoying Wine 4 Paws with her special "winery visits" collar (April 2019).

"Yeah, it does. I've been watching, hoping to see her. I just can't imagine. I had no idea the park was this big."

"Neither did I, and I've lived here for over twenty years."

Laurie still had flyers in her hand. She held them up, briefly. "I put them in mailboxes and talked to people as they came home for work and a few folks out walking their dogs. Everybody wants to tell me about the coyotes in the canyon."

"I know. Like we didn't know that."

"Really. It's not helpful. But they took my flyers."

"Good."

We were both quiet for a few moments.

"I can stay for another hour or so. May as well wait out the traffic," Laurie said.

"Thank you. I know this was a very long way for you to come."

"Not a problem. I can't imagine what you're going through. I want to help all I can."

Laurie was a very kind person—someone I'd known to drop everything to help dogs and people alike. She was after all, the person who allowed a fire-displaced Geraldine and over twenty rescue dogs to seek refuge at her ranch over Thanksgiving. "Thanks. Yeah. I can't believe this myself."

"What are you going to do tonight?"

I explained Babs's instructions for the chicken stakeout. Laurie was a vegan, too, and I knew she'd understand my ethical dilemma.

"It does make sense," she said.

"I know. I just hate it."

"You do what you have to do."

Laurie stood and I took over her boulder sitting spot. I spread the blanket over the damp boulder to provide cushion, hoping that would somehow alleviate what was sure to be crushing back pain. I tore the plastic wrap off the still-warm whole chicken and put the bag at my feet, apologizing again to the poor bird. I had one of Poppy's favorite squeak toys—a fabric steak, ironically—so I gave that a few squeaks (*Can you hear it, Poppy?*) and set that next to me.

Chris pulled up with Roe and Percival both in the car with him.

"I figured they need a walk. May as well walk them around this neighborhood. Maybe Poppy will come out if she smells them," he said.

"That's a great idea. I can walk with you," Laurie said as she immediately went to the car to love on Percival. Laurie is friends with Vanessa, who had been Percival's foster mom when Percival was rescued from a testing laboratory six years ago, so Laurie had actually known Percival a few months longer than we had. And Percival is a consummate charmer who loves all humans.

Chris and Roe and Laurie and Percival strolled down Via La Paloma, flyers in hand, and then turned to walk down the next street over, Via Zapata. I settled in on my boulder, cell phone in hand, as the sun went down. Babs called a half hour in on my watch.

"Did you get the chicken?" she asked.

"I did." I did not explain my moral dilemma to her. I had done what she advised.

"What are you doing now?"

"Sitting on a boulder with a bag of chicken and a squeak toy of Poppy's. I'm at the end of the street where we know she entered the wilderness park. Just sitting and watching."

"That's good."

"Did you call everybody back in?"

"Yes. Most everybody has gone home. Chris and one friend are out walking the neighborhood with our two dogs, handing out more flyers."

"What neighborhood?"

"This one. Where Poppy was running around yesterday."

"Is Poppy bonded to your two other dogs?"

"To Roe a little bit. But they've only spent about two weeks together."

"Would she come to him if she smelled him or saw him?"

I had to think about that. I hoped she would, but was that just hope based on desperation? Was there any reason to think she would? She played with Roe, cuddled with him, and enjoyed her walks side by side with him. Was that enough? And Roe was not alone. Roe was with Chris, who Poppy was still nervous around, and Laurie, who Poppy didn't know at all. Percival was a wild card in this whole thing, but I had to admit, it was unlikely Poppy would approach them or even allow herself to be seen by them. I'd messed up again.

"Not likely, I suppose."

"You need to call them back in. Don't have them out walking near the park, spreading scents. Poppy won't know where to go, even if she wanted to. Get them back and send them to another neighborhood."

"Okay." My voice was softer than normal and even I could hear my sadness. I hoped she didn't think I wasn't listening or wasn't appreciative of the advice. "It's hard. It feels like we're doing nothing. We just want to be doing something."

"You are doing something. You're setting things up to bring Poppy home. To help her find her own way. You're doing good. Just hang in there."

I texted Laurie and Chris and told them to come back to the boulder at what I was now thinking of as Poppy's home base on Via La Paloma.

Laurie texted: I have to head home anyway.

Chris: I'll take the Beagle Boys home. You going to be okay?

Me: I have no idea.

In ten minutes' time, they were gone, as was the daylight, and I remained, seated on my damp blanket on a boulder. The neighborhood lights were still on. Occasionally a car came down the street and turned into a driveway. A couple walked to the end of the street with their golden retriever on a leash. They glanced my way, but didn't seemed concerned with the crazy, wet, unshowered woman seated on a rock with rotisserie chicken at her feet. They may not have noticed the chicken, but their dog did. He pulled on his leash, straining to get to me and my bag of dog treasure. So, at least I knew the scent of the chicken was wafting as planned. The couple pulled the dog back to them and hurried along. Maybe they *were* concerned about the crazy boulder lady.

An hour passed. I'd been on my cell phone, responding to texts and emails and coordinating the volunteers for the next day. I'd be back in this same spot at sunrise, if not sooner, and Chris would sit watch in the wilderness park again, but at 10:00 A.M. the volunteers would meet up in my law office. Once again all my appointments had been canceled. BFP staff was coming with hundreds more flyers and large signs on tarps that we could hang near the busy Central Avenue intersection. Chris was at home making a large map, pinpointing where Poppy had run into the canyon, where she was when the GPS tracker died, and where she may have been spotted at the homeless encampment. On the map he divided up all the neighborhoods surrounding the wilderness park so we could send out teams to canvass the homes with flyers. Several other folks, some known to me and some not, volunteered to come help, and I accepted all offers of help but remembered to ask that no one chase her or hike the canyon. Anyone. Anytime. *Just watch for her, please.*

I stood up. The blanket was not enough padding for my rear end, and the dampness had begun to soak through my faux yoga pants. I stretched and twisted and tried to coax my back into relaxing, or at least to subdue the throbbing. I could tell exactly which vertebra was my cantankerous T12 by the pain. I wasn't supposed to be walking around, but I had to do something, so stretching would have to do.

My phone rang. When I saw Babs's name on the screen I sat back down quickly like I'd been caught.

"How's it going?" she said.

"I'm still here, just sitting and waiting. I haven't seen anything."

"What's the neighborhood like? Are there people out? Cars coming by?"

"A little. It's starting to quiet down."

"That's good. She's not likely to come out when there is activity."

"True. So I should just stay here?"

"As long as you can. You won't likely see her, but she may see you. She may be watching you now, trying to figure out if it's safe to come out. We just want sightings at this point."

"Okay." I didn't just want a sighting. I wanted Poppy. I wanted to be home, curled up in bed with her curled up on my pillow sleeping next to me. It's the vision I held most strongly. Poppy—returned to her safe space, alive and well.

Babs must have heard the doubt and pain in my voice. "Dogs like patterns. She will settle into a pattern, a routine. We need to find out her routine, or where she's found a safe spot—and she will. Then we give her time, patience, and a safe setting so she is comfortable exposing herself to you. That's how this works. That's why we need as many eyes watching for her as possible.

Remember, this is a marathon, not a sprint. It could take days, or weeks or even longer."

"I can't sit out here for days or weeks."

"I know. That's where the volunteers come in. Do you have more people to help tomorrow?"

"Yes, a lot more, I think."

"Good, that's what we need. Get everyone in that neighborhood to know this dog and be ready to call you the moment she's spotted. It's not just you sitting out there. You want the entire town on the lookout for this dog." Babs was encouraging, enthusiastic even. She believed we could find Poppy.

"Based on my Facebook responses, that's starting to happen." And it was. My social media posts were being shared repeatedly. Several clients who lived in the neighborhood let me know they were watching and had shared my posts. One of the employees at Ruff House, who'd been so careful and loving with Poppy on her first day there, shared the post on their page and printed out a flyer to hang on the bulletin board at Ruff House. And by now there were several hundred flyers posted, hung on streetlights, and handed out.

"That's good. Just remember sometimes this is as much about controlling the people as anything else. Be sure everyone knows their job is just to report sightings. Don't chase her. Don't try to catch her. Don't be a hero. They just need to call you and let you know where they saw her and, if possible, what direction she was headed."

"I'm trying to tell people that. It's hard, though. That's not the natural instinct."

"I know. But if approached, she's going to run."

"That's true."

"We don't want her running in a panic. She could run into trouble."

I pictured her bolting across the busy street again, or back into the canyons, running scared into a pack of coyotes. *Terrifying.* "Right. No. We don't want her running scared."

"If we figure out where she's hanging out, what her pattern is, we can set a trap. That's the goal here."

"Got it."

"Do you have the warming station supplies?"

"I do." Chris had brought me a waxed box, the kind that usually held vegetables, and another blanket of Poppy's, along with her toy. I'd been using the blanket on my lap, which I considered multitasking at that point—the blanket was keeping me less wet and absorbing my scent so I could leave it with the chicken in the warming box—a veritable cornucopia of comforting smells to draw out my little Popstar. I hoped.

"Stay as long as you can. Then set up the warming station and go home and get some sleep. She won't be out in the middle of the night, and you've got to keep yourself strong. Be sure to get some rest."

Strong. Rest. These things seem impossible now.

By 10:00 P.M., I was chilled through. I'd been sitting for hours. If I were religious or even a spiritual person this would have been a good time for prayer. But I'm not. I tried just envisioning a safe and home-again Poppy—putting it out in the universe and all—but more often than not that made me cry, and wet tears on a cold face in the cold air is not a good thing.

Coyotes howled in the distance, and I tensed, imagining the worst. Then I tried to shake it off, remembering all I had learned about coyotes recently.

A year or so previously I had written a magazine article on coyotes, wolves, and foxes, and our tendency to treat them so very differently from dogs even though they were all part of the *Canis* genus. I'd always enjoyed seeing the coyotes that roamed the hillside behind our Riverside townhome, though I was careful to never let my beagles in the backyard unattended. In working on the article, I had interviewed the executive director of Project Coyote, a nonprofit that works to promote coexistence with coyotes in urban and rural settings. I'd also read *Coyote America* by Dan Flores. I tried to think about what I'd learned: how coyotes were among the most persecuted species; how their curiosity and playfulness is often mistaken for aggressive, challenging behavior; and most importantly that night, how their howls were not screaming, murderous celebrations of the violent death of a small animal, but rather a means of communication among a pack. A language. One coyote could make multiple sounds as well. The howls I was hearing were not necessarily from an entire pack. I tried also to think of the trickster coyote stories and mythologies of Native Americans, the precursors to Wile E. Coyote cartoons. And I tried to remind myself that a coyote's diet was mostly gophers and rats, fruits and vegetables, and sometimes garbage left by humans, but not, despite humankind's opinions, our domesticated pets. Not normally. I tried to think all those things. I tried to be as brave as I wanted Poppy to be.

Besides, Babs had told me that "the littles," as she called small dogs, usually fared better when lost. "They're freaking fast, and agile. Not like the family pet lounging in its own backyard."

All I could do was hope Poppy's speed and her hiding skills were working to her advantage. And I hoped that somehow, she knew I was trying to find her—that I was doing everything I could.

And was I? Was I doing everything I could?

Chris texted, "You okay?"

"Cold. Tired. My butt is sore, and my back is killing me. But I'm here. Safe."

"You should come home. It's late. She's not going to be out now."

"Babs said I should stay as long as I could."

"She doesn't know you. She doesn't know you'd stay out all night for a dog."

"She also said Poppy wouldn't be out late at night and I should get some sleep."

"So come home."

"It's only 10:30."

"That's late at night."

"If it starts raining, I'll come home. My cell phone battery is almost dead."

"Okay, don't stay too much longer. Love you." He sent a string of emoticons—dogs, kissing faces, and a glass of wine.

"Love you too. Kiss Percy-pie and Roe-Roe for me." I sent back some emoticons—dogs, hearts, a cloud with a lightning bolt through it.

The neighborhood house lights went out one by one and a fog rolled in, giving the streetlight a muted, eerie glow. By 11:15 a light rain spat at me.

I walked up the trail with the warming box, the blanket, Poppy's steak toy, and the bag of chicken. I found a bush that would provide some cover from the rain and tucked the box under it, with the opening facing out to the trail.

I placed the blanket and the toy inside, and then ripped off some chicken (no bones) and placed that in the box as well. It looked oddly cozy and at the same time like a homemade monument, like one of those memorials on the side of a road where someone had died in a bike or car accident.

I could be feeding coyotes, but I told myself I was leaving messages for Poppy. *I'm here. I'm going to help you. Please come back.*

The rain came down harder. I packed up and moved to my car. Sitting in the rain, unable to see much through my window, the full futility of what I was doing settled on me. A gazillion acres of wilderness, and I've set out one box, with some shreds of chicken, near a neighborhood, on a cold, rainy night.

I started the car engine.

Babs and Mike have done this before. It is NOT futile. I had to believe. (You may have realized by now, believing positive, happy things is not naturally in my wheelhouse. I am, you might say, not a believer.)

Chris, Percival, and Roe were all asleep, sprawled out across our bed, when I arrived home. I stripped off my wet clothes, threw on a T-shirt, and slipped into the bed, angling my legs between the dogs and twisting into a moderately comfortable position on my side, facing Chris. Roe moved up against my legs, comforting me with his warmth and his doggy-ness. I drifted off to sleep just after 1:00 A.M.

Do I need to tell you what time I woke up? *Hello 4:00 A.M., my old friend.*

11
INSTRUCTIONS

I dressed in the dark, throwing on the same yoga pants, T-shirt, and sweat-shirt I'd been wearing. If Babs wanted my scent spread in one spot, this would surely help. No one else stirred, not even Percival—usually so happy to wake and demand belly rubs when anyone opens their eyes.

Thermos filled with black coffee in hand, I headed back to Via La Paloma.

The streets were quiet, with only a few cars out. Were people headed to work? I'd already forgotten what day it was. Thursday? Friday? I had canceled all appointments for the week, so I no longer had a work schedule to keep me on track. But Poppy had been missing for two nights, I knew that much. This was the third day—so Thursday. Third's a charm? Could that apply here? *So tired.*

I parked my car at the end of the cul-de-sac. Any neighbor paying attention would likely assume I'd spent the night there, and I couldn't help but feel I should have. I should have been doing something. Anything. Anything but sleeping in a warm, dry bed, while Poppy was lost in the cold, wet wilderness.

The boulder still seemed like the best spot to sit, so I again spread a blanket over the rock and another across my lap. I had grabbed the bag of chicken from the refrigerator at home, though cold it didn't seem to have the same wafting odor. That was good for me, but not so good for luring Poppy. I should have warmed it up at home. I opened it and set the bag down beside me. And then I waited.

And waited.

Everything was damp. The air was misty, and the sun rose slowly through the shrouded sky. I couldn't check the warming station until the sun was up and the humans were moving about—that would be the point at which Poppy was unlikely to appear. In the meantime, I was to sit and wait for her to appear. Babs had assured me Poppy would see me long before I'd see her. She could be watching me now, deciding whether to come out, whether she was ready to come home.

Come on out, baby. Come on, my little Popstar. Let's go home. It's okay, sweetie, please come on out.

If I think it hard enough, can I make it happen? Sure, right. Like life ever works like that.

This was a tough little dog. She'd already survived so much. And I knew she was wily—quick, smart, able to maneuver away or around any obstacle. I still believed she was out there, in that canyon somewhere. I had to believe that.

My dad texted me, saying good morning—it was 7:30 in Missouri. By then, he'd been up for hours too, I knew. He'd begun communicating mostly by text a few years ago when his hearing started going and phone calls got more difficult. Now that he was in a different time zone, texting had another advantage, since Dad was a very early morning person and I was a very late-night person.

Dad's text asked why I hadn't texted him lately. He probably had not expected me to reply so quickly, but I did. I told him about Poppy missing.

"You'll find her," he replied.

Encouraging, even though I knew that he, of course, had no way of knowing what the outcome would be. At least he wasn't telling me I was crazy, or talking about coyotes.

"I hope so."

"You will. Poor thing. You'll find her."

I wasn't sure if Poppy or I was the "poor thing." "We'll look as long as we have to," I texted back.

"Good. Keep me posted."

For not the first time, I was reminded how dogs were the thing my family members had most in common. This would be a time I could count on my family's support and encouragement, though no one was close enough to physically help. All of us were dog lovers. All of us connected with dogs, and we'd always had dogs, every one of us, during every stage of our lives. With all the marriages and divorces in my immediate family, I'd often joked that we didn't have a family tree so much as family groundcover. We spread out and expanded haphazardly but had no deep roots or sturdy branches. The common ground we did have, though, was dogs. It helped to know Dad was rooting for me, for Poppy.

As the sun rose, the neighbors came out walking their own dogs. Soon, cars left their driveways, lights were on, and the day began. I walked the trail up to where I'd left the warming box the night before. I still wasn't sure what I was supposed to find. What to even hope for? Poppy curled up sleeping in the box? That seemed unlikely.

Before I reached the warming station, I could see that the blanket I'd left had been pulled out and dragged about eight feet away. The fabric steak toy had also been taken out and dropped in the middle of the trail. By Poppy? How would I know? Poppy's habit was to take toys under my bed with her. She had a stash of under-bed toys in both Riverside and Paso Robles. She also had several of my shoes, shredded beyond repair, under the bed with her. While the wilderness park was a different environment altogether, it still seemed to me Poppy would have taken the toy with her to wherever she'd made her den. She'd take it under her new bed, so to speak.

The thought of that brought me fleeting comfort—Poppy, safe in a den, with a familiar toy for comfort. Only the toy was at my feet, not with my girl. I picked up the steak toy, shredded and wet, and walked to the box. The chicken was gone, of course, but there was no calling card to tell me whom I'd fed. No thank-you note. No request for seconds. I picked up the box and the blanket and brought them all back to my car.

I called Babs to let her know what I'd found.

"Do you have the trail camera set up?" She said.

The trail camera! "No. I forgot about that. I don't have one."

"Okay, yeah. Okay, well, the warming box isn't much use without the trail camera. You've got to get a trail camera and get that positioned so you can see the warming box. Then you'll know if she makes an appearance or if it's just coyotes. Remember, we're trying to find out where she's staying. Dogs like patterns. She'll settle into a pattern."

I didn't understand "trail camera" when she had said it to me the day before. Was this like an infrared camera? Night goggles? I must have just dropped the idea from my brain when I couldn't make sense of it.

"I don't know what that is or where to get one," I said. *Also, my dog is missing, and I don't have time for shopping!* I held that comment in. I was exhausted and she was helping me. I knew better than to let my frustration show.

"I'll text you a photo of what you need. Any sporting goods store will have it. Or Walmart. Possibly even a Best Buy."

These are not stores I frequent. I suspect my entering a sporting goods store would set off alarms, the same way my straying over to the petite section of a clothing store would. *Alarm! Alarm! Does Not Belong! Stranger Danger! Does Not Belong!* That is also what happens when I go to family get-togethers. Luckily, none of these things happen often.

The text came through. The trail camera looked like a toy: a 4" x 6" plastic rectangle covered in an army green camouflage print, with a hole—presumably the lens—at the top front and army green canvas straps to affix the camera to a tree or something on the "trail." The camera was motion activated and, as I could see by the packaging, used by hunters. *Great.* But I could see clearly how it would help in the search for Poppy. If I had strapped the camera to a nearby tree, pointed at the warming box, I would have known if I had made a sacrificial chicken offering to Poppy or to the coyotes. I would know if Poppy was sticking around this area. I would possibly know if she was still alive.

I had failed.

"It's alright. There's time," Babs said. "She's out there. Just get the camera today and we'll do it again tonight. What are you going to do now?"

"I thought I'd drive around a bit, look for her."

"No. Don't do that."

"Don't look for her?"

"You won't see her. Remember, you need to think like a dog. Think like Poppy. Think of it from her point of view. She'll be hiding. Especially if you're out driving around. Remember, she's frightened. Do you have any volunteer help today?"

"Yes. Six or eight people, I think. Maybe ten. Beagle Freedom Project is sending people. We're meeting at my office at ten."

"Great. That's good. But you've got to get control of the people. Make sure they understand what we're doing. Get lots and lots and lots of flyers made. Divide up the neighborhood around the wilderness park—miles around it if you can—and send people out plastering the neighborhoods with flyers. Get eyes on the flyers. I'll send you a diagram of how and where to hang the flyers so they get seen."

"Okay. I can do that. I'll get my office printing more flyers and I'll get a trail camera."

"Good. Remember, this is a marathon, not a sprint."

This explained why I felt like I'd ran twenty-six miles. Poppy had already been lost for over thirty-six hours. Wasn't that already more than a marathon? I didn't want to ask Babs what her timeline for "marathon" was. Days? Weeks? *Months?* It didn't matter. She had no way of knowing how long this particular marathon would run. And what if we never knew the ending? What if there was no victory tapeline to run through? *No. Can't think that. Poppy's out there.*

I texted Jessica with the photo of the trail camera, asking her to search for where we could buy one. "And print more flyers."

"More?" She texted back.

"Lots more."

Chris, Roe, and Percival were awake and fed by the time I got back home. I made some coffee and toast while I brought Chris up to speed.

"I printed out the map of the neighborhood and divided up the areas to assign to people. I'll print a few more. Are most of them coming in from LA?" Chris said.

"Some local—Cecilia's coming back. And I think Maria is close by. And Austin and Jessica of course. But BFP staff folks are all coming from LA. That's why we said 10:00 A.M."

By the time we arrived at my office Chris had printed out maps for each neighborhood area to be assigned, and made one large map (twelve 8.5" × 11" pages printed and taped together) that he taped to one of the large white erase boards in my conference room.

I wrote the office Wi-Fi password, my cell phone number, and Chris's cell phone number on the other white erase board, next to the map. As each volunteer came in, they wrote their name and cell phone number on the board. We were a strong, dedicated, and now organized team.

Bob and Brian, dads to BFP beloved beagles Abe and Davey, were among the first to arrive. They knew what I was going through. It was their Davey who'd been lost for a harrowing twelve hours shortly after his arrival at their home. I remembered that time well. Those hours had felt like days while the poor dog was missing, and I only had been watching the news unfold on the private Facebook page for BFP Fosters and Adopters. It was wonderful of them to "pay it forward" by coming out to help with the search for Poppy.

Cecilia and Maria, another BFP adopter, arrived soon after, adding their names and numbers to the white board.

Jessica and Austin were each on phones calling Walmarts, Big 5, and Bass sporting goods stores, with apparently no luck. The printers whirred and spat out flyers near each of them, as the coffeemaker spit out cup after cup of coffee.

Aaron arrived, ready to help again, and this time his wife, Deia, was with him.

This was truly a community of dog rescuers, helping one another whenever possible.

I grabbed two boxes of clear plastic sheet covers—the same ones we use to put clients' estate planning documents in before placing them in a binder for safekeeping.

"Thank you, guys, all for being here. We're waiting on the BFP staff people and they're on their way. In the meantime, I have a craft project for you. We need to put the flyers in these sheet covers to keep 'em dry. Put the opening at the bottom so the rain doesn't get in. Then tape the bottom closed when you hang it. Here's the instructions for how and where to place flyers." I handed out copies of Babs's placement diagrams.

At first, it seemed odd that Babs needed to give us instructions on hanging flyers. Just find a surface and tape, right? *Wrong.* She had detailed instructions for not just how but where to hang the flyers—how to get the most eyes on the flyers in the shortest amount of time. (I learned later that the flyers and instructions were actually Mike's.) Find neighborhood ingress and egress points and tape the flyers on poles at each corner of the intersection. Be sure to place them at eye level of someone in a car—not your eye level as you're standing. Lower. Find public group mailboxes and post there. If it's a cul-de-sac, post at the entry and at the end, you don't have to post along every light post. Post in Starbucks, fast-food places, grocery stores, anywhere there are lots of people. *Get eyes on the flyer so the entire town is watching for this dog.*

"This makes so much sense," Cecilia said.

"It does. Babs also suggested that if you see people out walking or can talk to anyone at the stores, have them take a photo of the flyer with their cell phone so they have the information. People will toss the flyers away, but the photo will stay on their phone. If we make it convenient for them, they're more likely to help," I said.

"Another great idea," Cecilia said.

Finally, all the way in from Los Angeles after a two-plus hour drive in the pouring rain, the BFP staff team arrived—this time it was Matt, Megan, and Nataly—bringing snacks, boxes of color flyers already printed, and boxes of supplies. They had tape, staple guns, markers, pens, and neon poster boards.

As everyone worked stuffing flyers and making posters, Chris took over to explain the maps and the various neighborhoods.

Teams of two—Bob and Brian, Aaron and Deia, Cecilia and Maria, Megan and Nataly, and Chris and I—chose the neighborhoods they'd each be canvasing.

"We can stuff these as we go," Deia said, grabbing a stack of flyers and sheet covers. "Let's get out there."

I knew the feeling. Sitting in an office conference room, like sitting in my car or even sitting on that boulder, did not feel like we were helping Poppy.

The instinct to head out walking and searching is strong. But I had to trust in Babs. She'd done this hundreds of times. I had to trust in the process. At least she *had* a process.

"That's fine. Take enough flyers and go. We have to remember the idea is to get thousands of eyes looking out for Poppy so we can figure out her patterns. If you hand out all the flyers or just want a break, find somewhere high on the perimeter of the park and sit to watch for her. Just sit." I hoped I had gotten that part right. I'd gotten so much wrong; I was doubting everything I thought.

"Don't chase her if you see her. Just call Teresa. Let her know where you spotted Poppy and what direction she's headed," Chris added.

Yes, that. That was the important part. But I saw more than one sideways glance. And I understood that too. It would be very hard to spot the missing beagle and not try to catch her. Even with all of Babs's coaching, I knew it would be hard for me to restrain myself. But I also knew how fast Poppy was, her gymnastic abilities to leap and twist and sail through the air, and I knew how fearful she still was. She would not likely be caught by human hands. Babs was right.

The teams, except for Matt, Chris, and I, set out to their neighborhoods, fully stacked with supplies, snacks, and water.

Matt and Chris worked on taping "LOST DOG" and my cell phone number on an eight-foot-wide bright blue tarp using wide white tape to spell out the letters. Matt then placed a large laminated photo of Poppy in the middle, taped on with the same white tape.

"We'll put this on a freeway overpass if we can. Or a wall or fence somewhere near the park. A freeway sign is how we eventually found Davey," Matt said.

"It's a great way of doing it. Hard not to notice that," I said.

"She's so cute," Matt said.

Walking away now. Not going to cry. She is really stinking cute. I went to my desk to order the trail camera on Amazon since it didn't seem Jessica and Austin were having any luck. There's an Amazon distribution center very nearby, so who knew, perhaps I could get same-day delivery. I also needed to return a few emails and keep my office running, or at least staggering along.

Once I finished with that, I posted an update on the search for Poppy to Facebook and Instagram, asking for more volunteers. As I hit "post," Jessica came to my doorway.

"We found a trail camera, but it's in Cerritos. We looked it up and it will take us about forty-five minutes to get there."

"If that's the closest one, go." I handed her a credit card.

"It's $80 and we still need to get the memory card and batteries."

"I'll get the card and batteries; you guys get the camera. We need it ready to go by dusk."

No sooner did Jessica leave than my phone rang. I had a moment of "Someone saw Poppy" excitement, since my cell phone number was now plastered throughout Riverside, but then I saw it was Babs.

"You need to change your Facebook post."

"Why?" I was trying not to whine. I just wanted to find my dog. "We still need more people helping."

"You asked people to search. We don't want people out there walking around."

"I thought I just said 'help.'" And really, was anyone parsing the language of my post? And yet I knew that anyone who wanted to help would think that meant actively walking around looking for Poppy. That's what I had thought 'help' meant too.

"It says 'search.' Just take it down and post that she's still lost. If anyone sees her they should call you. Make sure they don't chase her. Even calling out to her will scare her. Imagine a bunch of strangers walking toward you calling your name. It's scary. Especially if you were lost."

I dropped my head into my hand, elbow resting on my desk. "You'd think I'd know this by now. I'm sorry. I'm tired."

"I know. It's okay. Get some volunteers out to post flyers. If people want to help, that's what they can do."

"A bunch of them went out just a bit ago."

"Good. What are you doing now?"

She asked me this often, and I was usually doing the wrong thing. I hesitated before answering. *No time for ego—I had to find this dog.*

"Fixing my Facebook post?"

"Good. Then what?"

"I've got to pick up posters at the printer and get a memory card and batteries for the trail camera. We found one."

"Good. Then you need to go home and sleep. I'm sure you haven't been sleeping, and we need you rested."

Rest. Ha! "I haven't, but I don't think I can nap while everybody else is out walking the neighborhoods."

"That's exactly when you need to sleep. Here's the thing—you're the night shift. The volunteers will usually only be available during the day, and eventually they will lose interest and drop off. You'll have to keep going. Sleep now while you can."

Would they drop off? Would I keep going? How long could I keep going? The BFP people are devoted to these rescued dogs, but everyone has their own life and jobs and commitments. I'd probably have volunteers helping at least through the weekend—two, maybe three more days. Even Chris couldn't stay past Saturday. He had to be back at work Sunday afternoon—there was no one available to cover his shift in the winery tasting room. Would anyone be back on Monday? And how long could I stay out of my office? *One day at a time. I'd have to take this one day at a time. Maybe by Monday we won't need any more volunteers.*

Matt and Chris had finished the tarp sign—large, bright, and magnificently, brilliantly, waterproof—and Matt headed out to find a place to hang it.

"Babs is right," Chris said. "I'll go get the memory card and batteries, and whatever other running around needs to be done and you go home and sleep."

"I can't sleep," I said.

"You have to. You can't keep going like this."

"It's only been two days. I can keep going if I have to. And we're supposed to cover that neighborhood." I pointed to the map on the white board, and the section we'd agreed to cover.

"I'll go there. I can cover it. You need to rest."

I knew he was right. Babs was right. Everybody was right. "Okay. I'll go home for a bit. It just feels weird to do that. Wrong somehow."

"We'll all be sleeping when you're sitting watch tonight."

"I hope not. I hope we find her by then."

"I know, baby. I know."

At home I contemplated a shower before a nap and went into the bathroom. I first set my cell phone on the sink, then moved it closer to the shower—the top of the toilet tank. I turned the volume up. But when I turned the water on it seemed possible I wouldn't hear the phone ring over the sound of the water, or maybe I just wouldn't get to it in time. I turned the water off and returned to the bedroom. I couldn't risk such a stupid screw-up. My stink was part of the rescue plan, anyway.

I tossed and turned in bed, unable to block images of Poppy being chased by coyotes, running into the busy highways nearby, falling into the raging creek, or any number of horrid scenarios. I tried to think of her home, safe, curled up on the pillow next to my head as she'd been doing since soon after I brought her home. I wanted nothing more than to have Poppy back home, safe on this bed with me.

I had not allowed myself to think about anything after Poppy was back—where she would go then. Jessica was not likely to still want to adopt her, and BFP was not likely to allow her to (an escape artist dog is not an apartment dog). I couldn't think about that.

Roe curled up on the bed with me, and Percival lounged on the dog bed we called his "cloud bed." It was huge and fluffy and had a "hood" (a blanket attached on three sides) that he frequently burrowed under, leaving just the tip of his nose exposed, and sometimes not even that. I petted Roe and he stretched out gratefully and turned over on his back for belly rubs.

"You're a good boy, Roe-Roe. A very good boy." I rubbed his belly and choked back tears on instinct. But there was no reason for holding back tears, I realized. Home alone with just the dogs, I could let go and cry. Dogs were such understanding creatures. And I suspected Roe missed his little buddy, too.

🐾

I returned to my office at half past 2:00 P.M. Matt had come back from hanging the tarp and posting flyers.

"I went in the Nature Center and asked if I could hang the tarp sign on the building facing that busy road, but they said no. I shouldn't have asked!" Matt said.

"What's the expression—easier to beg forgiveness than ask permission? Something like that."

"Exactly. But I hung it on the fence. Still facing the street, just not up as high as I would have liked."

"That's still good. Thanks."

Matt was making a second, smaller sign. Chris had returned with the printed posters, the memory card, and the batteries. Jessica and Austin returned from Cerritos with the trail camera.

The camera still looked like a toy to me. But a complicated one. Austin offered to get it set up and I gladly agreed. I handed him the bag with the memory card and batteries.

Chris and I went to the conference room to look at the maps.

"Any word from anyone?" Chris said.

"Aaron and Deia are hiking out to the spot he was in yesterday to watch for her. They covered their area. But that's all I've heard."

Chris wrapped me in his arms and pulled me in close. "We'll find her. It's going to take time, but we'll find her."

I wiggled away from him. "I don't know. I hope so. But look at this," I pointed to the enormous map on the white board. "It's huge. She's this little, tiny, scared dog."

"She's smart, though. And you said yourself that she was quick and got away from you easily."

"Me, yes. I'm hardly as quick as a coyote."

"We've got to stay positive."

For most of our relationship, this was our thing. Chris stayed positive and I sunk into all the bad things that could happen. Still, I think of myself not so much as a pessimist as a realist. That shit can happen. That shit *did* happen.

"Okay. We should head out to our area." I scanned the map. "We're going back to the street where she entered the park, right?"

"That seems our best bet at this point. But I want to hike into the canyon again and sit near where we think the homeless encampment is."

"Show me where that is on this map so I can try to get oriented."

Chris circled a spot on the map. The homeless camp was southeast of where Poppy had first run into the wilderness park, and, not surprisingly, not close to any of the surrounding neighborhood housing.

"Okay, that's not as close as I thought."

"She may not have settled in yet."

"Show me on the map where she was when the GPS tracker battery died?"

Chris drew another dot. This one was north of where she'd entered the park. No pattern yet. No clear trail.

My phone rang. I answered quickly.

"It's Nataly. We just talked to a guy who says he saw Poppy this morning sitting on his neighbor's lawn!"

"What? He saw her?"

Chris turned from the map to me, eyes wide. Matt looked up from the floor where he'd been squatting to finish another sign.

"Yes! He's pretty sure it was her. He said it was about 6:00 A.M. this morning. She was sitting on the neighbor's lawn barking toward their front door. He says that neighbor has dogs, so she was probably barking at those dogs."

"We've never heard her bark. Did you talk to the neighbor?"

"We're headed over there now. Here's the address . . ."

I wrote the address on a scrap of paper. "Okay. We'll be right over. See if you can get the name and phone number of the guy you're talking to and of the neighbor at the house where she was spotted."

We ended the call and I looked at Chris. "She's still alive."

"Yes!" Chris hugged me again, and this time I didn't wiggle away.

"Here's the address. We should head over. Show me on the map where that is."

When Chris showed me, most of my hope and excitement evaporated.

"She would have had to cross Alessandro Boulevard to get to that neighborhood. That wasn't her."

"She could have done it in the middle of the night. And look," he pointed to the far eastern end of the map, "if she went all the way across the wilderness park and came out down here, she crosses over in a less populated part of Alessandro and is right back in wilderness. Then she comes out here and is in that neighborhood."

He had drawn a trail that seemed both incredibly far and unlikely. At least to me. "That's so far. Why would she do that?"

"She's scared. She doesn't know where she is. The guy said he's pretty sure it's her. And Megan and Nataly are in a neighborhood within the parameters of where Babs told us to send people. It's her. Poppy's out there."

"I'm going to call Babs. And then we'll go."

Matt spoke up. "I'm going to take this sign and meet up with Megan and Nataly over there. I think we know where the sign needs to go now."

Could the plan be working? It could. It was someone else's plan.

12

SIGNS

"Don't tell anyone the address," Babs said immediately.

Unsurprisingly, I was about to text the entire group with the address. At least this time I knew to call Babs first. That had to count as learning, right?

"If you give anyone the address, they will all want to run over there, and I guarantee you will scare Poppy away if she's still around. And this is a residential neighborhood, right? Lots of places to hide and lots of cars. We don't want her running scared," Babs said.

What she said always made so much sense. And it always went against my instincts. "Okay, right. But I can go over there, right?"

"Yep. Go talk to the neighbor. Find out if you can sit out on their front lawn tonight. If they don't want you there, sit on the public sidewalk."

"I'm sure the neighborhood would call the police if it comes to that," I said.

"I've had the police called on me many times. Take some flyers with you, explain to the police what you're doing. They'll leave you alone. You can even hand them some flyers. They're usually very helpful."

She was so matter-of-fact about my soon to be run-in with the police, almost as though it would be a rite of passage for any dog search and rescue person worth their rotisserie chicken. "Let's hope I can stay in the yard Poppy showed up in. So, same drill? Chicken, smelly clothes, sit, and wait?"

"Same drill. Get some chicken broth too. If you can sprinkle it around the yard. The wind will carry that scent too."

"Can I let the group know we had a sighting at least? I think everyone needs the encouragement."

"Absolutely. And if they want to focus on putting up signs in that neighborhood and for a two-mile radius out, that's great. Signs everywhere."

Wasn't there a song like that? "Signs, signs, everywhere a sign. Breaking up the scenery" and . . . Something with my mind? "Do this, don't do that? Can't you read the sign?" And why on earth am I thinking about what is surely an old song now? Apparently, my brain can't handle good news.

I sent a group text about the sighting, without the address. I included the information about the neighborhood and Babs's recommendations to paper the area with flyers, and reiterated the warning against attempting to catch or chase Poppy.

The group was excited and reenergized, but the logistics continued to be an issue. Some folks had to head back to LA, and Deia and Aaron were out in the canyon on the east end, which would be across Alessandro Boulevard from the neighborhood Poppy had popped up in, so they agreed to stay put to watch for her. By the time they hiked back out it would be sunset. We had no idea yet whether Poppy was returning to the wilderness park at night or was now roaming the residential area. We had no idea yet about anything. Except that as of 6:00 A.M. this morning, she was alive.

She was alive.

"Let's go, Chris," I said. "I really want to get over there."

"Okay. We'll go get you set up, then I'll go get more chicken and broth, and dinner for us. Beyond Burgers again?"

"I'm not hungry."

"You should eat. It's going to be a long night. And like Babs says, you're the night shift."

It was a little past 3:00 P.M. when we drove down Alessandro. The traffic was heavy, and I couldn't help but think of a little frightened dog trying to make her way across. Likely she did it in the middle of the night, but still, my brain saw eighteen-wheeler trucks headed to the distribution centers not far away, speeding Hondas, and SUVs driven by overworked, exhausted commuters. In my mind, none of them stopped for a little brown and white dog.

I followed Chris as he turned right on Trauitwein, another busy road. When my father and his second wife (my younger sister's mother) lived out in Lake Mathews—a very rural unincorporated area south of Riverside proper—Trautwein had nothing on it except what was then a Naugles fast-food restaurant and now was a Del Taco fast-food restaurant; it had been merely a road in and out of the Lake Mathews and Woodcrest neighborhoods. But now the corner of Alessandro and Trautwein had a large shopping center, complete with movie theaters, restaurants, Stein Mart, and a Stater Bros. grocery store. Another block down had BevMo, a gym, and Sprouts grocery store. So much activity. So many cars. Why would Poppy have come through here? What if she hadn't? What if it was a different dog spotted on the lawn? We'd never heard her bark. It may not have been her. We may be on the proverbial wild goose chase.

I shook my brain out of that thought. *We had a sighting. She was still alive. We would find her. We have Babs.*

Chris drove through the neighborhood behind the shopping centers, past the enormous "neighborhood" church, past another park, and into a typical Southern California neighborhood of stuccoed two-story houses close together with small manicured front lawns dotting a maze of streets, many of which were cul-de-sacs. I noted the "Lost Dog" signs that Megan, Nataly, and now Matt had been hanging up on light posts, mailboxes, and fences. They'd done just as Babs said—those signs were everywhere. It would be hard to come and go from this neighborhood without knowing one very cute beagle was missing.

Chris stopped on Dayton Street and got out of his car. I did the same and walked toward him.

"It suddenly dawns on me that I have to go ask those people if a very sketchy-looking, smelly, total stranger can sit out on their lawn with a bag of chicken and dirty clothes all night," I said.

"Let's hope they're dog lovers," Chris said.

"I love that you did not bother pretending I look fine."

"Ummmm . . . you look great?"

"Thanks for trying. Love you anyway."

We approached the door and I knocked.

A man in his early sixties answered. "You here about the dog?"

"Yes, she was here?" I said. Though why I was asking him that was unclear even to me. The people living in the house were not the ones who saw Poppy.

"Some folks came by earlier. We already have the flyer. I guess one of my neighbors saw the dog here. But we haven't seen any dogs. Just our own."

I could hear dogs barking and yipping. We heard them as we approached the house. From the sound of it, they had several small dogs. Good. Perhaps they'd be sympathetic.

"Yes, they called us after talking to your neighbor. It's our dog that's lost. Her name is Poppy."

Just then a young woman also appeared at the door. "It's your puppy? I'm so sorry. I hope you find her. We'll look for her. We have the flyer and I've seen them all around the neighborhood," she said.

"This is my daughter, Julia. And I'm Les."

"I'm Teresa. This is Chris. And thank you. We have lots of people helping. And we . . . well, I . . . um . . ." How does one ask to camp out on a stranger's lawn?

"We're working with a dog rescue expert and she thinks there's a chance Poppy will come back here tonight or tomorrow. We're wondering if you wouldn't mind if we sat on your lawn waiting for the dog," Chris said.

That. That is how one asks to sit on a stranger's lawn. Why won't my brain work? Thank Buddha for Chris.

"I have chicken and a toy of hers to try to tempt her back," I chimed in. *Thanks, brain!*

"Oh, that's great!" Julia said. "Yes, stay!"

We looked to her dad—all three of us—and I'm sure we looked like kids do when they're asking their parent if they can keep the stray puppy. Only we were the stray puppies. Sort of.

"Whatever you need. Not a problem. Use these chairs here," he pointed to the two rattan chairs with comfortable, padded cushions, sitting on their front porch. This stakeout would be much more comfortable than my time on the boulder. "We've got five rescue dogs of our own. We understand."

Good choice, Poppy. Good choice.

Chris and I got our blankets and the new trail camera out of my car, along with an umbrella and my journal. Chris left to get us dinner, and I set up camp. I upended what would be the warming box to create a side table between the two chairs. The rain had come and gone all day again, but their front entryway was covered so the chairs were dry. The lawn was still wet, and the air smelled of damp concrete, a change from the sodden earth and brush I'd been smelling.

The sun began its descent as I endeavored to journal about all that had gone on these last two days. Babs had told me not to make eye contact even if I saw Poppy. Let her find me. I thought if I concentrated on my journal, I could will that to happen. *Find me, Poppy. Find me.*

But I couldn't concentrate. I couldn't stop thinking of Alessandro Boulevard and how many hundreds of cars would be driving down that road now as people came home from work. I had to hope that much traffic would prevent her from even trying to cross. *Stay on whatever side of the highway you're on, baby girl.* Although the thought of her still in the wilderness park was also frightening. Who was I kidding? The thought of her anywhere but home was frightening.

Chris returned with yet another dinner of Carl's Jr. Beyond Burgers, fries, and iced tea, and we used my makeshift warming box-turned-side-table as the now dining table, eating and watching as the neighbors arrived home.

"What must we look like to them?" I said.

"I'm sure Les will get a few phone calls," Chris said.

"I don't know. People don't really know their neighbors these days. But yeah, I hope they call him and not the police."

"What would they report? Burger-eating non-burglars sitting on the front porch?"

"Non-burger-eating non-burglars? Un-Hamburglars? You know, because Beyond Burgers aren't hamburgers?"

"You are really tired, aren't you?" Chris patted my knee.

"I am. I'm also pretty sure I look like a homeless person at this point, but maybe the charges would be just loitering."

"Spoken like a lawyer."

"There's a complaint for everything. And someone to make it."

My phone rang, and as happened every time my phone rang in the last forty-eight hours, my heart raced. The screen showed it was Laurie.

"You had a sighting!" She was upbeat. I could hear the hope in her voice.

"Yeah. Megan and Nataly talked to a neighbor who saw her sitting in someone's front yard, barking. We're sitting in the same yard right now. Not barking though."

"Well, that's good. I talked to Mike Noon again. He said to call him. If you've had a sighting again that's very good. He can talk to you." She gave me Mike's number again.

"Okay, we've been talking to Babs. She's been really helpful."

"I don't know Babs. She's probably great. I just know whatever Mike says I would listen to without question."

I had listened to Babs without question, and if Laurie trusted Mike, I would listen to him as well. I needed experts.

Chris and I finished our burgers, and as we did so a car pulled into the driveway of the home where we were squatting. A woman with long, wavy dark hair, wearing a curve-hugging dress and heels, and clearly coming from work, got out of the car. She looked to be in her early forties. Les's wife? Julia's mom? A girlfriend? Whoever she was, I hoped Les had called her and warned her about the non-homeless but definitely vagrant-looking people sitting on their porch.

She smiled at us, said hello and a quick "I hope you find your dog," before disappearing into the home.

"So I guess he said something. Did she sound irritated to you? I thought she sounded irritated," I whispered to Chris.

"Not really. She just got home from work. Everybody's irritated when they get home from work."

Very true. I'd missed the last two and a half days of work and already had forgotten what it was like. I'd rather have the mild irritations of work than the nightmare we were currently living. Still, just as I'd done when I was going through cancer treatments, I thought how lucky I was I could take time off for my many personal emergencies. Being one's own boss has its perks. The fact that I'm earning zero dollars and still have a staff to pay (one of whom had also been out for two days searching for a lost beagle), however, is not one of those perks.

Ten minutes later another car pulled into the driveway and parked next to the first car. This time it was another man in his sixties, with long, straight dark hair, well past his shoulders. He was wearing a flannel shirt and jeans and carrying bags of take-out food. He too nodded at us, said hello and "I hope you find your dog," before slipping into the house.

"I wonder how many people live here?" Chris said.

"How many people he had to call? How many people we're annoying?"

"No. I just meant, is it two couples and Julia? Are they three single people and Julia living with her dad?"

"I don't know. I'd say it's Les, his girlfriend, his daughter, and a friend."

"They are all very nice people."

"They are." We sat silently for a few minutes. Then Chris stood up.

"I'm going to set up the trail camera. I'm thinking on that tree there," Chris pointed to the large tree that sat only about ten feet from the front door. "I can probably angle it to get a pretty good view of the entire lawn. That way if she comes back to visit their pups, the camera will pick it up no matter where she stops on the grass."

"Good idea. I'll call Mike."

But before either of us moved, the front door opened. The man with the long dark hair stepped out on to the porch and stood between our chairs.

"How long has your dog been missing?" he said.

"Two days now. She got spooked in the thunderstorm Tuesday night and ran into Sycamore Canyon."

"I had a dog get lost once. I know what you're going through. Heart-breaking. My dog, she was the sweetest little thing . . ."

Do not tell me you never found her! Do not tell me she was killed. Do not! I cannot handle a bad ending! I'm sure my face conveyed my thoughts as always, but it did not stop him.

"She was one of those long dogs. What do you call them? My wife loved that dog. You know, the weenie dog?"

I noticed the past tense. The dog was gone. No longer alive. I desperately wanted to change the subject, but I did not want to be disrespectful. I'd end up bursting into tears if I heard how she died, but still, I answered him. "A dachshund? Cute dogs. Ours is a beagle. So, also a hound."

"Yeah? Great dogs. I love beagles. We found her. She was at the pound. Or what do you call it? The animal shelter."

I wasn't sure if he meant when they originally adopted her it was from the animal shelter, or after she got lost they found her at the shelter. I fervently hoped for the latter.

"Oh, that's nice. Ours is a rescue too."

"Well I hope you find her. Ours was missing for twelve hours, or about that, and it was a long twelve hours. I thought for sure she was a goner. Because you know, there's coyotes in that park. And mountain lions even. And you have to worry about the hawks with the little dogs."

Great! Thanks! Why would you say that? Why does everyone keep telling us the obvious thing about a freaking wilderness park. Wil-der-ness. Wild. We get it. But hey, if I'm angry I won't cry.

"So you found your dog?"

"Oh, yeah, yeah. We found her. I hope you find yours."

"Thanks."

He was quiet momentarily but didn't seem to be going anywhere. Then he spoke up again.

"Has anybody seen her besides our neighbor this morning?"

Chris answered, "A hiker thinks he saw her by a homeless encampment in the wilderness park yesterday, but we couldn't find them or her."

"I know that group. They would know if there was anything unusual going on. They can be very helpful. A lot of them hang out to charge their phones at the Carl's Jr. you were just at." He pointed to our bag sitting on my makeshift dining room table. "You could bring them some flyers."

It had not occurred to me that homeless folks have phones. Or would need to charge them. Because I'm an idiot, and apparently a snob. "Okay, yeah. That's a good idea."

"If you give me some, I'll hand them out when I see them. I work with the homeless. Volunteer. A lot of them are vets. Good people."

Chris handed him a stack of flyers. "Thank you. That would be helpful."

We were all silent again. The missing dog. The coyotes. The homeless vets. The dark, misty night—the fog had begun to roll in. It was hard to know what to say in the midst of so much desolation. But he spoke again, more softly this time.

"There's an owl around here too. Big beautiful spotted owl. I talk to him."

Chris and I looked at each other. *He talks to owls?* He did not sound crazy. He sounded entirely believable. I had thought he was Native American, and maybe I was stereotyping Native Americans from childhood television shows (the non-woke kind), but it seemed entirely plausible to me that he could commune with owls. He had a sort of aura about him. Also, he loved animals and helped people, vets, and the homeless; this is someone I would and did instantly respect. I was all in. He could do this. Would it be okay to ask him to ask the owls to not pick on Poppy? Maybe even protect her? Like some sort of scene out of Narnia? Or, I suppose for kids these days, Harry Potter?

"He does his *hoot hoot* conversation"—he said "hoot hoot" in a higher pitch and with elongated vowels—"and I answer him. *Hooooot. Hooot.* I don't know if he understands me, but he seems to come back from time to time. I like talking to him."

"That's nice." *But you're not going to be able to tell him not to hurt Poppy.*

"Yeah, it's nice. But I still wouldn't let our small dogs out around him. We got five little guys in there," he pointed at the closed front door.

"I think maybe that's why Poppy appeared here. The dogs I mean. Not the owl."

"She picked a good house. Everybody here loves animals."

"I see that. I hope she picks it again."

"Me too."

The silence descended again for long enough that I began to wonder if the owl was going to make an appearance soon. That would be both cool (an owl!) and awful (Poppy is still out there and she seems so tiny!).

"You folks have a good night. We'll leave the door unlocked if you need to come in for the bathroom or anything, just help yourself."

"Thank you. Very much. Thanks. That's very kind."

He went back inside, and Chris and I turned to each other.

"Now we have owls to worry about too," I said.

"I totally believed him. Dude talks to owls."

"I believed him too. I wanted to ask him to ask the owls not to harm Poppy."

"Remember the owl with Daphne?"

I did. I had thought about that owl immediately. Chris and I had been in the hot tub in our backyard in Riverside. Daphne had come outside with us and was sniffing around, as beagles do. But suddenly she was looking up above our heads and her already big root beer candy eyes became enormous. She was backing away slowly but not taking her eyes off the spot above our heads. I followed her gaze and saw a very large owl on the roof right above us, eyeing Daphne with as much interest as she eyed him, but with a lot less fear. No, he looked to be mentally weighing her. I turned back to Daphne and did the same calculation the owl was likely doing. Could he pick her up? Would he dare try?

I didn't wait to find out. I leapt up out of the hot tub, stepped down and immediately slipped on the glazed terracotta patio tiles and crashed down, slamming my elbow on the stair for good measure.

The ruckus sent the owl into flight and Daphne into full beagle howl. We have not since let any of the dogs out on our back patio when we're in the hot tub and never without us.

"Poppy probably weighs ten pounds less than Daphne did. Great. Now I'm worried about owls too."

"I think she's still too big for an owl," Chris said, reasonably.

"I can't think about that."

"Fair enough. I'm going to get on that trail camera."

Chris stood and went about trying to set up a hunter's trail camera on a large, manicured tree in a very suburban neighborhood.

I called Mike and immediately began to recall Mike's own traumatic situation with his father, just released home on hospice, thinking maybe the phone ringing would disturb his father—somehow, I pictured this person I didn't know sitting in a dark room in a recliner next to his dying father's hospital bed in the living room of his home. Then I began to worry maybe Mike was available now because his father had already passed on. Then I began to worry what to say, should I ask about his dad? Should I not?

I worried about all of that in the time it took for two rings. Then Mike picked up.

"How's it going?"

I wasn't sure how to answer that. "Well, we had a sighting. So, it's going good. I think?"

"Sounded like a solid sighting. Tell me what happened."

I reiterated the story of the neighbor spotting Poppy. "We've never heard her bark, though, so I don't know if that was really her."

"She's going to be a different dog. Her behavior will be different out in the wild on her own than it was with you," Mike said.

"Yeah, that makes sense. My own behavior is already different."

"Like staying up late and getting up at the crack of dawn?"

"And not showering. Living off vegan fast food. Camping on a stranger's lawn. Those things."

Mike laughed. And though I didn't know him, I was glad I could make him laugh at a time like what he was then going through. "Not showering is good. It will help her find your scent."

"Great. I'll remember that when people start telling me I stink."

"It's all for the cause," he said. Then, "So what are you doing now?"

Ah, I knew this trick. This is what Babs did. Ask me what I'm doing so they could explain everything I'd gotten wrong. Which *would* be everything. But not this time! I had the trail camera, I had the chicken, the toy, and my own stink, and I wasn't out walking around. I was sitting, letting Poppy come to me. So I told him that, proudly.

"And Chris is setting up the trail camera. We've got it angled to be able to see the entire front yard."

"Chris?"

There was something about his tone. Something very Babs-like in the way he asked that question.

"My boyfriend?" Suddenly I was that twenty-something with the up-ticked vocals that ended every sentence as though it was a question.

"Is Poppy familiar with Chris? Would she come to Chris at home?"

Damn it. "Um, no. She's a little afraid of Chris."

"So what do you think she's going to do if she gets near you and sees Chris? Or if she smells him a mile away?"

"Not come near me?"

"Right. Chris needs to go home. Nothing personal, but he can't be there."

"Okay." I knew that. Why could I not remember that? Because I needed Chris, that's why. And speaking of need . . . "He needs to go home to our other dogs anyway."

"Get the trail camera set up. Send Chris home. Stay quiet, watch the neighborhood, and give me a call a little later. I'll give you more instructions for setting up the area to entice her back."

I needed to ask one more thing, but I also didn't want to hear what I knew would be the answer. But there was no point doing this all if I wasn't doing it right. I took a deep breath and ventured, "I'm sitting on their porch. It's set back some, so I'm blocked from the wind and out of the rain. But I can see the whole lawn. Is that okay, or should I be further out on the lawn?" In other words, can I be remotely comfortable and dry and somewhat hidden from the neighbors?

"Out of the wind? You want to be in the wind. We want the wind picking up the scent and carrying it right on up Poppy's nostrils. A porch can create an eddy, with the air just circling around in place. Move out into the breeze."

No. No, I could not be comfortable. "I was hoping to stay dry. That has not been an option."

"Stay out in the breeze as long as you can. If you can't take it, go back on the porch. Something is better than nothing."

If I can't take it? No, damn it. I can take it. I'll take it. I need to find my baby girl. Challenge accepted!

We ended the call and I told Chris he needed to go and why.

"Yeah, I thought that might happen. I'm not insulted. If it were Percival, they'd be sending you home."

"Hard to imagine Percival running away, but yeah. Probably that one would be on you. Though I like to think after six years Percival at least likes me enough to come to me if he were cold and hungry and I had blankets and chicken."

"You'd like to think that," Chris said, but with a smile.

"Hey!"

"I'm kidding. He would. But Percival is never going to leave the comfort of beds, and twice-daily meals, snacks, and regular massages every morning and every night. Poor Popstar didn't know what she would be missing."

"She probably knows now."

Chris left and I moved my chair out onto the lawn, put on gloves, and wrapped myself more tightly in the dank blanket.

The neighborhood began to settle down.

There were fewer cars coming down the streets, most folks having already arrived home from work. I could hear a television inside the house I sat in front of, and music playing from a garage across the street. I was sure the music was too loud for Poppy to comfortably appear, and definitely too loud for me, since I considered most music "noise" and had a low tolerance for any noise not made by an animal. It looked like a guy was working on his truck in his very well-lit garage, blasting his heavy metal music (again, all music, save for Jimmy Buffett, whom I adore, is "heavy metal music" to me.) *How long would that go on?*

I removed my right glove and tried to return to my journaling, but writing about Poppy being lost only increased my anxiety. I wanted to be doing something to find her, and sitting in a stranger's front yard, wrapped in blankets, with a baseball cap over my greasy hair, and a bag of rotisserie animal parts at my feet did not feel like I was doing anything, except maybe acting out some weird satanic ritual. I tried looking at Facebook on my phone but quickly decided to avoid all the posts asking me if we'd found Poppy yet. I checked emails but found I couldn't concentrate, and I didn't want to return anyone's messages.

I called Mike again.

"Give me some hope."

"It's way too soon to be losing hope," he said in that deep, calm, listen-to-me voice of his.

"It's been over forty-eight hours."

"That's nothing. We find 'em weeks, months, years later."

There it was again. The marathon. I'd be sitting on boulders and lawns for weeks. Months. YEARS. And I would. I knew that. I would keep looking for her. "I just want to feel like I'm doing something. I want to be doing something."

"You need to listen."

Geez, dude. I just met you. I've listened to everything you've said. What do you mean listen? I listen to you more than I listen to my own family members! Okay, well, that was a low bar. But still. "I am listening. What haven't I listened to?"

"No. Not to me. Sit and listen. Listen to what's going on in the neighborhood."

"Music. A television."

"Listen for other dogs barking. If you hear the neighborhood dogs barking, it's because something is passing through. A cat, a stray dog, your dog. Listen and pay attention."

"Okay. I can do that."

"You okay out there?"

"It's better than sitting on a boulder worrying I'd be a feast for a pack of coyotes. But it's cold. And I'm tired." *And I'm whining to a total stranger who is just trying to help me—and Poppy—out of the kindness of his heart. Pull it together.* "It's okay. I'll do what I need to do. It just feels so hopeless."

"It's not hopeless. Dogs are very resilient. And smart. She's figuring out a safe place to hang out."

"She crossed a major street."

"Not likely she did that during heavy traffic." He told me later that of course that did happen, but usually because some well-meaning but ill-informed person was chasing the dog and frightened them into a mindless haul-ass run of fear. I'm glad he didn't tell me that at the time, since it was all too easy to picture Poppy doing just that. She had only just begun to trust me. *And look what that got her.*

"It's quiet in the neighborhood now. Music has stopped. Lights are going out."

"That's good. She won't likely appear when there's activity. Your job now is to sit. Let her find you. What are you going to do if you spot her?"

This was a tough one. I knew the answer, I just didn't know if I could do it. "Stay seated? Let her come to me?"

"And if she doesn't?"

"Curse really loudly? Cry? Scream?"

"Only in your mind. Then just make a note of which way she goes. But don't chase her."

"Oh, wow, that will be hard."

"I know. But remember, if you chase her, she may head back across that boulevard."

Well done, Mike. Well done!

"Very convincing. I'll sit still."

"I helped a woman once who sat out waiting for her dog when she was eight months pregnant. Baby was sitting on her bladder and all, so eventually she had to get up to go pee. She went behind a bush, and when she came out, her dog was sniffing around where she'd just been waiting. He'd probably been three feet from her the whole time, just figuring out the situation."

"She got her dog!"

"Well, no. Once she made eye contact the dog bolted. But we knew where to set a trap and we caught him the next day. So don't think of it as not doing anything. You're doing exactly what you need to do."

"Good to know. I'll just think of Poppy hiding in one of these bushes here, checking me out. I won't give up." I couldn't imagine giving up. I didn't know how I'd be able to continue sitting stakeout night after night and dawn after dawn, but I would not give up on her.

"That's what I want to hear. Okay, you ready to set up the warming box?"

Mike described the same process Babs had, but with more detail. Or maybe repetition was finally soaking the message into my brain. He had me do the ol' wet finger trick to figure out which way the wind was blowing. I should be sitting upwind so the wind would carry the sent as far as possible. The wind was blowing in the direction of the wilderness park. Or at least I thought it was.

As directed, I sprinkled chicken broth over the bushes in front of the house and drenched the trunk of the tree where Chris had attached the trail camera. I placed my dirty sock in the tree branches, and put her toy, along with more chicken and the same blanket, in the warming box in the middle of the lawn.

Then I returned to my chair, hoping no one had seen me sprinkling liquids about and called the police. I likely looked like I was doing some sort of wiccan blessing . . . or curse. Or some adult version of toilet-papering a house. I remembered the time when I was about eight years old and we moved to a new neighborhood in Sylmar, California. The neighbor kids had welcomed us by attempting to toilet paper our house. No sooner had the first roll of toilet paper been thrown up into one of the olive trees in the front yard than our solid black German shepherd, Thunder, welcomed them by leaping the backyard fence and chasing them off, nipping one kid in the rear end for good measure. That was how we met our neighbors. And how we learned the back fence was not high enough for Thunder. But our house was never toilet-papered again. This time, though, I wanted the dog to come running—and I wouldn't even mind if she nipped me in the butt.

I sat in my chair, unable to see much more than twenty feet or so through the shroud of mist. I pulled the blanket tighter and let my head drop down. Maybe I could nap. If I'm not supposed to make eye contact or any quick movements if I saw her, maybe it would be a good idea to nap.

Nice try. I couldn't, of course, sleep. Not any more than I'd been able to sleep in the comfort of my own bed lately. I just sat in the stillness.

The front door opened, and Julia stepped out. "I wanted to tell you that I'll be up and leaving early in the morning. I'm a nursing student. But we'll put coffee on for you. If you need anything, just come in the house."

"Thanks. I'll leave around midnight and be back about 4:00 A.M. I think."

"Okay. I hope you find her. I really do. Good night." She waved.

I sat, waiting. Ten minutes, fifteen, a half hour. I'd stay until midnight. Longer if I could. If it didn't rain more.

The night got quieter. The neighborhood went to sleep.

I looked down the street and imagined Poppy walking toward me, her long legs and cute prance on full display. I imagined her seeing me and running toward me, doing her dancing wigglebutt thing before leaping into my lap. Though I knew that wasn't what was expected, I needed to believe that could happen, so I continued to stare down the street, watching the fog roll through.

A dog barked. Then another.

And after a pause, another.

It's what Mike said! The dogs are barking at something. Another dog? Poppy?

I strained to see through the fog, as the barking got closer. Dogs in nearby houses had joined the choruses. Whatever they were barking at was moving this direction. That was easy to tell, just as Mike had said.

I sat, still, listening. *Don't move. Don't chase her. Let her come to you.*

The dogs' barking grew more frantic.

13

SIGHTINGS

❖

I tried to keep my head down, avoiding any eye contact, but as the dogs in Les's house began to bark too, I couldn't resist. Whatever it was, it had come closer to me. I looked up.

Nothing.

I turned my head to the left and looked down the street, where I imagined she would be coming from, even though the dogs barking were to my right. To my mind, albeit a mind terrible with directions, if she came from the wilderness park she'd be coming from the left. But there was nothing—just the fog slinking down the street, caressing the trees, and slipping around the streetlights.

I turned my head right and strained to see anything through the thickening miasma.

Was that movement? Did something just move? Stay calm. Don't get up. Don't. Get. Up.

I leaned forward but averted my eyes, once again willing her to appear. I could almost feel her, so strong was my vision of her popping up into my lap.

There was movement, and a flash of white dashed behind a bush right alongside the driveway, not twenty feet from me.

Every muscle in my body tensed. This was more self-control than I thought I was capable of. Shouldn't I at least call to her? Talk quietly? *No. That is not what Mike and Babs have been telling me.* I looked down at the bag of chicken beside my chair. *I should have opened it more. Can she smell it? The broth! The broth was in the bushes—she smelled that. That's what was bringing her. She'd come out of hiding for that. Wouldn't she? She had to be hungry by now.*

The bush moved.

And then it meowed.

Shit.

A black and white cat stepped out, clearly headed to my bag of chicken. I reached for the chicken and the cat leapt in the air. Apparently in his concentration on the chicken he had not noticed the strange human wrapped in dew-covered blankets sitting on a damp rattan chair, smelling like chicken and sweat. I'd done a better job of staying still than I'd thought.

The cat walked around me, giving me and the chicken a wide berth, and then trotted down the street, disappearing into the mist.

I really thought it would be Poppy. I'd pictured a reunion for so long and so intensely, I was sure it would happen. I wanted to scream. Instead I slumped in my chair, trying to convince myself this was all worthwhile.

The cat, I knew, was likely to return the moment I left. The chicken I left in the warming box would surely be gone. But the trail camera was set up, so I'd at least be able to tell if this was the cat or Poppy. Or a coyote. That was still possible, even in a suburban neighborhood. I looked back at the camera Chris had set up and wondered if it had taken a photo when the cat walked by. There was no way to check just then, but a cat photo in the morning would tell us we'd set it up properly.

I stayed in my chair until half past midnight, wretched and waiting. I hated the thought of giving up, and yet the wait seemed futile. Surely, she was curled up somewhere sleeping by now if she was still . . . no, not going there. She's curled up, dry, warm, sleeping. Somewhere safe.

Eventually, I had to go to the bathroom. I knew the front door was unlocked—Julia had said it was. But I just couldn't see walking into a stranger's home, even strangers I already knew to be very kind, and using their bathroom at this late hour. And did the rest of the house know that Julia had invited me to do that? Maybe. Probably. I think the gentleman who communed with his owl friend also said we could come in the house.

I was also cold, and that could not be fixed by using their bathroom.

I folded up my blankets, moved the chair back to the entryway, and took the bag of chicken over to the warming box.

I tore off some additional chicken breast, careful not to leave any bones, and once again apologized to the chicken and thanked her for the sacrifice she had had no choice in.

"Here you go, kitty. Please leave a little for Poppy."

I went home wondering if owls also ate chicken and if we'd see an owl on the trail camera, because clearly there was a regular owl visitor. And just as clearly, I needed sleep.

🐾

Again, I woke at 4:00 A.M. without the necessity of an alarm. Was Poppy still doing that? If my body was remembering and waking at four, was Poppy also?

I slipped out of bed and threw on jeans, a T-shirt, and another sweatshirt after realizing the one from the night before had not dried since I'd left it in a puddle on the floor. I reached in the dresser for a clean pair of socks. I'd use the ones from the day before as another "scent" distributor. They'd be hanging in trees somewhere soon. Roe lifted his head and looked at me. Even in the dark I could tell his expression was one of bewilderment. *Now? You're getting up now? Is there a walk involved? Breakfast?*

I petted his head and kissed his forehead. "Sorry, buddy. Believe me, I'd rather we were all staying in the nice warm bed."

"Me too. Do you want me to come with you?" Although I was tired enough to believe Roe was talking, I did know that was Chris.

"Is that Roe or you talking?" I asked, playing along. Chris and I had a habit of "talking" for our dogs, and each dog had its own voice. Roe's was deep, like his howl, and slower than the more excited voices of Percival and Poppy, because Roe was a calm and serious dog.

"Me. Though I'm sure Roe would go with you, too," Chris said.

"No. You're not supposed to be sitting out there, remember? Stay home. Sleep. Take care of these two. You'll have the day shift. Or, the daylight shift I suppose."

"Love you."

"Love you, too."

Downstairs, I threw my blanket in the dryer while I made coffee and filled a travel mug. I grabbed a banana, a protein bar, and Michelle's raincoat and headed back out.

Even at 4:30 in the morning, there was traffic on Alessandro, causing me to simultaneously hope Poppy did not again cross this street and that I would see proof she was still alive on the trail camera. Or even better, she'd be sitting on the lawn, waiting for me.

The neighborhood was as dark and quiet as it had been four hours before as I parked in the same spot across the street from Les's house. Poppy was not sitting on the lawn waiting for me, and I could not yet check the trail camera to see if she'd been there at all, since I'd need my laptop for that. I checked the warming box. The chicken was still there. Even the cat hadn't come back for it.

I set up my encampment on the lawn again, and sat, sipping coffee, waiting.

After ten minutes, Julia came out the front door, dressed in nursing whites, with a heavy coat. "I knew you'd be here. Did you see your baby?"

"Not so far. No."

"You'll find her. You will."

"Thank you. I hope so."

"I made coffee. There's a fresh pot. Do you want me to get you some?"

Wow, these were nice people. "No, I have some. But thank you. That's very kind."

"It's there if you want some later. Just head straight in. I've got to leave. Good luck. I'm praying for her safe return."

Julia left, and I wondered how many others would be driving down the street soon. These early hours were completely foreign to me. I had no idea how much traffic or life there was before 9:00 A.M. Would the cars prevent Poppy from coming out?

My father texted again, asking if we'd found Poppy yet. I was definitely up early if I was getting my dad's texts in real time. I liked hearing from him, knowing he cared about Poppy, too.

I responded, "Not yet."

"You will. Keep searching."

"I will. I have to."

"I know. I would do the same."

"Love you."

"Love you, too."

A simple, but comforting exchange.

It took another hour before anyone else drove down the street, but depressingly, Poppy did not appear. The sun rose, lights in the houses came on, and people walking dogs started to populate the streets. The half inch of coffee in my travel mug grew cold.

She wasn't coming out now. She would be too frightened. I knew that. What I didn't know was what to do next.

So I texted with Babs.

Babs: It's okay. It's still early. We'll figure this out. You've had sightings, that's a good thing.

Teresa: I know. It is. I just didn't expect her to travel so far. Cross a street like that.

Babs: They try to find their way back. You just need to help her find her way to you.

Teresa: Okay. I'm trying.

Babs: When a dog gets loose from their own home—someone leaves a gate open or something—I always tell the owners to be sure to leave a door open, leave the dog a way home. I've known it to happen that the dog returns to the house within few hours, but by then everyone had left searching for the dog. You can see the dog on the security camera, sitting, waiting, but no one is home to let the poor guy in. You're staying put, letting her find her way to you.

Leave a door open. Let them find their way back.

Teresa: I'm trying.

Babs: You're doing great. We'll find her.

🐾

I took down the trail camera, bagged up the chicken, picked up the warming box and loaded up my car before returning to place the chair back on the porch. I wished I had thought enough to bring a note of thanks. I had their address—I could send a proper thank-you later. Or would I be back that night, sitting again?

I drove around the neighborhood, slowly, looking for a little white blur slipping between the houses, or a tan and white backside seated on someone else's front lawn, barking at their dogs. When I spotted a woman out walking her two dogs I pulled over and got out of the car with a flyer.

"Hi. Have you seen this dog? I'm looking for her," I handed the woman a flyer.

She looked at the flyer and back up at me with *that* look—there was the head tilt, the squinted eyes, the downturned mouth. "I'm so sorry. How terrible. I haven't seen her, but I'll hold on to this. I'll keep an eye out."

It was my turn to squint my eyes. I tried to hold back tears—the sympathy was hard for me. Thankfully, I had sunglasses on, though why I cared if a stranger saw me crying over my lost dog was probably something to contemplate later. "Thank you."

"I'm sure you miss her. She's very cute. I'll keep looking."

"Thank you," was all I could muster.

I drove around for another twenty minutes. Signs were plastered everywhere. Megan, Nataly, and Matt had done a great job. Austin and Jessica had come back and placed a hot pink poster board sign at the nearby park, and a few more signs in the medians on the main thoroughfare.

The traffic increased enough that again I hoped Poppy would not be out and about. I drove to Starbucks in the nearby shopping center, both for a coffee and to put up a sign on the community billboard. Then I went to McDonald's and put a sign on the door.

A guard was in the parking lot. I remembered Mike telling me to find a guard at this shopping center and give him the flyer—have him take a photo with his phone. Guards see a lot and they have time on their hands. I waved to the guard and he walked toward me. I handed him the flyer.

"She was seen yesterday not far from here. Could you keep an eye out for her? If you take a photo of the flyer it will be easier to hold on to."

"This your dog?" he said. I was happy to see he did take a photo of the flyer. He also folded it and put it in his pocket while we talked.

"Yes. Her name is Poppy. She's been gone a few days, but we've had sightings."

"That's too bad. I'm sorry about that, ma'am. Dogs are so good. Best friends. Like they say. I'll watch for her. If she's around here, I'll see her. Maybe coming for some good breakfast food."

I smiled. Poppy popping up for a Sausage Egg McMuffin was a nice thought. "Maybe so. Thank you."

"Don't lose hope." He sounded like my dad.

I sat in my car, sipping my coffee. Would I lose hope? Had I lost hope? We'd searched for three nights now and this would be the third full day. That seemed like a lot of time and no time at all. I knew dogs went missing, and survived, a lot longer than that. But Poppy was terrified of everything, she was lost in a wilderness park, and the weather had been dreadful. I couldn't give up on her, and I still had the weekend ahead of me where at least work wouldn't be a concern—well, client appointments wouldn't be a concern. The fact that I was now three days behind would still be a concern. Even in non-emergency weeks I typically worked one day on the weekend, just to get caught up. The joys of being a sole practitioner never end. So, yes, one day at a time I'd keep going. I'd keep searching. Somehow.

At home, Chris had fed and walked Percival and Roe, and taken a shower himself.

"Here's the trail camera. I doubt there's anything on the memory card, since the warming box still had the chicken in it, but can you check?" I said. "I'm going to hop in the shower. Today's volunteers are meeting at my office at ten."

"Yeah, I'll check it. Why don't you get some sleep? I can handle the meeting and volunteer assignments."

"I can't seem to sleep. But let me take a shower, and then I'll try to nap."

I stood in the hot shower, washing away three days of sweat and grime, thinking about our plan for the day. (Yeah, I know. Plans are my kryptonite. But if I focus on the logistics, I can avoid the emotions, you get that, right? Breaking down in the shower is too cliché even for me.)

Did we have enough volunteers? Did we have any? No one from Beagle Freedom Project staff could come out because they had a rescue that day—four dogs rescued from a laboratory. Some of my fellow BFP fosters and adopters who saw my social media posts had said they would be there. And a few acquaintances and strangers did as well. But I wouldn't know who would come through until ten. I had to be thankful for whoever showed up. So far, we'd had a lot of help.

Amazing to think what so many people were willing to do for just one dog. We could each go down to the shelter or any number of rescue groups and save a dog, or we could be out searching and helping any number of stray dogs, and yet we would all be focused on this one dog. Poppy was both a very unlucky and yet astoundingly lucky dog.

I felt an intense commitment to this dog. And to BFP. And to all these people helping or wanting to help. Thinking of that rallied my spirits. So yes, maybe a nap, and then back at it. Chris could handle organizing the volunteers.

My phone rang five minutes after I stepped out of the shower.

"Hi. My name is Jennifer. I'm calling about your dog."

I thought I'd put my emotions firmly in check, but they were racing to the stage now. "Have you seen her?" I asked, quickly, probably loudly.

"Yes. But don't get too excited. She came up to our back door, but when my husband opened the door to let her in, she ran off."

"But you saw her? She's alive!" Happiness now danced with excitement, metaphorically, since I was standing there wrapped only in a towel, with wet hair dripping.

"Yes, my husband is 100 percent positive it's the same dog. But listen, we live up against Sycamore Canyon Wilderness Park. We're at the end of a cul-de-sac. When she left, she ran into the wilderness park and that's not good."

Happiness and excitement needed to slow their roll. "No, I know. But that's where she's been the last few days. So this is good news. Can I get your address?"

She gave me her address. "But she's not here anymore."

"I know. I know. We're just trying to figure out her pattern. Thank you. And you have my phone number. Please call if you see her again."

"Oh, absolutely. Good luck."

Jennifer probably thought I was nuts to be so happy the dog ran into the wilderness park. But I'd known that part. I was happy about the "100 percent positive" part—and the fact that she was alive. I threw on my bathrobe and ran downstairs to Chris.

"I know where that is. Ironwood. It's not far from the homeless encampment place. I'll show you on the map," he said.

We both ran back upstairs to our office and Chris's computer. Roe and Percival raced upstairs with us, joining in the excitement as dogs are wont to do. No reason needed—if the humans are excited, the dogs are excited.

"I'm calling Mike," I said. I knew from our texting that morning that Babs was working another rescue where she was physically involved in the process. I also knew from my texts and conversations with Mike and Babs that they knew each other well. Mike had mentored Babs on finding lost dogs. This explained why their advice and phrasing was basically the same. So, for a time anyway, Mike would be taking the lead on the search for Poppy. There was no drop off in communication, no contradictions, and no confusion. Mike and Babs worked together well and without ego. It was all about the dogs.

"Good idea. I'm going to find Jennifer's house on Google Maps," Chris said.

I put Mike on speaker phone.

"That's a good sighting. Where is it in relation to the other places she's been sighted?" Mike said.

"Back in the wilderness park. Chris thinks it's not too far from the homeless encampment where she may have been seen."

"That's good. Very good. Give me the address. I'll scope out the area from an aerial view. And by the way, don't give it to anybody else. Don't let a bunch of people head over there and scare her off."

I gave him the address. "Babs made sure of that yesterday when we had the sighting too. No massive crowds. Got it."

Chris had Google Maps up on his computer screen. He pointed to the address I'd just been given. "And this"—he moved his finger north—"is where the homeless encampment is, and this"—his finger moved north again and slightly east—"is where she was when the GPS battery died."

"Are they close?" Mike said.

"Not really, but she seems to be sticking to basically what is the middle of the park." I said.

"I've got it on my satellite map. The house she was at is just the kind of place we expect them to settle down. Humans tend to leave out food for their own pets and trash and whatnot. She can hop into a yard for meals or water, or to escape . . ." Kindly, he did not point out what she might be escaping. "And then hop back into the park to get away from the humans. She'll likely stay near the houses, but in the park. And that's an area in the park she could keep her back covered. You see how it's closed in on three sides by the houses?"

Chris flipped his map to the satellite view and showed me a wilderness cul-de-sac where the park dipped into the housing tract.

"Yes. We see that."

"Chris, can you make a map with pinpoints of where she's been? Put where you live, or the people who lost her, where she went into the park, where GPS showed she went, and these sightings?" Mike said. "We may be able to tell a pattern soon."

"Yeah, I can do that. I'm just supposed to meet the volunteers at ten at Teresa's office," Chris said.

"It's okay. I'm awake now. I'll go," I said.

"Okay, let's talk about those volunteers and what you're going to have them do," Mike said.

"Yep. Let's talk." *Give me the instructions—I will obey the commands. It's working.*

Mike described a stakeout that involved placing volunteers at various locations far out in the wilderness park to block off the opening if Poppy was still in the wilderness cul-de-sac behind Ironwood. "Their job is just to stand there so she isn't tempted to leave that area. We'll move in gradually and hopefully have some more sightings. But they need to be prepared to just watch and listen. No chasing. No walking around. We don't want her to bolt in fear." Mike sounded like he had as much faith in people as I did. Not his first dog rodeo, so to speak.

He rattled off places we should station folks, but he used words like "east" and "north," so I knew I'd be among his human disappointments.

"Any chance I could put you on speaker phone with the volunteers and have you explain this?" I said.

"Yep. I can do that. Just have a map with you."

"I'll finish this one and bring it. I think it will help people realize what we're doing," Chris said.

That would be great. I needed to be one of those people to realize what we were doing, because it didn't necessarily make sense to me. Weren't the places he wanted to station people much farther out than that little corner of the park near the houses? And when would we move in closer? I didn't understand completely.

But we had a plan. We had volunteers. And Poppy was still alive. I dried my hair as quickly as possible, threw on a baseball cap, and headed to the command station that once was my law office conference room.

We had a sighting.

14

DIRECTIONS

We'd had a sighting, and I was ready to go, but my positivity was quickly put at risk. At ten o'clock, my conference room was empty. There were no volunteers.

I once again wrote my name and phone number on the white board, with space underneath for the team that day, if we had one, to all list their names and numbers. The map from the day before was still taped on the board as well.

But there was no team. No one to follow Mike's instructions. Was it already happening? Was I, as both Babs and Mike warned, losing volunteers now at this crucial moment? Now, when the plan was coming together? I was not prepared to be abandoned. Was anyone ever?

A woman named Wendy, a complete stranger, was the only volunteer who had confirmed she was meeting us. She had somehow seen my Facebook posts and messaged me asking if I still needed help. When I said I did, she immediately said she'd be there. No questions. No hesitation. She was on her way.

Jessica and Austin were still available, though Austin would need to go to work that afternoon. Including Chris and me, that would be only five, and four of us were exhausted. I'd have to recruit more people. I texted Mike to let him know the call would be late and we wouldn't have many volunteers. And then I paced, trying to quell the panic.

Soon Wendy arrived, and I learned she'd driven from Los Angeles—sixty miles to help a stranger find a dog she'd never met. And she wasn't a BFP adopter or foster, though she knew of them. She was simply a good soul who loved dogs and saw my post when it was shared by Valerie, the BFP board member I'd seen on the night I picked up Poppy. Wendy was tall and thin, with long, flowing red hair and a pale freckled face. She had a hippie vibe to her—peaceful, earnest, and ready to help. She was, in short and in the best way possible, another "crazy dog lady." My spirits buoyed.

Shortly after Wendy arrived, Jessica and Austin arrived. Then Chris appeared, bringing copies of his updated map showing Poppy's recent sightings for everyone. He'd already emailed the map to Mike as well. By 10:45 A.M., while we may not have had the troops of previous days, we had a small but dedicated force ready to deploy.

On my cell phone speaker, Mike explained what we'd be doing. Using the map Chris had sent him, he described where he wanted people stationed in and around the park.

"We need a few more people," he said.

"I know. I'm going to see if I can get a few more. But Chris will go out and Jessica and Austin, and now Wendy's here," I said.

"I can hike. Send me where you need me," Wendy said.

Assignments were made and pointed out on the map, but Mike had a few more suggestions.

"Tape the flyers to your car windows. That's more eyes on the flyer and also if you're driving slowly or driving where you're not supposed to be, it sort of explains why."

Where would we be driving that we shouldn't be? Into the park? I'd find out soon enough.

"Also, if you go back out to the houses, hold the flyers up to the security cameras anywhere you see them—those Nest camera things or whatever they are. The cameras will alert the homeowners and they'll see it on camera. That way you know it's being seen."

Wow. That makes so much sense. I hadn't been going door to door, but others had. Maybe they already knew that. The information in my head, like the days, were all blurring together.

Wendy and Chris left to take up their posts, and I headed to my office to see if I could recruit a few more volunteers. Jessica followed me.

"Hey, um, I think we're going to go over to Mission Grove, the neighborhood where they saw her this morning? We'll put up more signs and hold them up to cameras and stuff. But I can't hike anymore. I'm really sore," Jessica said.

"That's a good idea."

I'd forgotten she'd been hurt on the very first night. I'd forgotten everything but Poppy. (I'm pretty certain I forgot to say thanks too. Ugh. Sometimes my focus can be an issue.)

Without Austin and Jessica in the wilderness park, we wouldn't have much of a perimeter set as Mike had been talking about.

They all left, headed to their assigned spots, but I stayed behind.

With everyone gone, I took a few moments to update social media with the morning's sightings and another request for volunteers. Then I returned a few work emails, trying to stave off the collapse of my law practice (and yeah, push away the nerves too. *Give me a problem I can solve*).

A few minutes later my cell phone rang.

"We're coming to help. We're in the car and we've got Rocket with us. Just tell me what you need. Point me in the right direction."

It was Curtis, on his way with his wife, Melody. They'd at least met Poppy, on the night she flew in from China and they carried her and her sister Miley from the van to the backyard where we all met them. It was Melody who had taken the photo when I first picked up Poppy. But I knew they'd do anything they could for any dog, any time. They were good people. And the best kind of dog people.

"I'm going to have Chris call you. He's better with directions and knows the game plan today."

"We'll be there in an hour, maybe a little longer. Someone saw her this morning? That's great news. We'll find her!"

It was great news. It was.

I grabbed my keys and my phone and noticed a Facebook message.

"I can't believe Jennifer saw her this morning!" The message was from Paige, a local dentist and the wife of our former district attorney. She'd been following my posts and sharing them regularly.

"Jennifer?"

"Sniff."

Sniff? Yes, I know it's sad, but I can't think about that right now. No tears!

"Jennifer who?"

"Jennifer and Stan Sniff. Isn't that who saw her this morning?"

OH! Later my mistake would be funny. Paige wasn't sniffing or tearing up. She was telling me that the Jennifer who called me this morning was Jennifer Sniff, wife of Stan Sniff, our recently retired sheriff. Which means . . . the man who identified Poppy as 100 percent the dog in the flyer was none other than the former sheriff. *Well done, Poppy.* Nice place to make an appearance. I'm going to trust Sheriff Sniff can ID a perpetrator, even one who only perpetrated heartbreak and random cuteness.

I left, headed for the wilderness park. I figured I'd hike out to the spot Jessica and Austin were assigned. Mike had told me to go home and sleep, but we didn't have enough people out watching for her and keeping her contained in the area we now knew she was. Maybe once Curtis and Melody got there, we would. And Aaron had texted that he was coming back later in the day. When others were out watching, then I could sleep.

The neighborhood where Poppy had been spotted was upscale, larger homes, with big lots abutting the wilderness park, just as Jennifer had pointed out. It was also quiet, not surprisingly given that this was midday during the work week. I drove the streets looking for an opening where I might be able to walk back through the homes to a canyon in the wilderness park. After several turns and circles through what seemed like cul-de-sac after cul-de-sac, I no longer knew which homes backed up to the park, so I headed back to Ironwood Drive. Along the way I spotted an opening between two homes and parked my car. I sat and stared into the park until eventually a truck pulled into one of the driveways and two men in heavy work boots, flannel shirts, and jeans got out. One of them grabbed a toolbox and they headed to the back of the house, through the side gate.

If they were working outside, that would be enough to keep Poppy away. Even Chris, standing upright, still scared Poppy. And what made me think Poppy would use an opening just because it was visible to me? She's not walking around thinking, "What would make things easiest on this crazy foster lady?"

Think like a dog. What would a dog do? I remembered Babs's advice. We can't think like humans; we have to think like the dog. We have to go with a dog's instincts, not our own.

I thought I knew dogs. I'd had dogs my entire life. There were times when I thought dogs *were* my entire life, and my own life certainly wasn't complete without them, and yet I was coming up empty on how to think like Poppy in this situation. From what I knew of her, she would have been curled up hiding deep in the park, and clearly that was not going on. Girl was on the run.

I checked Google Maps to see if there was a park entrance somewhere nearby. The Canyon Crest Road entrance was not exactly nearby, but I could drive to it and hike in, eventually coming up behind these houses.

As I drove in that direction, I remembered that Mike did not want us at the Ironwood house or nearby. That might scare Poppy away. We wanted her to stay in that area so that we could set a trap. And I wasn't supposed to be walking through the park, spreading my damn scent, which, even with the shower that morning, was going to be fetid, thanks to my clothing. Maybe I'd just walk a little way in and sit and watch. Maybe there'd be a rock formation I could climb up and watch the area behind the houses. Maybe I'd fall and break my back again, but that wasn't high on my list of concerns at that moment.

My phone rang as I parked my car.

"I finished posting all my flyers. I'm trying to get to the trail I'm supposed to follow, but I can't find an entrance where Mike wants me to hike in," Wendy said.

"Are you on Alessandro Boulevard?"

"I think so. It's a busy street."

It was midday, maybe, but that was always a busy street in daytime. "Okay. I'll head over to you. There's a Farmer Boys hamburger place, can you find that? I'll meet you in the parking lot."

I texted Mike, asking for specifics.

"It looks like there is a trail in off Alessandro. And another one near a distribution center, north of Alessandro. If you can each walk in from one of those spots that would be good."

He texted a satellite map screenshot to me, with bright yellow lines drawn in and two arrows showing where he thought we should go.

I saw the Alessandro trailhead as I drove to meet Wendy, so that one would be easy. But the distribution center I was unsure of—just as I was unsure of "north." Luckily, as I looked in my rearview mirror to make a lane change, I noticed my car had a compass. On the right side of the mirror a red LED light said "E." Either I was on empty, or I was headed east. If I recalled my Girl Scout training, a left turn would have me going north. I turned slightly left and the letters turned to "NE." Either I was now "not empty" or I was headed in the right direction.

Wendy's car in the parking lot was easy to spot. She'd taped the "Lost Dog" signs to all four side windows and the back window. More advice Mike had given that morning. I realized I had forgotten to do that myself, so I quickly did.

"I saw the trail, I think. I can drive you to it and drop you off, because I don't think you can park nearby," I said.

"Okay. That's good. I drove around, but I don't know my way around and I just couldn't tell where to go." Wendy was not flustered in the least. She was focused and intent on being helpful.

"No worries. It's kind of a walk through a field, and I'm guessing then it heads into the wilderness park. Just hike in a bit and find a place to sit and watch."

"I can hike. I'm ready to go."

She looked ready to go. She had a safari hat, hiking shoes, and a warmth and determination that I envied. She also had on fresh lipstick and a coat of gloss. My kind of girl. I dropped her at the trail and she walked off, while I paused to marvel again at a total stranger willing to hike into a wilderness park to help save a little dog.

I couldn't pause for long. Chris called.

"I think I just saw her!"

"What? You saw Poppy?"

"I'm not sure. I did what Mike said. I was sitting up on a rock and I could see across to the neighborhood where she was this morning. I heard all the neighborhood dogs barking—just like he said—and when I looked I saw this white blur go speeding by. Super fast. So I don't know if it was her."

"Oh my god. It had to be her." I felt the urgency, but also extreme frustration. He'd seen her—maybe—but she was across the park from where he was, and I didn't even know where I was, let alone where Chris was.

"I think it was her," Chris said, with the same sense of urgency, but none of my frustration.

"Okay, can you call Mike and tell him where you think you saw her? I'm trying to go to the Ralph's distribution center and find a way into the park that way. Would that still be useful?"

"I think so. I'm west of that."

"West?" I repeated, hopelessly.

"To the left of the distribution center."

Buddha bless him for knowing me so well.

My car assured me I was heading north when I turned left off Alessandro. I could see many trucks parked at several distribution centers on my left (west?), but Mike seemed to think the opening to the trail was at the Ralph's grocery distribution center.

I drove for a mile without seeing so much as a Ralph's truck. I turned around and decided to pull into each of the distribution centers until I found one with an opening to the wilderness park, or at least a fence I could climb. The fact that I'm a middle-aged, sizeable woman with a broken back was not going to deter me, because despite all the evidence, I don't see myself that way, and this was no time to start.

Each distribution center was well fenced, some with cinder block walls and some with standard chain link, but chain link that was six to eight feet tall. I wasn't likely to get over that, and certainly not before I got caught. I couldn't remember the last time I climbed a fence, and it's possible I've *never* climbed a chain link fence, even as a kid with a healthy spine who didn't even know the word "exhausted." I drove on, dodging trucks as I pulled in and out of each center, driving to the back or as far back as I could go before being stopped by a gate or too many eighteen-wheelers to pass. I was defeated at every point.

I texted Mike. "I can't find a way in."

He texted another satellite map, this one with orange lines in a shape that looked . . . Well, it looked like a penis.

"This is where we want to keep her. We want people stationed along the area I drew. Anywhere you can get to."

"I can't tell where any of that is."

"Do you see where the line I drew loops down, to a tip?"

Like a pubescent boy, I giggled. I'd already thought it looked like a penis, and now he'd said "tip." I was so overwrought by my lack of ability to find a way into the wilderness park that I laughed at my own stupid, nonfunctioning mind. But that wasn't embarrassing enough. I actually heard myself say, "The tip of the penis?"

Mike was quiet. *Sure, right. I don't know him. We've never met.*

"Sorry," I said. "It's kind of shaped like a penis."

"That's not what I was drawing." Fortunately, he laughed. "But sure. At the tip there is more or less where Poppy has been hanging out, we think. It makes a nice cul-de-sac where, if we can get folks stationed around the opening and walking in slowly, we can contain her back there."

"Yeah, the walking in part is where I'm having trouble. I dropped Wendy off Alessandro. And Curtis and Melody are out there somewhere. And Chris."

"See if you can find out where everyone is. I can try to direct from here. Soon we'll be losing light." There were times in this search when the clock seemed never to move, and there were times when an hour flew by in a minute. This was the latter. I'd wasted over an hour trying to find my way into the wilderness park through the distribution centers.

I sent a group text, and Curtis was quick to respond. He texted me a satellite photo of the park on which he had made a u-shaped drawing in orange. He pinpointed where Chris spotted Poppy, where he and Melody were stationed, and then wrote across the bottom area "Polly's Area." His drawing was nearly identical to Mike's.

I had two thoughts. One was that I needed to let Curtis know the dog he's spent days searching for is named Poppy not Polly (and gosh, I hoped that didn't make a difference to him). And the second was that I really, really wished I had a good sense of direction. I ignored the first thought and texted Curtis's map to Mike.

I continued to try to find anywhere I could access the wilderness park until Chris called me. He'd tried to hike to where he saw Poppy along the fence but couldn't cross the creek—still raging courtesy of the rainstorm we'd had for days. He hiked back out and had to take an Uber back to where his car was parked. I asked him to text Mike and find out where he should go.

"I can't figure any of this out. I'm over in the distribution center, dodging eighteen-wheelers, trying to find an opening to get into the park. I can't get in anywhere and I'm sure I'm not supposed to be driving back here. And I don't understand where anybody is, or where Poppy is, or what Mike wants us to do. I don't even know where I am."

I was right on the edge of breaking down. *I hate not knowing how to do something, and I hate feeling stupid, and I hate losing, and I hate breaking a commitment, and I made a commitment to this dog. And I hate everything. She's so close and we can't get her, and it's all going to be because I have no sense of direction.*

Chris was quick to recognize my escalating panic. "I'll talk to Mike. I'll coordinate everybody. Do you remember the first night when we went over to the houses on Speyside Road?"

"I remember that name."

"It's where we went with Michelle. Where the neighbor came out asking what we were doing. Drive over there. That's near where I saw her, and you're not far from there."

I would have sworn I was very, very far from that street. "I'm not? God, I really have no idea where I am. I'll put it in Google Maps and get there that way."

"That's good. I'll talk to Mike and let you know what he says."

I had been literally driving around in circles, until I'd pulled over along a wall at the far end of a truck service center. I dropped my face into my hands and rubbed my eyes. I rotated my head around trying to loosen up my neck and let out a large exhale of air. *Keep going.*

My phone pinged with a text from Curtis. He and Melody had to leave. They had to be home to feed and medicate their own dogs. They still had to hike back out, and then they were likely looking at a two-hour drive.

"We'll be back tomorrow," he said.

"Thank you. Thank you so much."

"Hang in there. We'll find her. She's out there."

Before I had time to consider that we were down to only one person actually out in the park, Wendy texted me. She'd followed the trail as far as she was comfortable but came upon a group of homeless men, one of whom began to follow her. He shouted asking if she wanted help. She had politely, but firmly, told him no and turned around and headed back to Alessandro.

"I'll come pick you up and take you back to your car. I can't find how to get into the park from here anyway. We're going to another area."

As I drove to Wendy, I could see Mike was right, we were losing light. In a half hour, maybe an hour, it would be too dark to see much of anything.

Back at the Farmer Boys parking lot with Wendy, I got another call from Mike.

"I talked to Chris. He's a good guy," Mike said.

"I know. He is."

"He's worried about you. Says you're tired and stressed. Have you slept?"

"Not a lot."

"Remember, you're the night shift. Let him do the day shift."

"I got excited when we had the sightings."

"I know. Remember it's about controlling the people as much as anything. That includes yourself."

"Got it." And I did. I just couldn't sleep.

"So it's getting dark. Chris says there's a good vantage point over on this Speyside Road. You should head over there. Just park at the end of the street and watch for any signs of movement. If you see her and you see which way she's headed, that will help us. Just remember, don't call to her. Don't scare her."

"I don't want to scare her. I imagine she's scared enough."

"You still have any volunteers helping?"

"Wendy is here with me, but she's got to head back to LA soon. And Jessica and Austin were out."

"Jessica and Austin?"

"Yes. My paralegal and her fiancé."

"Didn't you tell me that's who was walking the dog when she got loose?"

"Yes."

"Don't have them out looking for the dog."

"They weren't. They were posting flyers and signs everywhere. But they have been helping."

"No. They're the ones most likely to do something stupid."

Had I mentioned their ages? Was he saying this because they are of the much-maligned millennial age group? "They're actually both pretty smart. I wouldn't think they'd do anything stupid."

"I'm not saying they're stupid, but guilt weighs heavily in a situation like this. They might try to do something heroic to redeem themselves. They'll be more likely to chase Poppy or get overly excited and send her running. Keep them away from the search. Flyers and errands and whatnot is fine. They can get coffee or pizza for the volunteers. Hang flyers everywhere. Check the shelters. All fine. Not out in the wilderness park."

I hadn't thought of that. I wondered if *I* would be able to stay calm and not chase. That would likely be hard for Jessica and Austin, too. "Okay. That makes sense. It's all so counterintuitive, but it makes sense."

Every step of this had been counterintuitive. But we were getting more and more sightings. We knew she was alive. And for reasons I could not fully explain even to myself, I fervently believed in Mike and Babs. Their advice and their calm, firm guidance, along with Chris's support and strength, was keeping me going.

Chris texted he'd meet me at Speyside, and Jessica and Austin would as well. Wendy followed me in her own car.

As I drove toward Speyside, an SUV pulled up next to me, honking. The woman driving was smiling and pointing to my car. Then she held up a copy of the "Lost Dog" flyer we'd made.

My mind spun. *Did she have Poppy? Did she know where Poppy was? What was she doing? Who was she? And she's going to drive me off the road.*

15

INSTINCTS

❧

I swerved back into my lane and turned back to look in front of me just in time to see that the stoplight had changed to red. I hit my brakes.

At the stoplight she came up next to me and rolled down her window, so I did the same.

"I came out to help you!" she said.

I had no idea who this person was or how she knew about Poppy or how she got a flyer, but I was aware of the lengths people will go to help an animal.

"Okay, just follow me. There's a car behind me following as well."

When the light turned green, I accelerated faster than I otherwise might have, hoping that Wendy would too, and the new volunteer would be able to quickly change lanes and get behind Wendy.

That didn't work so well. My next turn came up much more quickly than expected and I made a sharp, much too fast left turn. There may have been a screech of tire and some rubber left behind.

To my surprise, both women in the cars behind me did the same thing. *Outta the way people, we have a dog to find!*

Our caravan of middle-aged dog rescue women in SUVs zigzagged through a neighborhood I would have sworn was nowhere near the wilderness park or even Riverside. Without Google Maps, I'd be in Kansas by now.

Chris, Jessica, and Austin were already at the end of Speyside Road, standing at the fence looking out over the wilderness park, which, to me, had suddenly appeared out of nowhere.

Our new volunteer got out and introduced herself to us all. Her name was Karen, and Karen had a lot to say.

Maybe because we'd all been at this for days or, in Wendy's case, one very long day, but Karen's energy level was way above ours and way above what the situation needed. She insisted we needed a drone. Someone should get a drone. She could get a drone, fly it over the canyon, and find the dog. Easy peasy. A drone. Get a drone.

"Wouldn't the drone scare the dog?" Jessica said—wisely, I thought.

"Nah. They think it's a bird."

This seemed unlikely. And I suspected Poppy would be frightened of a large "bird" flying over her as well. But at any rate we didn't have a drone. "No drones. Sorry. We're just going to watch for her and track where she goes. No drones, no yelling, no chasing."

"Nah, man. Just call her. Talk to her. What's her name? Doesn't matter. I'll call her in her language."

Karen begin to howl at the moon. Well, out into the canyon, but that was merely a technicality. She tilted her head back and howled *"Arrrr—arrr—arrr—ooooooooo"* several times. A dog barked in response.

"There she is! See!"

I did not see. "We've never heard her bark. I don't know what she sounds like, but I don't think that was her." The dog that had responded was clearly a bigger dog with a much deeper bark. And it was a bark, not a beagle howl. Besides, there was no way Poppy was just sitting in the park waiting for some random stranger to howl at her. Was there?

Karen howled again.

"Okay, please, stop. You're going to scare her away." I said.

"Nah, man, you gotta let her know you're here."

How to explain that my scent was going to do that? Or the chicken. Or that we weren't letting her know we were here, we were just trying to find where she'd set up camp. I couldn't, but it didn't matter. Karen was not listening.

Karen was now telling us about her psychic abilities and where she "felt" Poppy was. She was not our first psychic. People on Facebook told us they saw her near "trees," "something blue," and "near an orange tree." I am a cynic about those sorts of things, sure, but these guesses all seemed particularly lame. Since Poppy was lost in a wilderness park, "trees" seemed a given. The sky was blue, and I was pretty sure she was under it, and Riverside is a city steeped in citrus heritage. Besides the actual orange tree groves, the streets had names like Orange, Lime, and Lemon. The neighborhood she'd appeared in on Wednesday morning was called Orangecrest. Citrus was a given. The psychics lacked imagination.

Karen was a more aggressive psychic. Karen pointed into the finger of the fifteen-hundred-acre wilderness park where we happened to be standing and said, "She's over there. Right there."

This made me wonder why Karen needed to follow my car to the place her psychic abilities had already told her about, and why she bothered howling first. But, I got distracted. By a hawk.

Wendy—with her peaceful, gentle energy—had walked away from Karen and her manic, loud energy. Wendy was standing under a tree looking up at a large, regal bird that I quickly realized was a red-tailed hawk. It was no more than six feet above Wendy's head.

At least it's not a vulture. I studied the hawk. Could it pick up a beagle? Even a tiny one? Much like with the owl that eyed Daphne, it seemed clear it could at least injure a dog. I remembered Babs's comment on that first day—"to Poppy, everyone is a predator." I hoped those instincts would serve her well.

I snapped a quick photo of the hawk—he was a good-looking animal—and realized we had lost almost all light. The hawk was a silhouette in my photo.

"I'm going to have to go. But I have your number," Karen waved the flyer at me. "I'll text you tomorrow and see if you need help."

As quickly as she appeared, Karen was gone. Wendy left soon after. And then Jessica and Austin. Chris and I remained at the fence, staring out into the darkness of the wilderness park, still hoping for a flash of white.

"What now?" Chris said.

"I have no idea. I have no idea what just happened. Who was that woman?"

"You don't know her?"

"No. She flagged me down on the street on the way here."

"She seemed determined to help," Chris said, perhaps a tad sarcastically.

"Was that what she was doing?"

"That's what she thinks she was doing. But that wasn't Poppy barking."

"As desperate as I am to find her, even I can't convince myself that giant bark came from my little Popstar. But to answer your question. I don't know. I don't know what to do now. Except call Mike." And I did just that.

Mike was his usual steady, calm self. "We don't have anything much to go on right now. I'd say either go back to the place you were the other night—the place she went into the park, or someplace close to where she was spotted this morning. What does your gut tell you?"

I had to think about that. But was my head supposed to be involved if I was listening to my gut? My head was trying to figure out if either of those two spots were near each other or near where Chris may have seen Poppy this afternoon. My gut just wanted to throw up. Chris tried to explain to me where the spots were in relation to each other, but I was so turned around from the drive to this spot on Speyside Road none of it made sense. I'm not sure if it was my gut or just the only thing my tired, stressed-out brain understood, but I chose to go back to Via La Paloma, the place she'd first run into the wilderness park. Maybe it was ridiculous, but I hoped she was trying to make her way back out.

Help her find her way back.

On my drive there, I told Mike about the barking drone woman, worried she may have scared Poppy off.

"Was her name Karen?" Mike said.

"Yes. How'd you know that?" *How did he know so much?*

"You gave a pretty good description. I'm pretty sure she and I had a run-in on Facebook over her techniques. She called me an asshole, as I recall."

"You're not an asshole."

"Oh, I can be. Especially when a dog's life is at stake."

I felt better about my lack of appreciation for Karen's "help."

🐾

Chris parked at the beginning of Via La Paloma, and I assumed my usual position on the boulder at the end of the cul-de-sac. Chris set up the trail camera, strapping it to a tree, pointed in the direction of the trail that led up and into the wilderness park, then retreated to his car. I'd set up the warming station just off the trail. By then it was completely dark, and a light mist covered every surface, including me. There was no movement. No sound, except the trees blowing in the wind, leaves shifting and falling with the light rain that had picked up.

I texted Chris, "You should go home and feed Roe and Percival. Make sure they're okay."

"I was thinking that. We both should. It's raining now. She won't be out."

"I'm going to stay a little longer."

"Sit in your car at least."

After Chris left I stayed on the boulder, but soon the rain picked up and I had to move into my car. The car windows fogged up in a matter of minutes, eliminating my view of the hillside. I knew that Poppy was not likely to be out in that weather, and I knew that I couldn't see her even if she was. And in the rain would she see or smell me? And yet, I couldn't bring myself to leave. To do nothing.

So I did what I had come to do in the last few days when I was feeling lost or hopeless. I texted Mike.

"If it's raining, go home," he responded.

"And do what?"

"Sleep?"

"Not likely."

"Know anyone who is a member of that golf course nearby?"

Mike must have been looking at the satellite map again. I felt certain no one was at the Canyon Crest Country Club in this weather, but why would he want to know that? "Probably. Why?"

"Get someone to go there early in the morning. Find the greenskeepers and give them flyers. Dogs often show up at golf courses."

"I don't think Poppy is really the golfing type." I texted "LOL" but I wasn't really LOL'ing. I was WTF'ing.

"Grass, water, often food. Greenskeepers see all kinds of animals, and they know when and where they show up. Great source of info. And if you can have someone park their car in the parking lot near the entrance with the flyers in the windows, you'll get that many more eyes on it."

He was right. The golf course was not far. And a part of it, the second hole, came up to the wilderness park. Poppy could get there without crossing a busy street. And she'd actually been close to there when I had taken her to Michelle's house, which backs up to the sliver of the wilderness park that then meets up with the golf course. But if Poppy went to the main part of the course, near the clubhouse (and food smells), she'd have to cross Canyon Crest Drive, another main thoroughfare. I realized that me not wanting her to cross busy streets did not mean she wouldn't do that, and in fact I knew she'd already done it a few times. It just meant it was very difficult for me to focus on anything that involved that scenario. My mind wanted to run off screaming in another direction.

"Okay. I can do that."

Mike must have sensed the weariness in my voice. "Coyotes and stray dogs both love golf courses. If there's a healthy rabbit population in and around the golf course, coyotes have plenty to eat, you've got nothing to worry about. Maintenance doesn't usually do anything about coyotes because the 'yotes control the bird and rodent population, and they're gone by the time golfers show up. But little dogs can hide in small places where coyotes can't get them. It's not worth the trouble. If your dinner's going to bite you back, you're going to another restaurant."

I laughed, much to my own surprise.

"I once helped a pro ball player out in Denver for spring training. His little dog got out and was spotted on the golf course nearby, then not seen again. I told him to start looking in holes in the ground. Guy found the dog in a rabbit hole very near where the dog had been sighted on the golf course."

"Alive and well?" I knew, or at least I sensed, by then that Mike would not tell me stories of dogs that did not make it. He was telling me the stories with happy endings to keep me going. But I needed that confirmation.

"Alive and well."

Poppy often strained to stick her head down rabbit holes and other small spaces when we took her on walks in Paso Robles. She and Roe wanted to explore every inch of land, and Roe definitely was searching for rabbits. Poppy, we'd always thought, was just doing what her adored big brother was doing. Maybe she'd found a safe place to duck into. And maybe it was near the golf course—one more place we'd need to focus our efforts.

Back at home, I returned to social media to find a member of the Canyon Crest Country Club to take some flyers and talk to greenskeepers in the morning. It took no more than ten minutes until a friend of a friend volunteered; she lived only five minutes away from me and offered to drive over and pick up the flyers that night.

So many people—friends, acquaintances, clients, and strangers—had joined in the search for Poppy in big and small ways. Over the last few days, several clients who lived in the neighborhood around the wilderness park told me they've driven around looking for her and shared the flyers with their neighbors. My former writing instructor, now the director of the MFA program for UC Riverside's desert campus, drove around looking for her when he had to be in Riverside for meetings. I knew he too was a dog lover and that he meant it when he said the search for her stressed him out and had him heartbroken (so stressed he also stopped for doughnuts, he told me later). Hundreds of people had shared our social media posts. Another friend and fellow lawyer and dog lover, Ann-Marie, had continued to check for Poppy at both the Riverside and Moreno Valley animal shelters, which broke her heart repeatedly, but she did it. My friend Matt, whom I'd talked into rescuing both of his beagles—one of whom came from Charlotte and Meade Canine Rescue—had searched for her on his morning runs through the park. Justine and Wendy, two women who didn't know me or Poppy, spent hours hiking a wilderness park searching and sitting stakeout. And now another stranger had volunteered to meet me on a rainy night to get flyers and then wake up early on a Saturday morning to meet the groundskeepers at her country club.

This rescue nation, these are my people.

I decided I'd try to refresh. I'd eat, shower, get some sleep, and get back out there at four in the morning. I needed to do that for Poppy, and for all these people pulling for her. For us.

I knew by then that I did not need an alarm. I woke as usual at 4:00 a.m. As I stood and put on my jeans, Chris spoke.

"I'll go with you this time."

"You can't sleep?"

"No. I'll go and sit somewhere else."

Percival and Roe barely moved. They were not morning dogs (Roe had quickly adjusted to the joys of sleeping in on a pillow-top king mattress) and it was very dark out; they probably knew the drill by now. I petted their soft heads and promised them we'd be back for breakfast. Percival's tail thumped and Roe lifted his head for a moment (I think it was the word "breakfast"), but I'm sure they were back asleep before we even got downstairs.

Chris grabbed his laptop so we could look at the memory card in the trail camera after sunrise. I got my travel mug of coffee and a banana, and we headed out.

Stationed again at the boulder, I could see very little. There wasn't enough moonlight, and the streetlights weren't on. Poppy was mostly white, so I hoped I'd still be able to see her, however remote that possibility was. Hope seemed to be my strongest weapon in this search.

Chris had parked at the opposite end of the street. It was unlikely he could see much more than I could. My phone pinged with a text from him.

"Sitting in my car. I can't see much."

"I'm still sitting on the rock, but it's starting to rain."

"Maybe watch from your car?"

"Yeah. I'm going to have to."

I moved my car so it was facing up toward the trail and the warming box, which put me parked facing the wrong direction for that side of the street, but I didn't think parking enforcement would be out at 4:30 on a Saturday morning. If they were, I'd hand them a flyer.

Neighborhood dogs barked, and I immediately regretted sitting in my car. *Are they barking at Poppy? Is she walking around here?* I twisted in my seat trying to see anything at all on the hillside or in the neighborhood. She could just as easily trot down the sidewalk as come over the hill from the park. To my left I saw movement. And was that white? Was that a white animal?

Through the fog, trotting at a surprisingly quick pace, came a skunk.

It did have white on it; I'd gotten that part right. Pepé Le Pew crossed in front of my car, across the street, and on into the front yard of one of the nice homes on the other side of Via La Paloma, then into some bushes. I hoped for that homeowner's sake, as well as the skunk's, that they did not have a dog.

My phone pinged again with a text from Chris.

"2 Coyotes coming your way."

"What? Thankfully I moved to my car."

"They probably won't come near you, but they're walking that way."

"Walking toward my warming box, I'm sure."

I watched but saw nothing. No Poppy, no coyotes.

Five minutes later Chris texted again. "Another one. Walking the same direction."

"I haven't seen any coyotes. Just a skunk."

The rain stopped as the sun came up, and I returned to sitting on the wet rock, using the blanket as a cushion and protection from the dampness. I focused on the trail into the wilderness park, again willing her to appear. Visualization and all that. But there was nothing. And I realized that with Chris's sighting of three coyotes, it would be terrible if she did appear.

Time passed, lights in the homes began to turn on, and an older couple came out walking their little white, fluffy dog. A car came out of a garage and drove down Via La Paloma. It was Saturday morning, so the neighborhood was waking up perhaps a bit later than during the week, but it was clear there would soon be activity. My mornings were repeating themselves and so was the result. Poppy would not appear.

I checked the warming box.

The chicken was gone, and the blanket had been dragged out a couple of feet again. I walked up the trail a bit and retrieved the now soaking wet sock I had left in a bush. We had the camera this time. At least we'd know who ate the chicken.

I picked up the warming box and the blanket and headed back to my car.

Chris drove to my end of the street and took the camera down. He popped the memory card into his laptop and searched it as I climbed into his passenger seat.

"Coyotes."

"Coyotes ate the chicken?"

"There's quite a few of them." He turned the screen toward me and clicked through the photos. Coyotes had appeared throughout the night, sometimes a lone coyote, usually two, but at one frightening point there were five or six of them all near the warming box. Their eyes were flashes of light in the photos, adding a spooky element that was not needed.

Their appearance should not have surprised me. I sprinkled an entire carton of chicken broth in the bushes and left several chunks of rotisserie chicken in the box. I had set up an animal lure. I should not have been surprised, but I was. I was horrified. They looked so big! And this was a pack, a hunting pack. How on earth would Poppy stand a chance if she encountered this? She wouldn't.

I clicked through the photos again, terrified. Some of the photos had been taken during the time I was seated in my car. The coyotes had appeared right in front of me and I hadn't seen a thing.

"I'm going to delete this. You don't need to look at this." Chris said.

"I won't need to look at it again. That will be burned in my memory."

I returned to my car to follow my new routine: a text to Mike.

"Camera at Via La Paloma shows coyotes all night long. Including when I was sitting there (but didn't see them!). I assume she won't come out there with coyotes around."

He didn't respond, which also should not have surprised me since it was not quite 7:30 in the morning, but in a short time I'd gotten used to his almost immediate availability and wise counsel.

There was at least more help coming. Curtis and Melody were already driving out again. We had told them we would meet them at Starbucks and Chris could give the update. They were prepared to hike the wilderness park again. And, since it was Saturday, we had more volunteers available.

🐾

As Chris and I sat at Starbucks, waiting, I twisted the cardboard sleeve around my cup, shredded a napkin, stared at my watch.

"I can't stand just sitting here. It's too loud. It's too cold. We're not doing anything. I just think we need to *do* something."

"I know. You should probably go home and sleep. You're exhausted."

"I'm beyond exhausted, but I can't sleep. I need to do something." My voice caught. I took a sip of my coffee. "It feels so hopeless. Those coyotes were terrifying. I know everyone keeps telling us about the coyotes, and it's not like I didn't know they were there. I'd been blocking them out. But there were *so many* of them. It's hopeless."

"It's not. We had a sighting yesterday, and that was probably her I saw. She's still out there. But why don't you go home, take a nap. I'll meet Curtis and Melody and show them where they need to be. And I can feed the dogs when I get home."

"I don't know about a nap. But my car needs gas. I'll go do that, maybe drive around some more. And I'll meet you at my office at ten. I think we have six or so people showing up today."

"I can get the construction fencing too. Home Depot isn't far."

"I had forgotten about that." Mike had told us to get the orange webbed temporary construction fencing in case we can get her secluded in a small area. We could use the fencing to close in on her. "It feels like we'd have to get enough to fence off fifteen hundred acres at this point. And the dio-something earth. We need to get that."

"Diatomaceous earth? For what?"

"I don't remember. Tracking? I suck. I can't remember anything. Mike said to get that dia-earth stuff when we went to get the fencing. I don't remember why."

Chris grabbed my hands across the table and squeezed. "We'll find her."

We'll find her, we'll find her, we'll find her. That's what everyone keeps telling me. That's what my dad keeps texting. That's what I keep telling myself. But will we?

As I filled my car at the nearest gas station, I raged internally. In my head I cursed the station owner for taking advantage of their location to gouge on the prices. I cursed the landlord for their leasing prices that probably added to the price per gallon; I hated on the gas station owner for their capitalism, and every stupid car owner anywhere near me for having a better life than I did at that moment. I was aware of my irrational state, and I gave not one rat's ass. Everything and everyone sucked. I slammed the fuel dispenser back into its holder and noted the $56.76 I'd just spent. *Fuck.*

I reconsidered going home to get some sleep. My nerves were fraying, that was obvious. My anger and frustration were building to perhaps a dangerous point. Maybe it was the coyotes; maybe it was the lack of sleep for four days. I think had someone spoken to me at the gas station I would have had some insane outburst of anger or tears, depending on what the hapless soul said to me. But I knew going home would be useless. I knew I wouldn't sleep.

I drove to the trailhead off Via Vista—the one closest to the homes where Poppy had been spotted the morning before—and walked in for a bit. The skies had cleared and were now bright blue with storybook puffy white clouds. But it was still cold, and the wind added a chill.

I didn't get far before I saw two coyotes, lying in the grass, sunning themselves. One coyote stood and looked toward me. He looked healthy, not thin, and his eyes and coat were shining gold in the sunlight. I could see why they were referred to as "sun dogs" by native Americans. How beautiful those coyotes would be in any other scenario. But right then, they were the last thing I wanted to see.

One coyote took a step toward me. Everything I'd learned about coyotes in my research for the article I wrote and, more recently, from Mike evaporated from my brain. I didn't raise my arms and shoo him away or make loud noises, though I'd read plenty about "hazing" coyotes when encountered. I didn't even do the algebra on my size versus the size of these two coyotes, or our relative weights. And the math on who could run faster didn't need to be done (I'm neither a sprinter nor a marathoner). I'd been thinking of packs of attacking coyotes for days now and just that morning witnessed an actual pack of them on the trail camera photos. Logical or not, fair or not, they had become my mental enemy. I turned around and headed back to my car, slowly but deliberately.

The wind was sharp, cold, and stinging. The liquid dripping from my eyes could have been from the wind, or it could have been tears—tears of frustration, tears of sadness, tears of rage and exhaustion. It could have been my last ounce of energy.

Instead of going home and napping, like everyone kept telling me to do, I went to my office. If I was going to have to keep spending my early mornings and late nights in the wilderness or strangers' yards, I was going to have to get some work done whenever I could (and the pull of problems I could solve was strong). My law office had all but shut down for three full days, with only my administrative assistant answering phones and rearranging my appointments. I had about enough energy and brain power to go through my mail, some of it junk, some of it things I really needed to pay attention to. I delegated what I could, responded to some of it, pushed the rest aside.

Mike texted just after 9:00 A.M. "You're right. She'll steer clear of an area with 'yotes. How are you holding up? What time are people coming this morning?"

"I'm kind of crashing today." I texted back. "Losing hope and dissolving into tears. There were so many coyotes. People meeting at my office again at 10:00 A.M. I'm already here." I immediately felt ridiculous for complaining to him. *I'm sitting waiting for a dog to show up. He's sitting by his dying father's bedside.*

I sent a second text, letting him know I was not completely useless and could focus on the task at hand. "I sent someone to the golf club. I found someone to go to both animal shelters for me. And Chris will go to Home

Depot to get the fencing. 2 others are out posting flyers and will hike in to sit and watch."

"I get it. This is a horrible roller coaster ride. When she's safely back with you, please feel free to fall apart. Until then, stay focused and strong. This is not a sprint. We have recovered dogs in far worse situations, who have been out far longer and in crazier terrain."

"That's good to hear."

"Stay fed, hydrated, and rested. Coming up short on any of those three doesn't work. The camera showed 'yotes, but it DIDN'T show her. If it had shown her then 'yotes, that would be incredibly concerning."

"True. I just feel like putting chicken and broth there made it a coyote hangout and now she won't come there. So now I have no idea what to do/where to go. Just sitting around directing people and hoping for a call feels so useless."

"But you've had calls. It's working. We're narrowing down her pattern."

I contemplated a reply that wouldn't sound ungrateful. He was right. I knew that. This was just so damn hard. Before I replied, he texted a photo of a dog collar.

"This collar belonged to a dog who was taken in by a rescue only to be mishandled at the vet. Their cheap little leads and lack of attention enabled her to escape. She ran directly into and across busy streets with people chasing her all the way. Ultimately, she found herself in a semi-rural area filled to capacity with 'yotes. Early one morning, a neighbor reported to the rescue hearing the worst 'yote event ever. I pushed the rescue to search with a ton of people fanned out as she could be injured and suffering. For two days I didn't get responses from them. I pushed harder and received confirmation from them of her death. I asked if they recovered anything. Their answer was again, it was confirmed to be her."

Why is he telling me this?! And oh god, that collar!

"Twenty-eight days later that same 'dead' dog walked into my trap! Skinny, dehydrated, and tired, but no signs of a struggle or attack anywhere. Turns out they were too sickened by the thought of having to go and identify remains, they just never did. I keep her collar in my van as a reminder. No matter what we think, what people tell us, or what we may hear, you don't give up until you find a body or absolute irrefutable evidence. They need us, as scared as they are, as much as they evade us, they need us to never give up."

The collar was pink and white gingham with a felt daisy attached. If it had been a pink and white collar with a poppy attached, I would have been a blubbering idiot. As it was, I was merely a blubbering fool.

Then Mike texted a photo. A photo of a very cute blond pit bull mix, smiling at the camera. He captioned it "The most amazing-looking dead dog ever!"

"You kept her?"

"Hell yeah, I kept her."

"Awesome."

My optimism was returning, if not my energy. I had an idea.

"Can you talk to the group of folks arriving at 10 again? Chris will be here to help with the directions, but I just don't trust myself to cover all the instructions right now. And, I think it would be really helpful for the group to hear you."

"Absolutely."

"Thank you."

"Thank you" seems not nearly enough. And yet I wondered if I'd said it enough.

16

TEAMS

The volunteers began arriving at my office promptly at ten. This time Mike and Jeanne Kataoka, fellow BFP rescuers and vegans, as well as former patrons of Chris's wine store, joined us. Jeanne is an ordained animal chaplain, and they'd first learned of BFP when Percival and I were part of a talk at her spiritual center. They'd adopted two BFP dogs since that time. Mary and Liza, sisters and more BFP rescue family, arrived soon after with their two adorable blind beagles. And Jessica and Austin returned for another day. Once again, everyone put their name and phone number on the white board, and I created a group text message, allowing us to coordinate efforts.

By 10:15 Mike was on my speaker phone. He explained the idea of the perimeter and the area on which we should focus, while Chris handed out the maps. The map now included nine points—everything from Jessica and Austin's apartment to where she'd entered the park, where the GPS died, where I'd been stationed with the warming box off Via Paloma, where she'd appeared on Les's lawn, the sighting at the sheriff's house, where Chris was seated when he thought he saw Poppy, and where that possible sighting was. I could not see a pattern. To me, it looked like Poppy was still running scared and darting all over the wilderness park. And the #5 spot on the map, the one at Les's house, was far south and across Alessandro Boulevard—I could hardly stand to consider that. But Mike seemed to feel she was settling into a pattern. Based on the sightings and the topography, he said she was likely to be near where she'd appeared the morning before, which he said was the southeast corner of the park (and I just had to take his word for that). We would focus on that area, near the sheriff's house, but also out in the wilderness park to form that perimeter and keep her contained in that wilderness cul-de-sac. The goal was another sighting so we could determine where to leave a humane trap.

I clung to the idea of a concrete goal. I tried to find encouragement that Mike saw a pattern even if I didn't. But I was too tired to make sense of most of it, and I could see from the looks on the faces of the volunteers that they were also perhaps confused about how we set this perimeter. They were not clear on the plan. And I knew from recent experience it was hard to be sitting and waiting and not out walking and searching.

"Mike, maybe you can explain . . ." My phone rang before I could finish the thought. Without thinking, I hit the button rejecting the call and instantly regretted it. "Shit. Mike, my phone rang and it could have been someone calling about Poppy. I'm going to hang up with you to call them back. Chris, can you call him on your phone?"

I moved into my office and hit "call back," cursing myself for not answering previously, and hoping someone would answer. Someone did.

"Hi. I'm sorry, I just missed your call."

"Yeah, I was calling about your dog. She was in my yard this morning."

"Oh my god. Okay, where? Was she okay?"

"She was in my neighbor's yard yesterday and ran over here then, too. I think my neighbor called you about that. I'm catty-corner to the Sniffs. She came up from the canyon, into my yard, but she ran off when she saw me. Fast little thing."

A neighbor! There is a pattern! She is *exactly* where Mike said she'd be.

I got the caller's name and address and rushed back into my conference room.

"Another sighting!"

People gasped, cheered, shouted, talked, and did a lot of oh-my-god-ing. Or maybe that was just my brain. But we were excited.

"It was just this morning. And the guy that called is right next door to the yard she was in yesterday!"

Mike's voice boomed through Chris's speaker phone, "That's it! We've got a pattern. We've got enough to set a trap. Everyone, listen up."

The room vibrated silently. I think every one of us wanted to rush out the door and drive over to the neighborhood where we now knew Poppy was. I knew that's exactly what Mike was trying to prevent. That would scare her off, and maybe for good. This is where controlling the people would really come into play, just as Mike and Babs had been talking about.

He tightened up the perimeter, moving people to spots further along that street and still out in the wilderness park, but a little closer in.

"Teresa, if you can get into a neighbor's backyard to watch, that's good. Just sit and watch. See where she's headed. You're the only one going to the house she was spotted at. Did he say you could go into his backyard?"

Darn it! "I forgot to ask. I'll call him back."

"Same drill, only this time you might be there awhile."

"And it will be daylight."

"More chicken. More chicken stock. I'll get a trap and head out there this afternoon. Find out if we can set a trap in his yard."

"Ok. I'll go call him back."

"And do you have the diatomaceous soil and the construction fencing? You'll need those."

"Chris was going to Home Depot after this. I'll send someone else."

Chris huddled over the maps with the rest of the volunteers, and they soon raced out to their cars and over to their assigned spots in the Mission Grove neighborhood where she'd been spotted.

I called Gordon, the gentleman whose house Poppy had now visited twice, and he readily agreed to let me camp out in his backyard and set whatever trap we needed. Whether it was all the coffee I'd had by then or the excitement of another recent sighting, I was wide awake and ready to go. *Hello, second (third, fourth, eighteenth) wind!*

Water bottle, snacks, blanket, and my journal were already in my car. I grabbed another water bottle from my office refrigerator and drove as calmly as I could to Gordon's house. Mike called me as I drove.

"Do not let them all hang out at that house. Don't give out the address."

"I know. They know the street, but they're spreading out. Chris is there with them. He gets it."

"I know he does. He's a good guy. His map has been extremely helpful." He paused. "What are you going to do if you see her?"

I knew this was a test. I knew the answer too. Luckily, he wasn't asking me if I was capable of doing what I should do. "Nothing. I'll stay still. Watch to see where she goes and what she does. I'll wait for her to come to me."

"Good girl."

"Do I get a treat?"

"Sure. Have some rotisserie chicken."

"Ugh."

"And if you see her while you're driving down the street?"

That one I didn't know. What would I do? "Don't stop? Slow down? See if I can tell where she's headed?"

"You can guide her with your car. If she runs forward, just drive past her and wait. When she passes you again, pull up past her again. Don't follow behind her. If she's headed to traffic get in front of her and head her the other way. Keep playing leapfrog. Just keep in mind she's going to run *away* from you, not to you. And don't call out to her. She's running scared."

"Let's just hope I see her in the backyard and not out in the highway."

"Looks like that's where she's hanging out."

When I arrived at Gordon's house, Chris greeted me in the street with matters well in hand. Gordon had told him that another nearby neighbor sighted Poppy on Lakewood Drive. The finger of wilderness park that came into this housing complex was bordered by Firwood to the south, where Gordon's house was; Ironwood to the west, where the sheriff and his wife lived; and Lakewood to the north, where Poppy had now also been sighted. To the east this sliver of wilderness park opened to the larger wilderness canyon area and eventually, far to the east, the distribution centers I'd been lost in. She was staying in that smaller area, bordering all the homes, just as Mike had predicted.

Mary and Liza had gone to Lakewood, with Austin in the backyard of a house at the end of Firwood with an eastern exposure, and the Kataokas went a few more houses down, rounding the cul-de-sac, facing southeast into a property owned by the Metropolitan Water District with an expanse of dirt. No trees, no bushes, no rocks. If Poppy popped up there, she'd be easy to spot. These houses all had large yards, and they all faced the canyon. They also all had neighbors willing to help us find a lost dog.

Chris had also let Curtis and Melody know of the sighting, and they'd agreed to hike in toward the line of homes to find a vantage point from the east, looking west. I'd be in Gordon's backyard, facing north. We had the perimeter set.

The rain had again stopped, and the sky had cleared up to a bright blue with only a few cottony, nonthreatening clouds and a vivid sun. A clear view on a clear day.

Gordon, a tall gray-haired man, walked me through his side gate, around to his backyard.

"She was right up here," he pointed to a sliding glass door off his patio. "But when she saw me, she ran. Slipped right through that fence." He pointed to the fence around the pool, and I shuddered, too easily envisioning her slipping and falling in. Luckily, he continued describing her flight. "Then as quickly as she went in, she was out the fence over there and ran down the hill into the canyon there. She's quick. And she'll need to be—lots of coyotes out there."

"I know. Thanks. I'm going to go down there and sit watching for her."

"Call me if you need anything. You're welcome to stay as long as you need."

I walked down the sloping yard, still muddy from the thunderstorms. The hillside had gnarled trees, with gray-brown leaves and exposed roots, and only a patch or two of grass. This did not seem to be an area where anyone spent much time. The main attraction was a large oak tree. The metal fence separating the yard from the wilderness park was only about four feet high and rusted, with a large gap in the corner where the fence did not meet the side wall. Poppy could easily slip through the opening. She probably could hop over the fence as well. She was a springy little thing. We'd seen her hop from the floor to a dining room tabletop without needing a running start. Sometimes this happened when breakfast was on the table.

I spread out the blanket in a spot near the big oak but still in the sun, sat down, propped up my water bottle in the dirt next to me, and opened my journal. If I was going to be there for hours, and if I was going to stay calm and let her come to me, I needed to distract myself. I thought I could write down what had been going on, and particularly all the advice Babs and Mike had given me. So much useful information that anyone who lost a dog would need. I hoped I could pay it forward one day.

After writing a few pages, I put the journal down and leaned back on my elbows, face up to the sky. The sunshine was soothing, seeping into my clothing and skin and warming me for the first time in four days. I took my sweatshirt off and pushed up the sleeves on my shirt. I could stay here. I was comfortable and the neighborhood was quiet. I could see into several neighbors' backyards and down into the wilderness park. Directly in front of me was a huddle of trees and bushes that formed what looked like a cave. Was that where Poppy slept? Hidden in the bushes, tucked up near the houses, at the edge of the wilderness? Like Mike had said? The spot seemed almost safe, cozy. Almost.

My phone rang and I saw Chris's number pop up.

"Hey."

"We just saw her!" He was the most excited he'd been in days. "We all saw her. And it was definitely her!"

"Where? Which way was she going?"

"Toward you, I think. We all saw her. Austin saw her first, she went speeding by and passed where the Kataokas are, too. She was racing along the backyards, but behind a chain link fence, out in the Water District area. I saw her stop and put her little paws up on a wall, looking for a way through, I think. Then she was gone again, coming back this way, buzzing along the fence. She must have found an opening and slipped through—which is good. She's not in the water district property anymore. She's probably coming your way."

No one was chasing her, which was good. They'd listened to Mike. I pictured our little Poppy with her paws up on a wall, with that inquisitive look in her dark eyes. I hoped I'd see that very scene live at the wall in front of me, right where the opening was. Any moment now. But I had to stay calm.

"Okay, call Mike. Let him know. I'm going to sit quietly and watch for her like he told me."

I opened the bag of chicken and set it down closer to the fence line. *Wind, do your thing. Carry that scent.* I waved my sweatshirt in the wind a bit. I'd been wearing it for most of the four days, so Buddha only knew what it smelled like, but whatever the scent was, it was mine. Then I concentrated on slowing my heart rate back down to normal. Deep cleansing breaths and all that.

More than an hour went by with no sighting. No sounds. As far as I knew, Poppy had not come near me. But then, I hadn't seen those coyotes that morning either, and they had definitely been there. All six of them.

Just after 1 P.M., I moved my blanket under the shade of the tree. The direct sunlight was too much after two hours. It felt both strange and comforting to be so quiet, so calm in the sun. We'd had two sightings that day alone, which caused bursts of excitement, followed by lulls. I felt in my now sun-warmed bones that we were getting close, but what did "close" mean in the context of a marathon?

Mary and Liza texted that their dogs were restless, and they needed to get out of the sun too. They'd drive around and post more flyers. I asked if they could get some chicken too. I was down to slim remains, and we had to bait the trap.

Jeanne and Mike had to leave by 3:00 P.M. Austin and Jessica didn't have much more time either, as Austin needed to work that afternoon. Curtis and Melody were still out in the wilderness park, but since I knew they would have the long drive back and would need to get home to their dogs, I was worried we'd have no volunteers by the time Poppy showed up again. Despite the back-to-back sightings, our stakeouts had quickly gotten boring. And I'm sure it's hard to convince yourself you are helping if all you're doing is sitting in someone's backyard. I knew that feeling too well. But in a couple of hours

Mike would arrive with the trap. And the trap could do more than any of us could. The trap could catch Poppy. The trap *would* catch Poppy.

Chris texted, "I'm going to get us lunch while Austin is still here watching."

"Good idea. This could be a very long day. Get me an iced tea, too."

By the time Chris got back, I had nearly fallen asleep in my little I-only-look-homeless setup. I walked back up the hill of Gordon's backyard and around to the side gate. Gordon had left it unlocked for me to come and go as I needed, but this was the first time I'd left my camp.

I took the bag with the Del Taco bean burrito (no cheese) and fries, and a giant iced tea from Chris.

"Do you want to just sit and eat it here?" he said.

I did. I wanted to sit with Chris. I wanted to just sit normally and talk for a moment. Well, not exactly normally, we'd be in his car or on a curb. What was ten minutes? Was she going to appear and leave again in the ten minutes I left to have lunch?

"Yeah. Quickly. But yeah, let's just sit on the curb. You can tell me about seeing her. In all the sightings and all my time sitting stakeout, I have yet to see her myself."

We sat and ate, and I sucked down my iced tea, as Chris told me about seeing Poppy.

"She slowed down eventually, but she had some serious speed."

"So everyone keeps telling me. Did she seem okay? Not injured?"

"She seemed fine. Definitely not injured."

Over Chris's shoulder I saw movement. I leaned forward to look down the street.

"Do you see something?" Chris asked.

"I thought I saw a dog."

We both turned to look. There was no dog, and it wasn't hard to figure out I'd been concentrating so hard on seeing Poppy that I was likely going to hallucinate dogs.

But then a dog, small, white, with brown patches, trotted across the street at the open end of the cul-de-sac, five or six houses down.

"Jesus Christ!" Chris said.

"Okay, I'm going to drive down there. Just like Mike said. I'll drive down and get her to head back down this way. Or just see where she's going."

I hurried to my car and drove slowly down the street, only my heart was racing. I no longer saw the dog, but I knew she'd turned right at the end of Firwood, so I did too.

Two houses down on the left a man was out mowing his lawn. The little dog was sitting in his driveway, watching. I drove closer. The man stopped the mower and called the dog over to him. The dog came right up to him and sat. He handed the dog a treat from his pocket. I saw then that the dog was smaller than Poppy and had pointed ears that went straight up, where Poppy had the typical floppy beagle ears. This dog also had a docked tail.

Not my girl.

For the second time that afternoon, I had to take deep breaths to return my heart rate to normal. This wasn't a marathon; this was a damn decathalon on steroids.

I drove back to Gordon's house and Chris.

"Not her. But you know how we always think Poppy has Jack Russell terrier in her?"

"Yes."

"That dog was a Jack Russell. They really do look alike."

"I'm sorry. I was really hopeful."

"Me too. The trick now will be to stay hopeful. Tell me again how she looked?"

Chris smiled and gave me a kiss. "She was good. She looked good. She's trying to find her way back."

That's what I needed to hear. *Poppy was good.* "Well, I better go help her then," I said, rising.

I resumed my watch in Gordon's backyard. Chris sat in his car, texting with the volunteers to coordinate where everyone was before he chose a spot to resume his own stakeout.

Only fifteen minutes passed before my phone rang.

"Hi, yeah, you need to come out front and bring your ID," Chris said.

"My ID? Like my driver's license? Okay. Why?"

"Somebody called the cops on us."

Babs had mentioned the likelihood of police. I would have thought it would have happened during one of my late night or earlier morning sit-ins, but I suppose no one was up to see me then. No wonder crimes happen at night. "Oh. Great. Okay. I'm going to call Gordon too, so he can vouch for us."

Gordon easily agreed to meet us out front. "I guess this means I have good neighbors. Looking out for the neighborhood, anyway."

"True. I'm sure we do look sketchy."

In just the time it took me to walk up the backyard hill and out the side gate, Gordon was out front and Chris had already explained our purpose to the two officers, one of whom was now holding a flyer.

Gordon vouched for us, but the police were no longer concerned. One of them had seen the posting on the Nextdoor site, and they'd both noticed all the flyers as they drove in to answer the call. Most important, they both loved dogs.

They left, wishing us good luck finding her, and keeping the flyer.

I looked at Gordon. "Since I've already disturbed you, could I possibly use your restroom?" The iced tea had gone right through me. This time I had no choice but to go into a stranger's home to use their bathroom. Thank goodness modern suburban architecture always puts a half bathroom downstairs and usually not far from the entry.

When I came back out of the house, Mary and Liza and the Kataokas were all back, gathered near Chris. My phone rang before I got to their side of the street to see what was going on. It was Mike.

"Hey, Mike. You on your way?"

"My car broke down. I can't get there with the trap," Mike said. "My car won't even start."

I froze. Stunned. We were so close, and now, now something as mundane as car trouble is going to ruin everything?

We cannot catch a break.

17

PATTERNS

It was after 3:00 P.M. We needed the trap set up by sundown, and Mike lived about an hour away. I wanted to scream—not at Mike, at the universe, my old nemesis. But I stayed calm.

"Oh, I'm sorry. I hate car trouble. Are you home?" I said.

"Yeah. You know anyone who can pick up the trap in Costa Mesa and get it to you in time?"

"Maybe one of us can drive out? I think my volunteers are a little bored."

"We won't have time for that. We need to get this set up in an hour or so."

Right. Of course. A race against the sun—exactly what we needed.

"Okay. Let me think. There might be a BFP volunteer who lives out there. Let me think. What part of Costa Mesa do you live in?" I held the phone with one hand and my forehead with the other, as I paced.

"Not far from South Coast Plaza."

"Okay. I'll ask and call you back."

I walked over to where Chris and the others were, and Chris began to explain the new plans—what everyone would be doing that afternoon and who could be back tomorrow if need be.

"Hang on. Mike's car broke down. He can't get here with the trap. We need to pick it up from his house in Costa Mesa, like now. Who do we know in Costa Mesa or near there?"

"Well, my parents," Chris said.

True. I had not even thought of that. I had immediately thought of the dog rescue nation, but not of family. Chris's parents lived within a few miles of South Coast Plaza. But it was hard to imagine them driving to Costa Mesa, picking up a dog trap, and driving to Riverside. It was hard to imagine they'd even be home. Mostly, it was hard to imagine Chris calling and asking them for a favor. He hadn't spoken to them in over a year.

"Yeah. That's probably not going to work." But I did consider, for the briefest of moments, that maybe this would break the impasse.

As ideas and names were bandied about, and the timing on driving there and back discussed, it hit me. I looked at Chris.

"Shawna and Eli live in Costa Mesa." My sister and brother-in-law. Exhausted or not, it says a lot about our familial relationships that Chris's family wasn't an option, and it had taken me ten minutes to realize I had a sibling within a few miles of where I needed a favor. I was not in the habit of asking for help, and certainly not asking family members. Making matters worse, my last conversation with her had not been a nice one.

Well, I couldn't ask for help for me, but I could darn sure ask for help for a dog.

I called my sister. To my surprise, she answered. She wasn't available to help, but quickly suggested her husband, Eli, might be.

I called Eli, whom I'd known since he was seventeen years old and first dated my sister in high school. He was generally reliable, resourceful, and smart. And more to the point at hand, not one to hold petty grievances. I explained what I needed and without asking questions he simply agreed to do it. I gave him Mike's number and hung up. The love of dogs ran strong in my family. For all the time I thought that was all that did run strong among us, sometimes that is enough.

I called Mike and gave him Eli's name and number, and if he realized I had been slow to remember I had a sister and brother-in-law who were his neighbors, he didn't say anything.

I returned to my encampment in Gordon's backyard, but this time I was too antsy to sit. Instead, I used my phone camera and took video of the yard, narrating as I went, "Here's where the fence divides the yard from the wilderness park." I zoomed in on the opening where the fence did not meet the wall, "And here is where I assume she gets in. Here's the hill up to the house—she ran up there and then back down"—I panned back down to my encampment—"so this is where I've been hanging out."

I texted the video to Mike. "Thought you'd like to see this. Maybe we can figure out where to set up the trap?"

"Good idea. Let me look."

A few minutes later he texted back: "See if you can find someplace relatively flat. Near the fence is good, but we need flat ground."

"Okay. I think it's flat down by the fence. I'll clear a space."

"When Eli gets here I'll teach him to set the trap. When he gets there, you can call me and I'll walk you through it again."

"Got it."

"This is good. We've got a pattern. We may not get her tonight, but we'll get her."

This was the first time I felt as certain as he did. *We'll get her.* Still, I nervously watched the sun slipping lower as I waited for Eli.

Eli and Chris carried the trap down the hill toward me, and I directed them to what I thought was a flat area near the fence. The trap was bigger than I expected and less threatening than the word "trap" implied. It was a big, long, wire crate—not unlike the kind dogs are often in at home. We had a similar-looking, though newer, wire crate at home, and Poppy had willingly walked into it and curled up on the cushion a few times. The trap of course had no cushion, but still, I could imagine her walking into it without too much fear—especially if we put chicken in there.

They set the trap down and I called Mike, putting him on speaker phone.

"Which way is the wind blowing?" he said.

Eli licked his finger and put it up in the air.

"Does that actually work?" I said.

"I don't know. Isn't that what they do on TV all the time?" Eli was smiling. "It's blowing that way, I think."

"Which way is that way?" Mike said.

"West to east," Chris said.

"So my saying left to right is not going to help you?" I said.

"Maybe a little, since you sent me video. Find a spot where the wind can pick up the scent. Make sure the wind won't be blocked by that wall or even the tree."

The three of us walked around, trying to feel the breeze and a level space. Eventually we agreed on a spot not far from the spot I'd originally picked. Eli and Chris moved the trap, and I got Mike back on the phone as Eli went to work setting the trap.

"Pour some chicken broth all around that tree. Get some up in the branches and leaves so the wind really takes it," Mike said.

"Ok. We've got two cartons of broth to use," I said.

"Then head down to the fence and pour some there as well. But save some for the trap. Make it irresistible to her."

As I spread chicken broth around Gordon's yard and dripped it down the fence on the side facing the wilderness park, Eli finished setting up the trap. Mike instructed him to rub the trap back and forth in the ground so dirt covered the wire bottom, making it easier and presumably less intimidating for Poppy to walk into. Chris shredded chicken and placed it and my now very dirty sock inside the trap. I used the napkins left over from lunch to rub chicken broth all over the outside. And finally, Eli set the springing mechanism.

We looked at our handiwork. I could see her walking into it for the chicken. The door slamming shut would be terrifying, but she'd be safe. At least now if she appeared, we'd have a chance to catch her. We weren't just watching anymore.

"Don't check the trap until 10 or 10:30 tomorrow morning. She's been appearing in the yards in late morning." Mike said.

"That's because I've been out there in early morning," I said, with less hope and more sarcasm than I meant.

"Give her time to get in there. And you need to know, it may not be Poppy in the trap when you get there. We've caught raccoons, coyotes, stray cats, you name it. But the worst is a skunk."

"Oh, great. Hadn't thought about that." I said. That sounded exactly like my luck—after finally get the trap set, an angry skunk would climb in.

"Maybe Chris will have to handle that one," Mike said.

"Chris will be on the road," Chris said.

Chris had to return to Paso Robles the next morning to work. He would be taking Percival and Roe back home with him. There was no one left to cover for him. I was trying not to think about the fact that he was leaving. Another reason this trap *had* to work.

"I'll get somebody to help me. If she is in the trap, I can't carry her in the trap up that hill anyway, and I'm darn sure not taking her out of the trap until she's home behind two gates and a front door."

Chris, Eli, and I climbed back up the hill in Gordon's backyard. When we said goodbye to Eli and thanked him for helping, he hugged me and wished me luck.

I called and left a message for Gordon, letting him know about the trap and that I'd be back in the morning. Luckily, Gordon had no pets of his own, so we didn't have to be concerned they'd roam into the trap. Chris and I packed up my things and walked back up the hill, around the side yard, and to our cars. The sun was going down, and there was nothing more we could do. The volunteers had all left, each promising to come back the next day and, like me, undoubtedly hoping they wouldn't have to.

"Let's get home. I can make us a nice dinner. Something besides hamburgers," Chris said.

"And I can shower. Maybe I'll even sleep tonight. The trap makes me feel like we are at least doing something overnight."

"And it's no longer raining. It's getting better."

"What time do you have to leave in the morning?"

"Probably about six. I'll try not to wake you."

"I can't imagine I won't be awake."

We settled in at home. Chris made us a hearty pasta meal, and we spent some time cuddling on the couch with Percival and Roe, who had definitely been on the short end of the attention stick all week. My shoulders may have moved down slightly from their recent positions up by my ears.

At 8:15, my phone rang and an unknown local number showed on the screen. I answered, fully expecting a sales call.

A woman thought she saw Poppy at a park.

"Which park?" I asked. I now knew of far more parks in Riverside than I ever imagined I would.

"I don't know what it's called. It's the one with baseball fields and a hill? On Chicago and like Canyon Crest?"

"Andulka Park?"

Chris was shaking his head no.

No, it's not called Andulka? No, Poppy couldn't be there? I didn't understand what he was trying to tell me.

"I'm not sure. She was sitting up on the hill. A brown and white dog? Just sitting up there watching everybody. I couldn't get to her, I was just driving by last night. But then I saw your signs on my way home tonight so I called."

"So you saw her last night? Not tonight?"

"No, it was last night. I'm sorry. I didn't have a number to call last night. I didn't see her there today."

I got her name and number and we hung up.

"That can't be," I said to Chris. Andulka Park was west of Jessica and Austin's apartment, where Poppy had originally gone missing, and all of her activity had been east or south of that. An appearance at Andulka Park did not fit the pattern. Not at all.

"She could get to Andulka Park, but that wasn't the direction we saw her headed, and that doesn't seem to fit where she's been," Chris said.

"No, it doesn't. That has to be a different dog." Wishful thinking? A refusal of reality? Or simple logic? I could no longer tell. We hadn't received any false alarm phone calls, which was surprising given the number of flyers we had up all over town. Babs had a point about not putting "reward" on the flyer. I'm sure we would have received many more calls with bad information had we done so. Instead, we'd only received calls with very, very good information and positive sightings.

I texted Mike and he replied, "Mark it on the map but stick with the plan. That's not likely her. And even if it was, that was last night. We know where she was today. Everybody saw her."

Mike's response relieved me enough that I accepted the glass of wine Chris poured for me. With all this up, down, slow, fast, she's there, she's not, we're close, we're not, she's running, she's hidden, she's here, she's there, madness, I needed that glass of wine. I'd been on high alert for far too long. But finally, I felt I could relax—at least a tiny bit.

I slept, but not as well as I had hoped. All I could think about was that trap and what might be in it—who I hoped would be in it. Still, six hours was more than I'd slept in any of the last several nights. I woke, feeling almost human, when Chris and the dogs were leaving. I kissed all three of them goodbye.

"She'll be there. You'll get her. And let me know the moment you do," Chris said.

"You'll probably hear me screaming. Even if you're already in Paso by then."

"Love you."

"Love you, too."

I tried going back to sleep, but I couldn't. My mind wouldn't settle. I had time to kill. Mike had said I couldn't go to the trap until after ten. I thought about driving to the neighborhood and sitting watching the wilderness park again, but that seemed like admitting she wasn't in the trap. Not logical, I knew. But somehow it seemed like bad luck to act as though she were anywhere but in the trap. Sleep. I needed to go back to sleep to pass the time. Buddha knows I needed sleep.

Much to my surprise and relief, I eventually managed another hour of sleep before I got up and got coffee. I took my mug back upstairs and almost immediately as I settled in bed, propped up on pillows, my phone pinged with a text. It was Curtis.

"We're coming back out. Should we go to the same spot?"

"No. You don't need to. We have the trap set. Mike says I shouldn't go until 10 since her pattern has been to show up earlier than that and we can't scare her off. I've got to give her the time and space to wander into the trap." Again, she *had* to be in the trap. My mind was not allowing for other possibilities. Luckily, Curtis's was.

"But if she isn't in the trap, we need to have people already there. It takes us a while to get there."

"I know. But I'd hate for you to waste your time." *Because she's going to be in the trap.*

"If you have her by the time we get there, we'll be ecstatic to be there."

That was a good point. And I'd need help with the trap with Poppy in it. Curtis was a big, strong guy. He'd be great help. Again, my tendency to hyperfocus had almost caused a problem. "Okay. Yeah. Same place. Chris won't be there. He had to go back to Paso."

"I know. I can coordinate everybody if you'd like."

"That would be great. I'm so turned around on where everything is, and all I can think about is that trap."

"You focus on that. I'll round up more volunteers and get us positioned."

"Thanks. Really, Curtis. Thank you."

That's when I noticed that I had another text. A Riverside area code, but not a number I recognized.

I tapped on the text.

"Hello. I may have found your dog. Due to the late time I decided to text instead of call. Please contact me regarding the beagle. I do work tomorrow morning so please be patient if I take a bit of time to respond. If you call and I don't answer I'll call you back as soon as I can. :-)"

18

HEROICS

※

The message had been left at just after midnight. *How had I not heard that?* Of all the times to actually be asleep! He may have found my dog. *May.* What does that mean? Was she alive? Did he see her or does he have her? *No, she's in the trap!*

I hit "call back" and got his voice mail. The message box was full. *Are you kidding me?*

I texted. "I tried calling but your voice mail is full. Please call me as soon as you can about my dog."

A very long, grueling hour passed, during which I walked downstairs, stared at my phone, made toast, stared at my phone, ate toast, stared at my phone, walked back upstairs, stared at my phone, got dressed, stared at my phone, made up fifty-three more versions of what the call was about, and then, for good measure, stared at my phone.

Finally, the phone did what I'd been swearing at it to do. It rang.

The caller's name was Conor, and he was very calm. Not at all in the panic I was in.

"I was leaving my parents' house and I saw her running in the street."

Okay, so he saw her. Another sighting. "What street?"

"I don't know. My parents just moved there, but it's a big street, normally busy but this was late at night."

"Alessandro?"

"I don't know."

"By the shopping center or further down by the distribution centers? Like on your way to the 215 freeway?"

"Yeah, I was headed home. I'm in Moreno Valley."

That had to be Alessandro. Poppy was running from the neighborhood where she'd been first spotted, back across Alessandro to the wilderness park, and please Buddha, to the trap. That was her pattern. Well, except the trap part. *Another sighting and it fit the pattern.*

"She's really sweet," Conor said.

Wait, what?

How do you know she's sweet?

"Wait, you have her? You caught her?" My enthusiasm dampened. This was not going to be Poppy. There is no way he caught her.

"Oh yeah, she's right here with me."

Could it possibly be her? Wasn't she in the trap? My mind bounced from despair to hope, from the trap to the boulevard, and from sanity to chaos. But finally, I settled on one clear thought. "Can you text me a photo of her?"

"A photo? Sure."

In a matter of seconds he texted a photo of a very cute beagle. But it was not Poppy. This beagle's head was bigger, and she, whoever she was, had an air of confidence Poppy had never had. This beagle didn't look frightened of anything. *It's okay. Poppy is in the trap.*

He texted another photo from a different angle. I noticed the distinct white "horn" markings on top of her head. And was that the Elvis smirk—the little drunken lipstick smear—at her mouth? *It was!*

It is Poppy!

She was looking up, smiling, it seemed, and though she was a little dirty, she seemed no worse for the wear. In fact, she seemed *better*. She was standing there, next to a stranger, and his hand was on the side of her face. She was not flinching. She had not run away. She was being brave.

I sat down on the bed, astounded.

It's really her. She's alive. She's safe. She's fine.

I texted Conor, shaking and barely able to hold my phone and move my fingers, but I knew my voice would not be discernible by voice recognition through the choking back of tears.

"That's her! Address please?" was all I typed out. (Sorry, Conor—I was and am really thankful.)

He typed his address in Moreno Valley, the next city over and about a fifteen-minute drive from my house. "I don't mind driving her if you would like. Is there anything I can do to help her not escape again? I work at Petco, so I do have some discounts and such if you needed to get a harness or something. She even slipped out of the collar I put on her when I first caught her."

Oh, wow. Caught and then slipping out of a collar. I couldn't bear the thought. "I know you know this, but I have to say it, please keep her very secure. I'll be right over. I'll be right there. Keep her safe. Please. Thank you."

I called Chris and blurted it all out, crying and sniffing and, soon, laughing with joy.

Chris shouted "Yes!" in a way that likely scared Roe and Percival, but we had to trust they'd understand. "Call me when you have her. I can't believe someone caught her. This is the best!"

Next, I called Curtis, to save him the drive out to Riverside.

His joy nearly matched Chris's: "Best. News. Ever!"

"I know. Thank you so much."

"We're already on our way, so we'll still come out. We can help take the signs down. And I want to see that little girl!"

I texted Jessica as well. She would be as relieved as we were.

In the car, but before driving away (I had that much of my wits left), I called both Babs and Mike.

We were all excited and all three of us were talking at once, so the conversation sounded something like this:

"Holy shit! He caught her? . . . keep secure . . . no walks for two weeks . . . food . . . water . . . vet check . . . flight risk . . . sleep . . . contain . . . martingale collar . . . no harness is escape proof . . . get her home . . . just you . . . flight risk . . . escape artist . . . secure . . . holy shit!"

I laughed. "Okay, I'm going to have to ask you guys for one more text—my instructions for how to handle a recently captured escape artist. 'Cuz I'm not going to remember a thing you just said. All I can think about is getting my girl back."

"Fair enough," Mike said.

"Call us when you have her. This is awesome. Great job." Babs said.

For the rest of the drive, I alternated between bliss and bone-chilling fear something would happy to Poppy before I got there to get her back. And then I worried about getting her to my car and safely home. All I wanted was to be home, curled up on my bed, with her sharing my pillow and resting her head on my shoulder again. That was the vision that had kept me going these last five days, and that became my very intense focus as I drove.

I pulled into Conor's driveway, behind a car already parked there. I wanted to be as close to the door as possible to minimize the distance I had to carry her and therefore her chances of escaping again. There was no way I was walking her even two feet on a leash. I had the crate in the car and briefly considered carrying the crate into the house, putting her in it, and carrying the locked crate to my car, but I was too anxious to just get to the door and see her.

The front door had a heavy metal screen. Conor opened the door almost immediately, but I could see very little through that screen. He reached to open the screen.

"No, don't! I don't want her to get out again," I nearly yelled at the poor guy.

He chuckled at the crazy lady on his doorstep. "She's fine. She's in a crate."

He opened the screen door and I looked down. The crate was right there in the entryway, waiting.

My sweet, adorable, precious little Poppy Popstar was indeed in the crate, happily wagging her tail and doing her wigglebutt dance. She seemed to be smiling at me, though I knew in part that was her smeared lipstick marking.

"Oh my god," I bent down to her and stuck my fingers in the crate. "My baby girl. Poppy Popstar!" She immediately began to lick my fingers.

"She's really sweet. I put her in the crate to sleep last night, but she cried, so eventually I let her out and she slept on my pillow with me," Conor said.

"Probably the best night's sleep she's had all week. She's been missing for five nights. And yeah, she's used to sleeping on my bed, usually on my pillow."

"Do you want to let her out? I have dogs of my own. The house is safe, she won't escape."

I was sure that was true. Conor was obviously a dog person. I could hear his dogs off in another room, and the heavy screen door was closed tight, but still, I could not bring myself to risk it. "No. I'm really too freaked out for that. Let me get the crate out of my car and transfer her to that. Maybe then you can help me carry her in the crate to my car?"

"I get it. I can put her in the car in this crate. Just bring it back to me later."

I stood up. "Thank you. That would be great. So, where did you find her?"

"I was at my parents' house in Riverside. They just moved there, so I'm not familiar with the streets, but when I left, I saw all your signs. I knew someone was really missing that dog. And then when I turned on to a main street there, I don't know its name but it's a pretty busy street, several lanes . . ."

"Alessandro?" I don't know why I kept mentioning the same street to him, despite his repeated statements that he did not know the street name.

"Maybe. I think. I saw her running down the street and she was running with traffic, not across."

"Oh my god."

"So I used my car to kind of get her to run back into the neighborhood and out of the street. I'd sort of pull my car ahead of her and get her to turn . . ."

My head, my heart, my ears were not ready for this. I could not hear it. I blurted out, "Okay, I'm sorry. I can't hear this right now. It's giving me a heart attack, even though I know she's safe and right here. I'll want to hear it later, just not now. I'm sorry. I'm so sorry. But thank you. Thank you for all you did." I was sure I sounded crazy, but I hoped I did not sound ungrateful.

"Okay. Yeah. Okay. She's good though. She seems fine. I gave her food and water last night and a little this morning. She's good."

"She's very good. Thank you. Thank you so much."

Conor carried Poppy in the crate to my car and put her in the back seat. I snapped a quick photo of Poppy, thanked Conor again, and headed home. Until we were home, though, I couldn't relax. I couldn't fall apart the way I wanted to. I had to get home. Home with my girl.

Chris was of course the first person I called, confirming that I had Poppy and she was safe. I sent him the photo of Poppy in the crate. Then I called Mike and Babs. Again, the instructions and the excitement were too much, so I pulled over to concentrate on the call. Crashing my car after finally finding Poppy would not be a good outcome. It would be typical of my life, but when I can, I try to avoid the more obvious disasters.

"Take her straight home," Babs said.

"No walks for two weeks. She's had plenty of exercise. She needs to be home, resting and getting used to being with you," Mike said.

There were more instructions about martingale collars, upset stomach, and how she is likely to be a different dog.

"I can see that already. She slept on a bed with a total stranger. And a guy at that. She was afraid of even Chris still six days ago," I said.

"Yep. Probably figured out life with a human on a comfy bed isn't so bad," Babs said.

"She's seen things," I said.

Mike laughed. "She's probably seen a lot of things. We'll never know. But you know she's a smart, fast dog with escape skills, so you gotta look out for that. Take no chances."

"She's a survivor," Babs said.

"She is." I turned and looked at Poppy in the crate. She was looking right back at me, still sitting up, wagging her tail again. "Hang on a second." I texted them the photo. She was in the crate but still looked adorable.

"Awww. She's a cutie," Babs said.

"That's a cute dog. Get her home and you both get some sleep," Mike said.

"That is my plan."

Next, I texted the photo to Curtis. "I have her!"

"That is the best thing I've seen in a while!" He texted back. "We're all over near the house where the trap is, taking down all the signs. Can you bring her by so we can all see her?"

I really, really, really wanted to go home. But they deserved to see her, and I had to get the trap. "Yes, I'll be there in about ten minutes. But she's staying in her crate!"

"LOL. Absolutely."

"Can you text Kevin and BFP for me? Let them know she's safe."

"It'd be my honor."

❖

By the time I arrived at Gordon's house, Curtis and Melody were there along with the Kataokas, and Liza and Mary. Everyone took turns leaning in my car window to have a look at Poppy and inevitably stick their fingers in the crate. Poppy did not shy away at all. She continued to lick fingers, wag her tail, and look at us like she couldn't understand what all the fuss was about, but she was happy to be fussed over.

Curtis offered to get the trap.

"Okay. I should go with you, though. We've already had the cops called on us once. Plus it's a big trap." I looked back at Poppy, and then to the Kataokas. "Can you guys just keep an eye on her while we go do this?"

"Definitely. We'll stay right here with her."

Poppy was in a crate, in a car, with the doors closed (window down), yet we all still worried about an escape. I was certain I'd have PTSD from this for a while.

Jessica had texted back, relieved and happy for me and Poppy. She said she and Austin would start taking down the signs in their neighborhood. She'd wait to see Poppy at the office. I noted she couldn't bring herself to see Poppy just then. Jessica might have PTSD from this experience for a while too.

As Curtis and I walked behind Gordon's house and down the hill we joked about what we might find in the trap. Once Poppy had been found, I'd nearly forgotten the trap and all that Mike had warned me about

"Just please not a skunk," Curtis said.

"Oh, yeah. That would be a fitting way to end all of this. Though I feel like a trapped coyote would be bad too."

As we came down the hill, we could see the trap clearly. It was empty. My luck was changing. Curtis lifted it easily and carried it up the hill without my help, while I removed the trail camera and followed close behind.

Back at my car I learned that the group had come up with a plan for returning the equipment. Liza and Mary would take the trap and get it back to Mike, as they lived out in that direction. The Kataokas would take the crate back to Conor, as they did not live far from him and were excited to meet our hero. I suggested Liza and Mary take the diatomaceous earth to Mike as well. He could use it in his next search. (I had learned it was spread on the ground to track prints and determine if the dog had shown up in certain locations. We never needed it.) I handed Liza the trail camera as well.

"And give him this. I still have another one, and I'll give that to Babs. But I think he could use this. Help another lost dog."

"It's amazing what they do," Liza said.

I looked in my back seat, to Poppy, still happy, still wagging that tail. "It is. It really is amazing."

A lost dog. A storm. Six days. Five nights. Thousands of flyers. Several dozen volunteers. Two generals. Fifteen hundred acres. And now, at last—one happy beagle coming home with me.

19

REUNIONS

I pulled into my garage, with a dog curled up in a crate in my back seat.

I closed the garage door and got out of the car. My garage is detached, but there is a gated courtyard area between the garage and the townhome. Still, I needed to check that the gate wasn't somehow opened in the two hours I'd been gone, before I could let Poppy out. The gate was closed. I double-checked that it was locked. Then I triple-checked, pulling on the iron bars, shaking the gate. And despite the fact that I'd had four different beagles live in this townhome with me over the fourteen years I'd lived there, I checked the spacing of the bars on the gate to assure myself she could not slip through them.

I went back into the garage, opened my car door, and opened Poppy's crate.

"Come on, baby girl. You're home."

She looked at me, with her happy, eager expression, but made no move to come out of the crate.

"Poppy Popstar, let's go in. Let's get some breakfast, and a good, long nap. Okay? Come on baby girl, let's go."

Thump. Thump. Thump. Her tail was willing, but she was not moving.

"Okay, have it your way." I reached into her crate and she licked my hand. I scooped her up and pulled her out of the crate. As I held her up against my chest, she licked my face. And then I gave her many salty tears to lick away. She had lost weight, I could tell that much. And she was dirty, with a little cut near her mouth. But she seemed great otherwise. And she was clearly a much more confident dog.

Inside the house, it was obvious she knew where she was. She raced around the downstairs, then headed upstairs and straight to my bed. I followed her up.

She was curled up on my pillow, not yet asleep, but headed that way.

I took off my jacket, kicked off my shoes, and climbed into bed, exhausted and elated.

Poppy immediately moved over and licked my cheek. In moments we were both fast asleep, her head on my shoulder.

But for a brief visit to the vet to make sure she was healthy and unharmed, Poppy and I did not leave the house for twenty-four hours. We stayed in, slept, ate, slept some more. I did some laundry—sweatshirts, jeans, yoga pants, covered in mud and dog hair—and Poppy followed me up and down the stairs, never letting me out of her sight. Which was a good thing, because I certainly didn't want her out of mine.

I posted to Facebook and other social media, letting all know that Poppy had been found and thanking everyone for participating in the search. Beagle Freedom Project posted the news to the Fosters & Adopters Facebook page, where all rejoiced as if she was their own dog, because in a way, she was.

I fed Poppy small meals and gave her a warm bath, since she was as dirty as my yoga pants were. She stood still in the tub, watching me for reassurance. But once the water cooled, she was done. I could hardly blame her; she'd had enough cold water for a lifetime. I wrapped her in a big, fluffy towel and scooped her up.

"Baby girl, you are clean and safe. No more drama, 'kay?"

She licked my hand, which I took as agreement though I know very well that with a beagle, drama is guaranteed.

Monday afternoon (the Martin Luther King Jr. holiday), I left Poppy home sleeping (after carefully hiding all shoes, books, and magazines) and stopped by my office to pick up files. I had a week of work to catch up on and would be in my Paso Robles office for the next two weeks, which basically meant I grabbed every file on my desk, nervously counting down the minutes I'd been away from Poppy. I loaded up the file boxes in my car, sure I'd been gone way too long, and raced back home to make sure Poppy had not escaped. I called out to her frantically the minute I set foot in the door. She was on the couch, looking at me, wagging that busy tail of hers.

Mike and Babs had told me how Poppy was likely to behave and what I should do for her, but I was quickly realizing they'd forgotten to warn me about my own mental state—how I'd panic if she was out of eyesight, worry that I'd left a door open, convince myself there was no harness she couldn't escape, and envision coyotes, wolves, and owls stalking us both constantly. *Totally normal, I'm sure.*

❖

And now what?

Poppy was still our foster dog, and we still had a lease that allowed only two dogs in Paso and a homeowners' association bylaw that only allowed two dogs in Riverside. It seemed clear to me, though, that Poppy needed to stay with us awhile and get settled in. She was comfortable with us, and she'd been through a lot. Exactly what she'd been through, we'd never know, but we knew she covered many miles, slept outside in the cold and rain, and somewhere along the line lost her collar and GPS tracker. I didn't want to think about how that last part happened. She's deserved some rest and relaxation, some TLC and comfort. She'd be more comfortable with Roe and Percival in Paso Robles, I knew this.

I took her to Paso Robles Monday evening.

When she rejoined the Beagle Boys, crazy madness ensued. There was sniffing and rapid tail wagging, hopping about, circling, and then . . . mad zoomies. They gleefully chased each other around, tumbled over each other, raced through the doggie door out to the yard, back in, across the bed, back downstairs, around the couch, and finally, up on the couch, panting and looking very proud of themselves. They sniffed each other, and you could almost see Poppy communicating where she'd been, discussing her big adventure with her big brothers. It was hard not to notice how happy they all were together. Roe continued to be her guide, and though she was less frightened of most things, she still chose to hang out by his side and follow his lead on most everything. Poppy's presence seemed to get both of the Beagle Boys running and playing more than they would on their own.

We quickly noticed one other thing that had changed about Poppy—she now barked. Howled, actually. Just like a coyote. She tossed her little head back and let out the "aaahhhhhh . . . wooooooooo" at the moon, at moving leaves, when the neighbor's cat walked by. There was a little beagle in the noise, but it was hard to mistake the coyote sound. She'd seen things. She'd learned things.

Poppy was also always the first one up (though, thankfully, no longer at 4:00 A.M.), and she woke up extremely happy and perky. She'd paw at me for cuddles, then leap over Roe and off the bed, running through the bedroom and down the hall, circling back to stop in front of Percival, bowing down for play. He'd oblige, usually, but Roe stayed sleeping. Roe, older and more dignified, had quickly learned the joys of sleeping in. But Poppy made Percival younger. I was reminded of when we first adopted Percival, at about the same age Poppy was then—eighteen months or so. Percival tried so hard to get Daphne to play with him, but she seemed not to know how. Now, though, Poppy wanted to play, and Percival was happy to do so. Usually, Roe could not resist for too long. He'd stay sleeping, then slowly wake and look around, eventually jumping off the bed and chasing after Poppy. That was when Percival tagged out and returned to his beloved Chris.

"They kind of work as a great team, don't they?" Chris said one morning.

"They do indeed." I said. I got so much joy just from watching them.

Soon, though, we found ourselves faced with the exact same cluster of problems we'd had before she disappeared into the wilderness, plus a few more.

Poppy was still our foster pup, we still couldn't have three dogs, and I still wasn't dealing with that reality. We also learned that Poppy's run in the wilderness had turned her wild. She'd lost all housetraining skills she'd picked up, and she returned to shredding with a vengeance. Anytime she was without human supervision, she destroyed whatever she could reach, including a corner of carpet, the pee pads themselves, more books, two pairs of Chris's shoes, a bra, and a bathrobe (pulled down off the hook it hung on behind the bathroom door). Countless rolls of toilet paper and boxes of tissue likewise met their demise.

She was a lot of work. She had abundant energy. She was mischievous and destructive. But she was adorable, and cuddly, and happy, and I was connected to her in a way I knew I shouldn't be.

We needed to be her foster family, and only her foster. I hoped, though, that we'd have several months with Poppy—for her sake and ours. I clung to the fact that Percival had been with his foster mom for six months before we adopted him. And, inexplicably, I still had thoughts that somehow, magic would happen and we could adopt her. I didn't know what that magic was, and it was at odds with the logic of "two dogs plus one more" was more than two dogs, but the thought continued making its way around my brain, particularly every time Poppy jumped up into my lap, and certainly when she slept with her head on my shoulder.

Only four days after I returned to Paso Robles, Kevin called from BFP.

"We have an adopter for Poppy."

I was stunned. It was too soon. I wasn't ready. She wasn't ready. *No!*

Poppy had gotten a lot of social media attention from her big adventure, and she was freakin' adorable, so I should not have been surprised. But I was. I was surprised and heartbroken.

"It's too soon. She's not ready yet. She needs to stay with me longer," I said.

"I know. But they're worried she'll get too attached to you. Better to let her settle in with the adopters, where she'll be long-term."

Was it? Was that better? I was still so tired, so emotionally exhausted, I didn't trust my own thinking. Everything told me this was not right. She should not be adopted out this soon . . . or ever. She should stay with us. But I told myself they were the experts. They knew best. And, everyone had told me fostering was hard. So, this pain was normal. This is what I had to do.

It's hard to love them and help them, give them everything you can, and then say goodbye. But fostering saves lives and I knew that. And we had Roe.

We had made a commitment to Roe, and Roe needed us. I worked that over and over in my mind.

That night, I told Chris that Kevin would be driving up to pick up Poppy the next day.

"I was just starting to think we should adopt her," he said. "But we can't, I know."

"Can't we?"

He smiled at me, sadly. "I wish there was a way."

"I guess this is just one the universe will have to work out. The potential adopters are taking her on trial basis. If it doesn't work out . . ."

We both let that thought hang in the air. (You may recall, the universe does not usually work things out nicely for me.)

I held Poppy, petted her, and cried into her fur for most of the night. I didn't want to panic her or upset her in anyway, but I could not help myself. *We'd been through so much.*

When Kevin arrived the next afternoon, I tried to hold it together as best I could. I gathered Poppy's leash, a few of her favorite toys, and some treats. I carried her out to Kevin's car, kissing her head, kissing her little smirk. She licked my face and looked at me with that sweet, sweet, trusting face of hers.

I put her in the crate in Kevin's backseat.

Kevin hugged me. "She'll be okay. You did good."

I burst into heaving sobs as Kevin drove away with my Poppy Popstar. I fervently hoped whoever the lucky people were that adopted her would be very active posting photos and updates on the BFP Fosters & Adopters page. It was all I had.

For a week straight, I cried regularly and thought of her often. I missed her little face, her wigglebutt dance, her Elvis smirk; I even missed her early morning cuddle demands. My heart ached for everything about her. I'd see a shredded toy and start to cry—and then my shredded tissues would do me in again.

So I did the only thing I knew to do.

I put the word out with all my rescue friends—that mighty rescue nation—that I could foster short-term, transport, whatever was needed, and whatever would let me have a dog with me the two weeks a month I'd be in Riverside. Roe, of course, stayed in Paso Robles with Percival and Chris. The universe had done her thing there—the male dog I predicted, but leaving me with no travel buddy. (Roe was a country dog, there was no mistaking that.)

Roe's fur had grown back in, and with all the love, coconut oil, and supplements, he grew a very thick, soft, luxurious coat. In fact, he shed enough hair for six dogs, and yet his coat stayed thick. When he stood up, he left behind him the imprint of another entire dog in solid dog hair. And having understood he was adopted, and this was home, he now also howled, deeply, regularly, fervently. Just like our Daphne had. We loved everything about him. And he loved being in Paso Robles, with Chris and Percival.

🐾

In February, I threw a party in Riverside to thank everyone who had helped in the search for Poppy. Ruff House, the doggie day care and boarding facility that had helped to socialize Poppy and had posted flyers and on their social media page when she was lost, offered to let me hold the party in their training room, dogs welcome. I arranged for food and drink, even finding a Pinot Noir called Poppy with California poppies on the label. (Chris, like most wine aficionados, dislikes it when people buy wine for the label, but he gave me a pass on this one. Also, it was good wine.) In keeping with the theme of my life with Poppy, torrential downpour began the morning of the party and did not let up until an hour after it ended, at which time the clouds lifted, the sun shone, rainbows bowed, and I'm sure angels sung—just not during the party to thank a group of selfless dog lovers.

The weather caused flooding and street closures, and several folks I would have loved to have seen could not make it. But a hearty few gathered, and finally, I met Babs and Mike in person.

Mike was much like his voice, calm and rugged. His hands were rough, and his eyes were kind, just what you'd expect for a man dedicated to searching and rescuing lost dogs. He brought his girlfriend, Nicole, and he told me his father had passed away the week before.

Babs was smaller than I would have guessed—one who does such heroic deeds would seem larger than life, though. Her straight brown hair reached almost to her waist. She wore a constant smile. I learned at the party that in San Diego, where she lives, she is known as "Bring 'em home Babs"—an apt nickname to be sure.

Babs and Mike were happy to see each other, and I realized that probably did not happen often. They lived a couple hours' drive apart from each other. (A few weeks later I took them to lunch in a seaside town between where they each lived, to thank them further and to learn more about what they did and how they did it—much of what is included in the appendix to this book. You should read it. If you ever lose a dog, you'll want the information. Mike and Babs are what are known as "pet recovery specialists," but we all know that's a fancy name for "heroes.")

The Kataokas brought their two beagles to the party, both rescued from BFP, and Wendy came, bringing two current foster dogs—a fluffy little white terrier and a pit bull mix who charmed everyone with his boisterous affection—both available for adoption. Deia came, but without Aaron or River (Percival's brother). Cecilia, she who'd run private Uber services for Aaron and Chris in the first days of the search, made it as well. Jessica and Austin were not able to be at the party. They needed to be home with Baldur, the adorable little terrier/chihuahua/dachshund/something or other puppy they'd recently adopted from our local shelter. He was perfect for them, and they were blissfully happy to have him. I was delighted they'd adopted a rescue pup and had not been scared off by their experience with Poppy.

I had not heard from Poppy's adopters and had no way to contact them, so to my great disappointment and heartache, Poppy was not there to thank all these wonderful people who had done so much for her, and I was short one wigglebutt dance.

But we all met Conor—the young man who, against all odds, caught Poppy. By the time of the party, I could finally hear the story of how he found and astoundingly, miraculously, caught Poppy.

Conor, wearing a flannel shirt, jeans, and work boots, sat casually as he talked. He had the attention of the full room as he described the late night. He had been visiting his parents, and as he left his parents' home, he told us, he had noticed the signs for "Lost Dog" everywhere.

"I knew someone was really missing this dog, because I saw signs every-where. And she was really cute."

Thousands of eyes on the flyers, that's how you bring her home. I remember Babs saying that over and over again. I looked to Babs and smiled. She was smiling at Conor.

Conor continued, describing how he pulled out onto a busy road—he still didn't know the name of the street, but at least I didn't ask him again—and there she was. Running alongside traffic, going in the same direction. This was as much as I could hear when I first met Conor that morning, standing in his entryway with Poppy in a crate at my feet. I took a deep breath and listened as he continued.

"I honked to get the car next to me to see her, and he pulled off. Poppy was on the right-hand side, not on the sidewalk, still in the street but running alongside my car. I just drove in front of her, to sort of direct her and keep her from running back into traffic."

I remembered Mike and his careful instructions to me in case I saw Poppy while I was driving around. *Stay in front of her. Keep playing leapfrog.*

"I drove alongside of her, a little ahead, for probably like a quarter of a mile. Then I got to where there's like a big golf course there, and she went right, up into the neighborhood. So I followed her for like a mile, mile and a half. I tried to get out of my car to like get her, but she bolted, so I knew I couldn't do that. I just followed. Stopped, start, stop, start. Just tire her out. But she just kept going, kept going, kept going. Finally, she went into a cul-de-sac . . ."

As Conor talked, I kept trying to figure out where they were. Was she near where the trap was? Was this part of her pattern? Would we have caught her that morning if Conor hadn't?

He continued, leaning back against the window, calmly talking, as though he rescued dogs at midnight often which, as it turned out, he did. "I thought that would be my best chance to get her, in the cul-de-sac. So I drove into a driveway to cut her off, and so then she backed into a corner, on the side of someone's house. I grabbed a leash—I always have them in my car—made it into a slip lead, and she was stuck in that corner and she was not moving. I was worried I wasn't going to be able to grab her, like if I missed with the slip lead, so I kind of put it in front of her face to, you know, distract her, and then I grabbed her by the scruff when she was looking at the leash. Then I had to get the leash on her, but she would not move. She was not coming with me. So I picked her up, and she was totally okay with that for a few seconds, then as I started to walk back to my car with her, she got very not okay with it. She did like one attempt to bite back, and I don't blame her whatsoever. Then her other technique was, she just pooped all over me."

Most people in the room gasped at that point. But Mike and Babs both laughed the laugh of people who'd "been there, done that." They probably knew that was coming.

"Yeah, so all down my work shirt, everything like that. So I'm doing all this in front of somebody's house. At night. Late at night. Then I see somebody with a flashlight in the window like looking out."

Babs's laughter filled the room, and none of us had any doubt she'd done exactly this and more. I remembered how she and Mike assumed police stopping Chris and me at some point was inevitable, so what's a little upset neighbor action?

"I got Poppy in the car, and I started to drive out of the cul-de-sac. I had to come back around in front of the house, and I saw the guy had come out of his house and now he was out in the street. And at this point I have no shirt on, which does not help the situation. Now I'm a guy in a car who has been hanging out in front of his house, and I'm shirtless, with this scared dog in my car, so I just yelled out to him that I was chasing a dog and I found the dog. He didn't seem too happy, but he went back inside."

We were all laughing, safe in the knowledge that it had all turned out well. We were also very impressed with all this young man had gone through for this little dog.

I knew from all the flyers someone was really missing this dog.

I was still missing that dog. *I miss her so much.*

Conor continued, "So then I called my parents and asked if they could walk down the road and find the flyer. Because all I could see was that it was a beagle-ish dog, but I thought it might be the same one. They did and they sent me a photo of the flyer, and that was it. It was her. And that's when I called you."

He looked at me. Simple as that. He'd done the heroic thing, this kind, selfless thing, all for a dog.

We all applauded. What else was there to do? Except give him a new sweatshirt—I gave him a Beagle Freedom Project sweatshirt with the "Rescue. Rehab. Repeat." logo. And I gave him a check.

He never cashed it.

❧

Toward the end of the party, Curtis and Melody arrived. They drove through the hideous weather, for over two hours, on a Saturday, not because they wanted to party—I'm sure they would have much rather spent the stormy day at home cuddled up together with their own crew of rescue dogs—but because there was a dog in need. Curtis and Melody brought with them a new rescue dog, Junior, a very overweight beagle mix with a wound on his rear end that had been left untreated for so long it had been infested with maggots. Cleaned up at the shelter, pulled by one volunteer, and then transported from Los Angeles to Riverside by Curtis and Melody, Junior would spend a week recovering at home with me before I took him to Charlotte and Meade Canine Rescue.

Three weeks after the party and after Junior was safely ensconced at magical Meade Canine Rescue, I was again dogless in Riverside. I saw yet another face in a kennel staring up at me from my Facebook page (there is absolutely no pattern here; do not even think about it). He had a round face and those big beagle eyes, full of mischief and character. But he had a shortened snout and a hilarious underbite, with two sharp bottom teeth that peeked out from his jowls, giving him that look little kids make when they're trying to smile but don't quite have it down yet. I was smitten. Rescue nation kicked into gear again, and I agreed to foster Pickle the puggle short-term, just while I was in Riverside.

The next night Pickle slept on my bed with me, snoring louder than Daphne ever had, and taking up twice as much pillow as Poppy had, which I gladly let him do. Dogs will heal whatever ails me. Always.

The one advantage to fulfilling my foster duties and letting Poppy be adopted out was that I could continue to help other dogs. I could do short-term fosters every two weeks I was in Riverside, and I could transport dogs from Southern California to Central California and points in between. Dogs like Junior and Pickle would make it bearable for me. I wouldn't be dogless the weeks I was in Riverside, and I was helping these dogs on their journey to their forever families.

❧

But then the universe laughed at me again. (Did you see it coming this time? I did not.)

Two days before Pickle and I would be leaving to head up to Paso Robles (he to Meade Canine Rescue and I to Chris, Percival, and Roe), as I was working late in my office and Pickle was snoring away on the dog bed at my feet, I got a phone call.

The president of BFP was calling.

"Poppy's adopters have decided it's not working out. They have an older dog, and Poppy is just too much for him. They have to do right by their older family member. So . . . we're wondering if you'd like to adopt Poppy?"

My heart leapt in joy, somersaulted, and then slammed down and completely overpowered my brain. "Yes. Of course. We do. Yes." I responded instantly—pure emotion, no logic (hey, that's kind of fun! I should do that more often). I was ecstatic to have the chance to see Poppy again and, in a flash, decided it was fate, destiny, meant to be, all of that. I'd left it up to the universe, and the universe had delivered! Hallelujah, praise beagle!

Then reason began to creep in—we had a lease, we had a homeowners' association, we had Roe and Percival. But I swept that aside. "I have to talk to Chris first. I mean, yes, but let me talk to Chris. Can I call you back tomorrow?" I was prepared to break the lease, violate HOA rules, whatever it took. *Poppy was family.*

"Yes, that's fine. Poppy is with Kevin right now, but we'd need you to pick her up soon."

"I can pick her up on Saturday when I head up to Paso. I'll drive right through LA."

I was already mentally packing a bag for Poppy—her toys, some treats, a new squeak—with cursory thought to anything beyond the moment I'd pick her up again.

Chris surprised me with a shared enthusiasm.

"After all you two have been through, it's meant to be. Yes, we want her. Yes, we'll adopt her. I'd been thinking about it anyway," he said.

"You had? But she'd already been adopted."

"Well, before she was adopted, I thought about how we could maybe make it work with three dogs. And then when you started texting me about Pickle I was thinking about it again. I know how much you want a dog with you."

"So what's the thought?"

"I can talk to our landlord here. They probably don't care if we have two or three beagles. I don't think they cared at all when Poppy was here before. They even asked where Poppy went. And you're only here for two weeks. So it's three dogs for two weeks and two dogs for two weeks."

"True. But most landlords don't even like you to have one dog."

"They're not like most landlords."

And that was true. We lived in a paradise, nestled on a hilltop, surrounded by oaks and vineyards, where deer, rabbit, squirrels, and raccoons were regular visitors. Our neighbors—the landlord's granddaughter and her husband and daughter—had a dog and chickens and regularly snuck treats to our dogs through the fence.

"It can't hurt to ask. But what about here? In Riverside?"

"You're only there two weeks a month, and you'll only have one dog with you. When I visit for a weekend there will be three dogs, but they aren't living there. If we have to, Roe can go stay with Charlotte for that weekend."

"That's true. She's offered that. So in the short term we'd be fine."

"We're likely to be renting here awhile."

"And when we finally buy a place, it will have a yard big enough for ten dogs."

"Can we just ease into this? Three is good for now."

"Three is perfect. Though I'd adopt Pickle here in a heartbeat if four were an option."

Chris laughed. He could have screamed, but he laughed. Did I mention he's wonderful?

The landlord and her granddaughter next door had happily agreed to three dogs; it was so easy I wondered why we hadn't thought to ask before. When I returned to Paso Robles, Pickle came with me on his way to Charlotte's, and we stopped to pick up Poppy at Kevin's home in Los Angeles. Double the doggie travel companions!

Poppy met me at the door and immediately did her wigglebutt dance. She twisted back and forth, yipped, wiggled, danced, yapped, and jumped. Kevin's wife took Pickle for a walk (where she too fell in love with him) while I sat on their couch with Poppy curled into my lap.

"You're going home, baby girl. Home at last. For good this time."

She licked my hand and looked up at me with those deep brown, intense little eyes and her Elvis smirk. *How had I ever let her go?*

Poppy, in a crate, and Pickle, seat-belted in next to her on my back seat, sniffed at each other and wagged their tails, both happy dogs up for whatever came next. When we reached Paso Robles, we met Chris at the winery tasting room where he was working, and both dogs came in with me. They were both adorable characters, and Poppy, though still shy, seemed happy to see Chris. Pickle greeted everyone as if they had gathered specifically to meet him, the wine being just an afterthought. Charlotte met me there to pick up adorable Pickle the puggle. Though I was ecstatic to have Poppy back, I may have teared up a bit putting Pickle into Charlotte's car (where naturally he joined a half-dozen dogs already in the car). He'd get a great home, and soon, I knew. At least I had helped with that. I rubbed his big head, kissed his scrunched-up face, and wished him well.

Whatever sadness I felt dissipated quickly when I arrived at our Paso Robles home with Poppy. She squealed in delight when she saw Roe and Percival, and after a two-minute sniff fest, the three of them raced around the house, up the stairs, and out into the backyard. They raced back in, over the bed, around the bedroom, down the hall, down the stairs, back around the living room, and flying, like three furry arrows, they shot onto the couch. Poppy landed between her two brothers, and they settled in, leaving no room for any humans.

So this is what having three dogs will be like? I took my place in the armchair across the room and put my feet up on the ottoman. I looked across at the three beagles, now curled up, Poppy resting her head on Roe's haunches, sleeping soundly and contentedly.

Home.

EPILOGUE
HOME

⟨paw print⟩

"This is like your Christmas, isn't it?" Chris said. "Well, Christmas without the horrors?"

Poppy was in my lap as I sat in bed, one hand holding my first cup of morning coffee, and the other rubbing Poppy's pink belly. Roe was between my feet, still curled up and sleeping. Percival was, naturally, standing on Chris. "It's so much better. No stressing over gifts and where we're going, or not going, no cloud of doom hanging over me. Instead, it's all my favorite things with all my favorite people."

"By which you mean dogs."

"Yes. And the people who rescue them."

It was Sunday of Wine 4 Paws weekend in Paso Robles. Wine 4 Paws is a fundraiser for Woods Humane Society of San Luis Obispo County. Over one glorious weekend in April every year, forty or so wineries celebrate dogs and cats by donating their tasting room fees or a percentage of wine sales to Woods. And every year for the last six years, I've gone out wine tasting all weekend long with group of friends and our dogs. Because really, how much better could a weekend be?

This year we took Roe with us on Friday night, where we joined Chris working at the LXV Wine tasting room downtown, then made our way over to Chateau Lettau, where Roe howled along, loudly and enthusiastically, with the band playing there, and then to Thomas Hill Organics (some of the restaurants also donate from their sales) to dine on their dog-friendly patio. Roe and Daisy—my friend Judy's black Labrador mix—were each given a large marrow bone and blissfully sat under the table together gnawing on the bones, while the humans enjoyed vegan shepherd's pie.

Saturday was Percival's turn for an outing, since Chris could be with us for the day. We were pretty sure Roe mentioned the marrow bone to the other two dogs, and Percival probably had his hopes up. We did not disappoint. Cinquain Cellars was grilling hot dogs and were more than happy to offer one to our very interested beagle, and Paso Pups treats was outside Bon Niche winery, so of course he got to sample homemade dog biscuits. We taste wine, they taste treats; it's a fair deal. These treats—the bone marrow and the hot dog—didn't bother me nearly as much as buying the entire rotisserie chicken had, but it was not lost on me that I had some work to do on my ethical stance on veganism. Just not then. Not when these dogs were so happy.

And then it was Sunday. Poppy's big day out. She'd returned from what we now called her "big adventure" a different dog in many ways. She was more confident and more mature, and definitely now seemed to appreciate the comforts of a home and humans who provided her with regular meals and snacks. Chris said it was like we had sent her to an "Outward Hound" program. I couldn't help but laugh.

She was more confident, but there was still progress to be made. She was braver, no longer running from me or Chris, and happy to have her harness put on for walks. But strangers still intimidated her, and she was shy in new situations. We'd been gradually taking her out for short visits, trying to desensitize her and show her that people were okay (mostly) and there was fun to be had in this big, wide world.

We'd received her adoption papers and transferred her microchip into our name. We'd even bought a new GPS tracker for her. And so I took Poppy out for the Wine 4 Paws festivities—another big adventure, but this one would involve a leash, treats, a car ride between stops. It was also sunny and warm out, and she was accompanied by humans who love their wine almost as much as they love dogs.

Poppy stayed near me, but she seemed happy to be out and about. Maybe she knew this was part of the rescue nation she was with—Geraldine and Charlotte were both there. She was in a safe place, and she seemed to know that.

As I sat at the gorgeous Rava winery sipping sparkling wine, sun on my face, my rescue nation friends near, along with a half-dozen rescue dogs, I felt the same way—safe, comfortable. These people—the friends with me now, the friends I saw only when a dog was in need, even my social media friends—were important to me and in many ways like a family, or a community at least; people who were there when you needed them. Dogs have a way of finding their family. Perhaps they'd helped me find a family too.

I always believed that dogs come into our lives for a reason. Seamus had been there to show me how to make my way through cancer. Percival was there to finish the job Seamus started in turning Chris into a dog-loving human, which certainly makes our relationship easier. Percival was also the dog who inspired us to clean up the household products we used, switching to only cruelty-free brands. Daphne, my little personality doppelganger, had held a mirror up to me and just maybe we lightened each other up a bit. Roe, my little gift from the universe, is my reminder that sometimes the universe does me a favor.

And Poppy? Poppy got frightened and confused about home and people and where she was meant to be. So she bolted. She ran into the wilderness. I may have done much the same for most of my life. Her wilderness was literal, mine figurative. But we'd each encountered our own coyotes, hawks, and enemies, real or perceived. We'd each had trouble trusting humans. We each tested out many trails, hoping they led home. And people had surprised both of us. Strangers showed up, acquaintances showed up, friends and of course my rescue nation was there, but my family showed their support in the ways they could, and it was my brother-in-law, Eli, who'd come through, no questions asked, when we needed someone to pick up the crate from Mike. Maybe Poppy was here to show me the way out of my wilderness.

Leave a door open. Give them a way to find their way home.

My father had been gone for months, eventually leaving Missouri and set-tling back home—where he was born—in Georgia. We texted regularly. We texted more than we had talked when he was in California, and I could see he needed that as much as I did. Chris and I were making plans to visit him the following spring. My mother and stepfather, for the first time ever, were coming to visit me the following month, and my mother and I promised to talk about things we'd spent our entire lives not talking about. Maybe some losses are avoidable. Maybe they'd left some doors open that I hadn't seen.

Maybe I could find my way home.

❖

Months after the thank-you party, after Poppy was part of our family, and well into a time I could not imagine Poppy not being in our lives, I watched the video I took of Conor telling the party attendees how he caught Poppy that cold January night. As I listened, I realized for the first time that he had said "golf course." It occurred to me then that if Poppy was near the golf course, she had not been running on Alessandro, as I'd been so insistent about. She had been running on Canyon Crest Drive. Conor hadn't known the street names then because his parents had just moved to the neighborhood. Chances are he had visited his parents many times since then. *He'd know the street names now.*

I called him and asked.

"Of course, yeah. My parents live in the Mission Grove neighborhood, so I had come down Mission Grove Parkway onto Canyon Crest Drive, and that's where I saw her. Canyon Crest Drive goes right through the golf course, and right after that part is where she turned right."

He and I both had Google Maps open on our computers when we talked. I followed the trail he described—his parents lived one or two blocks over from Gordon and the yard where we'd set the trap for Poppy. Conor's route had fol-lowed Poppy's pattern, only he'd done it on surface streets and she'd been cut-ting through the canyon—just not on that night. On that night she'd gone on surface streets too. Had she gone to the golf course like Mike had mentioned?

I continued to follow along the map as Conor described where she went. I realized Poppy had run down Canyon Crest right past Via Conception, the street where my friend Michelle lived and where the photo of Poppy on our "Lost" flyer had been taken, and then she'd turned . . . *Oh my god.*

"Yeah," Conor said. "That's the street she turned on . . . Via Zapata. We went all the way to where it kind of curves around. There's two cul-de-sacs at the end there. Via Zapata and . . ."

Via La Paloma. The cul-de-sac where I'd sat for three of the five nights she'd been missing, with my bag of rotisserie chicken, my smelly socks, and my soggy blankets, waiting for my girl. *Poppy had returned to where she'd first gone into the wilderness park.*

Poppy had found her way back.

Doggone Helpful Tips for When Your Dog Is Gone

IMMEDIATE STEPS TO TAKE TO FIND A LOST DOG

1. Stop. Stop what you are doing. Stop chasing your dog, stop calling its name. Stop. Know that every part of this will go against your instincts. Your instincts are wrong and are fear-based. Stop and listen to the experts. Your dog's life may depend on it.

2. DO NOT CHASE YOUR DOG. This bears repeating. DO NOT CHASE YOUR DOG.

3. DO NOT CALL OUT YOUR DOG'S NAME. Your dog will hear the panic in your voice and think, "If he/she is scared, I'm scared. I better hide!"

4. Call in a pet recovery specialist. Someone like Babs Fry (619-249-2221), or Mike Noon (714-724-6712). They both work for free and can guide you by phone. Every circumstance is different, and they can tailor their advice to your dog's situation.

5. Give your dog a way to come home. Leave a door open—especially at night.

6. Do not run around spreading your scent throughout the neighborhood where your dog is lost. You want to establish one place where your scent is that your dog can find its way back to—that may be at home or it may be where your dog was lost (see #11 below). If your scent is all over several square miles, your dog may chase that scent and wander farther off.

7. Put out some dirty laundry that smells like you—socks, underwear, a T-shirt. (Not your whole laundry basket or bedsheets; dogs have a very strong sense of smell, and you don't want to startle them.) If you can hang a piece of dirty laundry in a tree or bush in front of your home, do so. The wind will carry the scent farther.

8. Get a PR campaign going—you want thousands of eyes on thousands of flyers. (See sample flyer.) Produce as many flyers as you can, and ask volunteers to hang them in the area the dog was last seen and for miles out from that spot. (See "Flyer Hanging 101.")

9. Put up big, bright posters where people are most likely to see them.

10. Do not have volunteers, however well meaning, out searching for your dog. You want people watching from a seated position, observing, and reporting sightings, but not chasing, not following, and not walking around. Activity will cause the dog to hide. A place with lots of humans roaming around will not be viewed as safe by your dog. Give your dog a chance to find its way to a safe spot.

11. Eventually, if your dog doesn't find its way back to your home, or if it was lost somewhere not familiar to it, your dog will establish a pattern. It will settle down in one locale. You'll learn where this is by the sightings reported to you by people seeing your signs. This may take a while. Do not give up.

12. Once a locale is established, go to that spot with smelly food and a piece of your dirty laundry and sit, waiting. Your only job is to give the dog a safe space in which to expose itself. Do not call to the dog; do not chase the dog. Do not make movement toward the dog if you see the dog. Just wait. Let the dog find you. They will see you and smell you, long before you see them. This is also where the warming box detailed below will be set up.

13. Eventually you'll find where the dog is and be able to set a humane trap.

14. Do not give up.

FLYERS

1. Make and place as many flyers as you can.
2. Use a photo with a side view of your missing dog, if possible. This is how most people will see your dog.
3. Do NOT offer a reward. You will only encourage people to chase your dog or provide false information that will waste your time.
4. Use one phone number only and post it clearly and visibly on the flyer. Make sure the phone can accept voice mail. Be sure to answer all calls, no matter what number they are coming from.
5. Keep the flyer simple (see sample): Lost Dog. [Insert photo.] Do Not Chase. Report Sightings. [Insert phone number.]
6. Put "Do NOT Chase" on the flyer.
7. You do not need to put the dog's entire story. People do not have time to read it. You want the message short and simple.
8. See "Flyer Hanging 101" for how and where to post.
9. If your search continues for a long while, you may want to post new flyers that say "Still Searching" so people know the search is ongoing and don't simply assume the flyers are old and the dog has been found.
10. Hang flyers at places that are heavily trafficked or have lots of people sitting around idly: coffee shops and coffee houses, community center or neighborhood bulletin boards, on the sides of community mailboxes (not federal mail boxes; that's illegal), entrances to parks and dog parks, supermarkets, big box stores.
11. Hang large banners on sides of buildings, fences, bridges (only if safe to do so and with permission).
12. If putting flyers on light poles, lampposts, or traffic lights, put multiple flyers along the street every three to four posts so drivers driving quickly will see them. Put multiple flyers at intersections with stop signs or traffic lights, where drivers are stopping and have more time to look.
13. Always hang flyers at eye level for drivers, so that they are seen when people are driving by.
14. Use polyurethane sheet protectors (available at your local office supply store) to protect your flyers from weather and moisture.

15. Use neon or bright-colored poster board with big block lettering for signs that can be seen and read from far away or if viewers are traveling fast (along roads, posted near dog parks, shopping centers, school fences, etc.).

16. After your dog is found, organize volunteers one last time to pick up all flyers and signs.

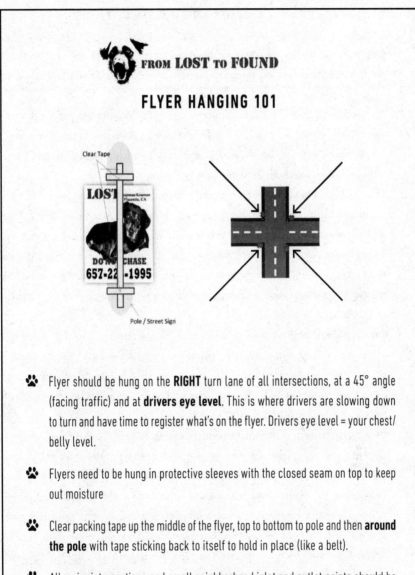

FROM **LOST** to **FOUND**

FLYER HANGING 101

🐾 Flyer should be hung on the **RIGHT** turn lane of all intersections, at a 45° angle (facing traffic) and at **drivers eye level**. This is where drivers are slowing down to turn and have time to register what's on the flyer. Drivers eye level = your chest/belly level.

🐾 Flyers need to be hung in protective sleeves with the closed seam on top to keep out moisture

🐾 Clear packing tape up the middle of the flyer, top to bottom to pole and then **around the pole** with tape sticking back to itself to hold in place (like a belt).

🐾 All major intersections and small neighborhood inlet and outlet points should be covered. Drop off at vets, pet stores, groomers, etc. in area.

🐾 While hanging flyers, have a pic of the flyer in your phone. Instead of giving passer by flyers, ask them to take a pick of your phone with theirs. This way they have the number at their finger tips in their phone.

COLLECTING AND ORGANIZING VOLUNTEERS

1. Use social media to put a call out for volunteers. Also look for local dog and pet interest groups on social media, as they can help keep a lookout, and many might be willing to come out and help.

2. Be specific in your calls for volunteers. Are you looking for people to canvass? Make signs? Sit as a lookout for extended periods of time? Remember, a volunteer might not be physically capable of handling one or more of these tasks, so allow for them to help in a way they can.

3. Have all your volunteers meet at a central location, ideally quiet and private enough so you can identify who are the volunteers, and with enough room to allow for the making of posters and flyers and to spread out maps of the dog's known vicinity.

4. When your volunteers arrive, have them all write their names and phone numbers down on either a piece of paper or a whiteboard. Once everyone has done this, have everyone take a photo of the list with their phones so everyone has the phone numbers.

5. Set up a single text chain with everyone's phone numbers, so that everyone can communicate with each other instantly. Emphasize that this text channel should only be used for communications directly related to finding the dog. Create a new text channel for each day you have volunteers, as the group of people involved may change day to day.

6. Don't get frustrated if your volunteers can only stay for a limited time or cannot assist on certain days or moving forward. Be grateful for their time and willingness to help at such a difficult time.

7. Before your volunteers arrive, have a loose game plan for who will do what and go where. This will shorten the time you need to explain and organize your volunteers and will help keep you focused on the task at hand and what needs to be done.

8. Break down your vicinity map into specific quadrants and assign your volunteers individual quadrants and sections with distinct borders, so they are not overlapping each other and you are canvassing a maximum amount of territory.

9. If a volunteer very quickly covers or finishes with a section, have them contact the text list to see if there are any areas that could use assistance or have not been covered as thoroughly.

10. Fewer people will volunteer in inclement weather; adjust your plans based on the number of volunteers and what the most vital tasks and regions are.

HOW TO CREATE AND PLACE A WARMING BOX FOR YOUR DOG

1. The primary dog owner or the person the dog was/is closest to should construct the warming box. The less human contact with the box, the better.
2. The warming box should be at least two times the size of your dog when he or she is lying down. Your dog should be able to crawl into the box comfortably and sleep inside if necessary.
3. Put clothing with your scent (socks and underwear are best), blankets with your dog's scent, and some of your dog's toys in the warming box.
4. Bait the warming box with rotisserie chicken (or some smelly food) to lure your dog.
5. If you have been tracking your dog with GPS or have had sightings, place the warming box at a place frequented numerous times by your dog, or in an area you believe your pet may be.
6. If possible, place the warming box upwind from where you think your dog may be, so that the wind will carry the scents to the dog.
7. Monitor the box in person from a distance for as long as you can, then set up a trail camera for overnight viewing, with a clear view of the box and of the most likely route of your dog.

Don't get frustrated! The warming box may attract other animals like skunks, coyotes, and other dogs, but it is still one of the best ways to lure your pet out for a sighting.

OTHER HELPFUL TIPS IN SEARCHING FOR YOUR DOG

1. Ask everyone you encounter to take a photo of the flyer with their cell phones. They will maintain the photo in their phone much longer than they will hang on to a piece of paper. In addition, the cell phone photo is much easier to access if they happen to see your dog while they're out walking or running errands.

2. If a homeowner is not home but they have a Ring or other doorbell camera, ring the doorbell and hold the flyer up in front of it. Even if they do not respond, they will have the image of the flyer and it will be harder for them to ignore than if you just leave a flyer in their door or mailbox.

3. Search on social media to find a dog recovery specialist near you. They may have supplies that you'll need, like a humane trap, in addition to advice.

4. Ask neighbors to check their home security cameras for sightings. Remember: you're trying to figure out the dog's pattern of behavior, so you know where to set a trap and/or where to sit calmly waiting for your dog to show.

5. Put the flyer on your car windows.

6. Ask friends to put the flyer on their car windows. If you can park a car (with the flyers in the windows) in heavily trafficked areas, do so. Golf courses, shopping centers, and entrances to parks are all good places to get lots of eyes on the flyers.

7. Security guards in parking lots, groundskeepers at golf courses, crosswalk attendants, and the like are all great resources—they know their areas and what's out of the ordinary, and they are typically present at dawn when a dog is most likely to be moving about.

8. Post to social media, asking neighbors to report sightings. Post on Nextdoor.com, your personal Facebook, lost dog Facebook groups in your area, Instagram, PawBoost.com, LostMyDoggie.com, PetFinder.com, FidoFinder.com, etc.

9. Homeless persons can be informative and often have cell phones. Provide them with flyers, inquire if they've seen your dog, and ask that they call you if they do.

10. Use a camping tarp and either duct tape or reflective tape to create a large lost dog sign with LOST DOG and your phone number as large as possible. If possible, blow up a photo of your dog to tape down in the middle. Hang this tarp sign around the busiest and most trafficked streets where the dog was seen (freeway overpasses and off-ramps are great for these, as are fences for parks and schools).

TOOLS YOU CAN USE IN YOUR SEARCH

1. Trail camera—It can watch for your dog when you can't.
2. Diatomaceous earth—You can spread it in an area you think your dog might be to see if paw prints are left. Identifying dog paw prints versus coyote prints might be difficult, however, so please work with a pet recovery specialist to identify the prints.
3. Construction fencing—for fencing off an area once you've located your dog.
4. Flyers—so many flyers!
5. Tarps—Large waterproof tarps make great backgrounds for large signs. Use white tape to spell out your "LOST DOG" message and phone number. Put a large photo of your dog in the center and cover with clear tape.
6. Neon poster board—to post signs that get attention.

❧

PLACING AND SETTING THE HUMANE TRAP

1. First and foremost, the trap should only be set up under the care and guidance of an animal rescue professional. Please do not attempt to set up a humane trap yourself without first consulting an animal rescue specialist.
2. Make sure all parts of the trap are working and unbroken. Before setting up the trap, test it several times to ensure all parts are working properly and that the door closes when pressure is applied to the floor.
3. Set up the trap upwind from where you expect your dog to enter or encounter the trap.
4. Place the trap on level ground and cover the bottom/floor of the trap with a layer of dirt, so that the animal will not feel or sense the bars when entering the trap. Make sure it is enough dirt to cover the bars, but not so much that it affects the mechanism of the trap.
5. Rub all sides, bars, and the mechanism of the trap with chicken skin and/or grease. Not only will the scent attract your dog to the trap, but the grease

and oil from the chicken will lubricate the components of the trap to allow it to work better. Just make sure you do not get any pieces of the chicken into the mechanism of the trap.

6. Place a small amount of chicken meat at the end of the trap farthest away from the opening, so that your dog will have to come all the way into the trap to sniff at or eat the meat.

7. You can also bait the trap with some of the same items of clothing you were using in your warming box, to bring your scent to the trap.

8. Create a trail of chicken broth starting from the entrance of the trap and extending thirty to fifty feet toward where you anticipate your pet approaching the trap.

9. Sprinkle the trunks and bases of any trees along this path and around the trap with the remaining chicken broth, to lure your dog and make this area as interesting as possible.

10. Set up your trail camera to record both the trap and this path leading to the trap. Try to set up as wide an angle as possible so you can see your dog approach from any direction and help you reposition the trap if they are not lured into it the first time.

11. Your final action should be setting the trap and making sure it is properly triggered.

12. Do not set up camp near the trap and watch it. If baited and triggered properly and with the trail camera working, there is no reason for you to stand watch over the trap. Go home and get a good's night sleep.

13. Do not get frustrated if you do not capture your pet on the first try. As long as you have a recognizable pattern or routine for your pet, continue to set up the trap. Be patient that it will do its job.

PREPARE FOR THE UNTHINKABLE

None of us plan to lose our pets, and yet 15 percent of pets go missing every year. Some things you can do to prepare in case your pet goes missing:

1. Microchip your pets. If Conor had not seen all of our flyers once he caught Poppy, our best chance for being reunited was the microchip in Poppy.
2. GPS trackers with phone apps are wonderful and very useful when your pet first goes missing. But don't make the mistake I made in constantly updating to determine where your pet is—that drains the battery. Use it sparingly to determine your pet's travel pattern rather than their exact location at any one point in time.
3. Have a photo of your dog from a side view. You likely have lots of photos of your dog on your phone, but they are probably looking straight at you or curled up sleeping. The photo you'll want on the flyer is from a side view.
4. If you can help find a lost dog, please volunteer. Karma and all. (But remember—don't chase a loose dog!)

WHAT YOU SHOULD KNOW ABOUT COYOTES

Please check out ProjectCoyote.org for valuable information on understanding and coexisting with coyotes. This information is provided, with permission, from their materials.

Normal Urban Coyote Behavior
- Active in the daytime and nighttime.
- Most active at dusk and dawn.
- Coyotes' primary food sources in cities include rats, gophers, insects, and fruit. But human and pet foods (and water) may attract coyotes, so eliminate these attractants to reduce negative encounters.
- Watching you (and your dog) in plain view or from a camouflaged position (like dogs, coyotes are curious).
- Sitting on a hill in plain view.
- Relaxing or playing in a field or other grassy area.
- Walking and not paying attention to you.
- Following you and your dog with curiosity from a comfortable distance.
- Hunting gophers in fields and meadows.
- "Bluff charging" your dog away from den/territory/food or pups during rearing season (spring and summer).
- Standing his or her ground unfazed by your attempts to scare him/her away, during pup-rearing season (spring and summer).
- Waiting at stop lights to cross busy streets.
- Dashing across a trail.
- More than one coyote relaxing together or greeting each other.
- Hearing coyotes howling and yipping (they are greeting, communicating, and defining territories).

When to Take Action
- If a coyote approaches to a proximity that you feel is uncomfortable, and you can make and maintain eye contact, do not turn and run, but haze the coyote (see below).
- When a coyote seems interested in the food you are carrying, even if he doesn't approach, but hangs around appearing to wait for a handout.

- When a coyote is in your yard, unless you think there could be a den on your property. If you think there is a den on your property, please call a wildlife expert.

Quick Coyote Hazing Tools
- Surprise with a pop-up umbrella or simple noisemaker (shake a penny in a shiny soda can).
- Wave your arms overhead, make direct eye contact, and yell, "Go away, coyote!" Don't stop until the coyote leaves.
- Pick up your small dog or put your large dog behind you before you haze so that the coyote focuses on you and your message.
- Stand your ground. Make eye contact. Advance toward the coyote with your hazing tools if there is hesitation on the part of the coyote. Haze until the coyote retreats. Allow room for the coyote(s) to escape.
- Make sure the coyote is focused on you as the source of danger or discomfort. Do not haze from buildings or your car, where the coyote can't see you clearly.
- If you see more than one coyote, continue your hazing efforts; multiple animals will most likely respond to the same hazing techniques at the same time.
- Make it multisensory. Use tools that scare with sound, light, and motion. Variety is essential. Coyotes can learn to recognize and avoid individual people, so the more often a coyote has a negative experience with various hazing tools and different people, the faster he will change his behavior to avoid human contact.
- Hazing should be exaggerated, assertive, and consistent. Communities should always maintain some level of hazing using a variety of tools so that coyotes do not return to unacceptable behavior over time.
- Coyotes have routine habits. Make note of when and where you encounter them. Ask neighbors in those areas to help you scare the coyote or avoid those areas.
- Think prevention first! Coyote pups begin coming out of dens in the early summer, and parents are very protective. Keep pets close and don't let them roam.

**OPEN SPACES AND URBAN AREAS BELONG TO
ALL OF US—PEOPLE, DOGS, AND WILDLIFE.**

**LIVING WELL WITH OUR WILD NEIGHBORS
IS A COMMUNITY EFFORT.**

WHAT TO DO WHEN YOUR DOG IS BACK HOME

1. Feed only small meals and small amounts of water over time. If your dog eats or drinks too much too quickly, it will all come right back up.

2. Keep your dog safe, secure, and at home for a while (a week if they were missing for more than a few days). They will have had plenty of exercise. They need rest and security.

3. Only transport your dog in a car when tethered or, even better, crated.

4. Do take your dog to the veterinarian to be checked for injuries, parasites, and illness. Some illnesses may not show up for 48 hours. Keep a close watch on your dog.

5. Do not take your dog out anywhere off leash—your dog is a flight risk.

6. Enjoy the reunion and spoil them with love.

A Note about Fostering

Fostering animals, whether short- or long-term, helps save lives. If you are interested in fostering, here's some important information:

- Fostering a pet can be a great idea if you already have pets but want to help save other animals or when you aren't ready to commit to a pet full time for any variety of reasons.
- Contact your local rescue groups (an internet search will likely reveal many) and find out what they need and what they expect. Rescue groups can vary in how they utilize fosters and what their requirements are, but all of them want and need volunteers to take in animals on a temporary basis.
- Make sure it's a reputable rescue you're dealing with and you are comfortable with the people in charge.
- Fostering can be for a few days, weeks, months, or until the pet is adopted. That's between you and the rescue, and often depends on the animal's needs.
- Generally, you need safe, clean, and secure housing for the animal (and that will vary with the type of animal), transportation, kindness, and patience to become a foster animal parent.

- Rescues usually take animals from city and county shelters to save them from euthanasia. The rescue may not know much about the pet. You'll be helping to learn what the animal is like and what type of home he or she should have. That means you're going to have to expect some surprises. That's where the kindness and patience come in.
- The dog or cat will likely need socialization and some time to adjust to their new circumstances. (More kindness and patience needed!)
- Fostering can involve a lot of cleanup. The pet may or may not be house-trained, but it will likely be stressed, and in unfamiliar circumstances "potty" mistakes are bound to happen.
- The rescue remains the legal owner of the animal and makes all decisions regarding the animal's care, future adoption, and health. Generally, they will consult with the foster parent, but the rescue has the last word. They also pay for the health care and other needs of the pet.
- You may be asked to bring the pet to adoption events or to meet with potential adopters. Be clear up front if this is something you can or cannot do.
- Fostering is always bittersweet—you help save a life, and then you let them go on to their new life. As is said in the rescue world, "Your heart breaks a little so theirs will never break again."

P.S. Foster "failing" is never a bad thing.

Acknowledgments

This book tells of many heroes, some of whom are mentioned, none of whom I could ever thank enough. But I'd like to try.

A lifetime of thank yous to Babs Fry, Mike Noon, and Conor Parker—dog lovers, heroes to me, to Poppy, and to so many others. You are spectacular human beings who I am lucky to have met. There truly would be no book without you, and there may not have been a Poppy by my side as I wrote this. I learned so much from you about commitment, perseverance, and always leaving a way home, for which I will always be grateful.

More thanks to the many kind and selfless people who came out to help find Poppy, who followed the plan even when it may not have made sense at the time, who never gave up, who walked for miles or sat for hours, who hung flyers, made social media posts, and watched, prayed and hoped for Poppy. Special thanks to Jessica Buck, Austin Blackwell, Michelle Ouellette, Aaron and Deia Schumann, Justine (whose last name I never learned), Kevin McManus, Megan Dunn, Nataly Sich, Angela Lira, Valerie Kelly, Maria Selby, Liza Franzen, Mary Pryor, Bob & Brian (aka Abe & Davey's dads), Wendy Baker, Matt Rossell, Laurie Gentry, Cecilia Ruiz, Curtis and Melody, Mike and Jeanne Kataoka, Ann-Marie Fritz, Matt Friedlander, and Paige Zellerbach.

ACKNOWLEDGMENTS

To what felt like the entire city of Riverside, California, and specifically the neighbors around Sycamore Canyon Wilderness Park and Mission Grove, who kept a vigilant watch for Poppy and allowed me to sit stakeout in their yards, I give a heartfelt thanks. Eternal gratitude goes especially to George, Les, and Michelle on Dayton Street, Jennifer and Stan Sniff, the neighbors on Via La Paloma (yes, I'm the crazy lady you saw for several late nights and early mornings at the end of your cul-de-sac), and Gordon and all of his neighbors on Firwood (even the one who called the cops on us). An extra thank you to Ruff House Pet Resort for their care of Poppy, their help with the search, and the use of their training room to honor some of the search volunteers.

I told Chris on about day three of the search for Poppy that if the story had a happy ending I would be writing this book, because the information and knowledge that Mike and Babs have needs to be shared as far and as wide as possible. I was lucky to find an agent who believed that too, and I thank Sheree Bykofsky for her diligent search to find *Poppy in the Wild* a home. That home was with Jessica Case and Pegasus Books, true dog and book lovers, which of course makes for the perfect home, for which I am both lucky and grateful. The copyediting stage is my least favorite part of publishing, but Daniel O'Connor, your suggestions improved the book, and particularly the appendix, and I am thankful for that. And more thanks to David Carriere, publicist, dog lover, and enthusiastic supporter from early on.

Writing is a solitary endeavor, but talking about writing, getting encouragement to write, and celebrating writing goals is not. I am lucky to have the support of fellow writers and brilliant editors Joeli Yaguda, Amy Wiley, and Sara J. Henry, who saw early drafts of this manuscript for what it could be and helped me get it there (sometimes kicking and screaming). I also raise a glass in thanks to my longtime writing cohorts, partners in wine and writing retreats, and fellow travelers through ebb and flow, Jane Gideon and Lori Lacefield: may we one day return to Maui, and may your rum always be safe from thieves.

I also give my sincere thanks to Steve Kettman and Sarah Ringler, cofounders of the Wellstone Center in the Redwoods, who hosted me for a blissful week-long writing retreat where I finished this manuscript. Your home, the environment you create, and your love of writing and writers was and is inspirational.

My rescue nation must always be thanked for all they do for dogs, and beagles in particular, but also for how they inspire me—Charlotte Meade, Geraldine Gilliland, Laurie Gentry (again!), Judy Scheffel, Karal Gregory, Julie Levine, and Bridget Blitsch. Keep doing all you do, because you're simply amazing.

And finally, and for always, an eternal debt of gratitude to Chris Kern, who wasn't a dog guy when we met but has become a dog god. When I think of all we've been through together these last sixteen years, I know I couldn't have done it with anybody else, nor would I have wanted to.